W9-DHP-520

BASKETBALL METHODS

Health, Physical Education, and Recreation Series

Edited by DR. N. P. NEILSON

THE STANFORD CHAMPIONS, 1936, 1937, 1938.

24 LEE, 26 STOEFEN, 7 LUISETTI, 37 MOORE, BUNN, 23 TURNER, 36 CALDERWOOD, 28 ZONNE.

BASKETBALL METHODS

by John W. Bunn

Dean of Men, Stanford University · Formerly
Director of Basketball, Stanford University

NEW YORK

THE MACMILLAN COMPANY

1939

PRINTED IN THE UNITED STATES OF AMERICA
AMERICAN BOOK—STRATFORD PRESS, INC., NEW YORK

FOREWORD

This treatise on basketball methods is the first of a new series of college textbooks in the fields of health education, physical education and recreation to be published by The Macmillan Company. The company plans to publish, from time to time, other volumes by competent authors, according to the need for and value of such productions.

John Bunn, formerly Basketball Coach and now Dean of Men at Stanford University, is the author of this book. He knows well the game of basketball as a player, as an attentive student under a famous coach, as a successful coach of championship teams, and as an instructor of students in classes on basketball methods. His philosophy of making the game fun for the players, his knowledge of the game, his technical skill, and his ability to establish personal, friendly, and informal relations with his players helped materially to make him one of the successful basketball coaches of the country. He is a member of the National Association of Basketball Coaches and Vice-Chairman of the National Basketball Rules Committee.

Textbooks are needed in the field of methods of teaching. Up to the present time, few textbooks in this special area have been available. Such textbooks may be used in the program of professional education of physical education teachers during their pre-service and their in-service preparation. *Basketball Methods*, therefore, is a timely contribution and should meet the needs not only of those instructors who teach courses in basketball or basketball methods in teacher training institutions, but also of high school and college coaches and of the students and players themselves.

N. P. Neilson, Editor

Washington, D. C.
May 9, 1939

v

PREFACE

THIS book is written for three reasons.

First, there is need for a book on basketball methods which not only will be an aid to a beginner in learning to play basketball, but also will serve as a ready reference and guide to the coach—the high school coach in particular—in the organization and direction of the play of his team. There are many good treatises on techniques and styles of play in general, but few writers have attempted to present their material in the form and order in which they present it to their squads. Experience at coaching schools and in coaching has taught me that both coaches and players are vitally interested, not in techniques alone, but in the reasons for them as well; not in just a set of plays or dangling examples, but in the whole system of play and the method of its presentation to a squad; not in a group of slogans, but in sound principles and the practice which shows their application. In other words, those seeking information about playing and coaching basketball want an ordered procedure, a reasoned sequence of principles, practices, patterns, programs, and proofs which will provide them with a complete and logical picture of the methods of leading a squad throughout a season of play. They may not desire to follow the procedure exactly, but more than likely it will serve as a useful guide to them in working out their own system of play and practice.

It is the purpose of this book, *Basketball Methods*, to meet this demand honestly, in a direct and even dogmatic fashion. If the attempt has been successful, then those who have so willingly expressed their desires and criticisms are hereby thanked. If it does not fulfill this need, then the author only is to blame for his inability to interpret intelligently and to express clearly those helpful suggestions.

Second, there has been published only one other book which represents the game of basketball on the Pacific Coast. This present book strives to give the game in this particular section its rightful place in the basketball world.

And finally, this book, by presenting some of the experiences and ideas that have seemed to be profitable to me as a coach of college boys, is the realization of a desire to contribute something that may be useful to others. Because the book sets forth and attempts to justify the philosophy and methods used in my everyday coaching work, many parts of it are dogmatic, others are argumentative, but all methods and procedures are accompanied by a statement of the reasons that determined them.

If it were not for the inspiration and sound basic basketball knowledge which I received from my old coach and friend, Dr. Forrest C. Allen, who is responsible for my interest in coaching and particularly for my joy in working with young men; if it were not for the hearty and enthusiastic coöperation which I received from my boys, who taught me more than I shall ever be able to pass on; if it were not for the very sane attitude toward sport held by Dr. Thomas A. Storey, and the realization of his perfect confidence in my ability; if it were not for the encouraging support of my many friends during fair weather and foul and for the kicks in the back that I received from the few, which made me fight to show them how wrong they really were, the following pages could not have been written. To them all I humbly make acknowledgment and offer my thanks.

JOHN W. BUNN

STANFORD UNIVERSITY, CALIF.
May, 1939

CONTENTS

PART I

BASIC PRINCIPLES

PART II

INDIVIDUAL TECHNIQUES

CONTENTS

PART III

TEAM PLAY

ILLUSTRATIONS

DIAGRAMS

PART I

BASIC PRINCIPLES

LEGEND

PATH OF BALL

PATH OF PLAYER

DRIBBLE

OFFENSIVE PLAYER

DEFENSIVE PLAYER

START OF BALL

SCREEN

PIVOT

This Key Refers to the Diagrams Scattered throughout the Book

CHAPTER I

A COACHING AND SPORT PHILOSOPHY

EVERY coach of basketball or of any kind of sport has his own ideas of how that sport should be conducted. He has a plan for coaching players and for his relations with these players. He knows what kind of an attitude he would like these players to assume toward the game and what part he would like them to play in the whole scheme of things. His convictions on these points represent his philosophy of sport.

It is the purpose of this chapter to set forth a philosophy of basketball, the coaching of it, and the player's and coach's relation to it. This philosophy will give the basis for an understanding of the principles and practices that are presented in this book. The chapters which follow represent an attempt to show how this philosophy has actually worked. Its success is proved by the players' ready acceptance of it, the acclaim of the public, and the record and enjoyment of the teams that adopted this way of playing.

1. No Secrets About Coaching.

In the first place there are no secrets about the art of coaching. Everyone has access to the laws of learning. Neither is there any corner on the knowledge of the techniques of playing the game. In spite of the fact that many coaches confer in low tones about their strategies and camouflage their manuscripts with superfluous materials, the information about the game is quite well disseminated. Of course, some coaches are better teachers than others and some players are both more capable and more apt pupils than others. But these facts do not change the statement that there are no secrets about coaching or about the techniques and strategies

3

of the game. A secret practice may be held, but this is not for the purpose of hiding secrets from the public or from opponents. It is done mainly to stimulate players, a common psychological trick. Secret practice, even for this purpose, is of doubtful value.

About the only requisites for success that I have ever discovered are the ability to select players who are potential champions and a willingness to practice consistently and diligently. It was a revelation to me to learn that even our finest artists, who have been endowed with great native capacity, spend hours upon hours in diligent practice. This is also the formula which must be employed for success in sport.

2. Game Should Be Fun.

Next, games should be fun for those who play them. If the game is serious, monotonous business, neither the desired mental hygiene for the player nor the successful and satisfactory outcome of the game itself will be accomplished. It is the responsibility of the coach to make the game fun for the players. If the coach has done his part, then a player who does not get fun out of a game should not play the game. Winning a game is not alone sufficient to make it fun. There have been many teams which, in spite of the fact that they were winning, or were champions, did not care whether they played another game.

Practice should be enjoyable. Making games out of drills helps to put fun into practice. The relations between players and coach should be informal. The players should be reluctant to quit practice. At the end of a season they should be eager to play more. They should be joyous, happy, and carefree during practice and games. These are evidences that the game is being conducted on the proper basis and that it is fun.

It is not fun when a player is driven to his task, when he is forced to play until his feet are blistered and his muscles cry with pain. (There is little excuse for sore muscles in basketball.) It is not fun when practice is carried on for four or five hours a day and for seven days a week. It is not fun if only the flesh and not the spirit can enter into the play.

3. Freedom in Play.

The greatest freedom should be encouraged among the players. They should be urged to use their own personal initiative when they play. This does not mean that there is to be no organization to the game. There must be a pattern by which the players are guided and general principles which help them in making their decisions. But these should not be rigid, formal grooves with no flexibility or possibility of variation. Certainly, if a sport has educational value of an intellectual nature, that value comes out of this principle: *Give the player an opportunity to think for himself and invite him to make his own decisions.*

4. Democracy in Control.

There should be democracy in the control of the sport. At a time when the principles and practices of a democratic way of living seem to need support, certainly in the conduct of our sports we can give an opportunity for this kind of experience. Since we learn by doing, all of our educational procedures should afford practice in democratic living.

Too many of our athletic teams are ruled by an iron will and a mailed fist. This system may win more championships and build a doubtful reputation for the coach, but it is not educational from a democratic point of view, and it is not satisfying to the players.

If the greatest possible all-round development is to be achieved, the players should share in all the plans and decisions regarding the team. The coach should welcome criticisms and suggestions concerning the type of play to be used, the strategies to be employed, the schedules to be played, and the personnel of the squad and team. A domineering, dictatorial, "Beau Geste" attitude should not be assumed. Independent thinking and action should be encouraged, and when decisions are made, all should coöperate enthusiastically in their execution.

This philosophy also recognizes the value of having students handle the details of athletic management. Such a policy provides opportunity for valuable experiences for many who are not able to earn a place on a team. It encourages further student participation and control in the activities that should be for, of, and by the students.

5. Aggressive Endeavor Should Be Encouraged.

Aggressive basketball is advocated because it encourages the greatest freedom of play and has proved to be the most fun for the players. It has likewise proved to be the most successful. (See Chapter VI, *Strategical Situations.*)

The spirit of youth is a daring, chance-taking spirit. The role of the entrepreneur and the pioneer has ever been the dominating force in the development of our nation. This characteristic is fundamental in our American life. It led our forefathers to discover and settle America; it carried Lindbergh and Corrigan across the Atlantic, Hughes around the world, and Byrd to the Antarctic. Why should this spirit be stifled in basketball by forcing boys to play a conservative, careful, mechanical, ball-control, stereotyped game?

Once the aggressive game is adopted, coaches must accept the fact that more mistakes will be made than when a cautious, unadventurous game is played. The aggressive game is faster and more difficult to play; consequently more mistakes should be expected. Contrary to the current idea, there is no positive correlation between the number of mistakes a team makes and the outcome of the game. How often have coaches been heard to remark, after losing a game, "We made too many mistakes"? This is a popular refrain. Actually the opposite is true. Statistics recorded for the past five years prove that the team which made the most mistakes usually won the game. These statistics hold true for the conservative team as well as for the aggressive, ball-hawking team.

In 1933, when Stanford had a losing team, it made fewer mistakes than its opponents who won. In 1938, with a winning team, it made more mistakes than its opponents who lost. In 1938 University of Southern California won one game out of four from Stanford. In the game that University of Southern California won, its team made more mistakes than Stanford. In the three games

University of Southern California lost, Stanford made more mistakes. This instance is cited because University of Southern California played a conservative, ball-control type of game.

Again, to show that aggressiveness and gambling really pay dividends, a study was made of the methods of scoring by the Stanford team for 1938. Aggressive play would here be indicated by scores from the fast break, from interceptions and recoveries (stealing the ball and forcing the play), partly from rebounds where four players are used with reckless abandon for rebound work, and from long shots. It was found that more scores were made from the fast break (28 per cent of the total) than from any other method. Sixteen per cent were made from long shots, 30 feet or more from the basket; 15 per cent were made on rebounds, and 9 per cent from interceptions and recoveries. This constitutes 68 per cent of the field goals made, which certainly argues in favor of the aggressive game. At least, it shows positive results.

The testimony of the players themselves is of considerable importance. Only comments from those who had been dyed-in-the-wool conservatives in their play are presented. Their reactions are represented by the following typical remarks: "It is more strenuous to play aggressively, but it is much more fun to feel that you can take a chance." "Once you get into condition, you don't notice this aggressive game." "I like the aggressive game better because everyone gets an equal chance to score." "You get to score more in the aggressive game, and it's more fun when you score." "I always thought the fast aggressive game was a wild, unorganized game, but it takes more organizing and more careful timing than the other [conservative ball-control game]." These are all comments from boys who, before going to college and before playing the aggressive game, had been star players on high school teams that played a conservative ball-control type of game.

6. Emphasize Team Effort.

Team effort, not individual starring, should be the goal of every player on the squad. Team games offer one of the greatest fields for experience in coöperative and harmonious group living. When team effort is the rule, there is always a higher morale within the group. This will be found among the players on the bench as well as among those on the floor. And the real test comes when a team is losing, not winning. Morale often takes care of itself, at least bad morale is not evident, when a team wins; but a team that can maintain its morale when it loses is really the worthwhile team.

Seldom do selfishness or petty grievances creep into a group if the interest is in the team. The greatest individual accomplishments are made possible by the help of the team. The player who is a star performer, but who modestly credits his team with his success, will never give concern to a coach. While the scoring exploits of Hank Luisetti of Stanford stand out as an all-time record, the boy will be forever revered by his teammates as a great all-round team player. He was one who placed team above self. His teammates adored him, not because of his scoring prowess, but in spite of it. His scoring record may be eclipsed, but his unselfish team play can never be outdone.

This idea of team coöperation should involve not only the offense but the defense as well. That is why a team defense as against a man-to-man or a zone defense (Chapter XXIII) is advocated. In offense, no effort is made to specialize. All players are taught to play everywhere. A uniform pattern of offense is presented (Chapter XVII) which encourages all-round team play and not specific, individual tasks.

7. Coach-Player Relationship.

Finally, the coach-player relationship should be personal, friendly, reciprocal, and democratic. No boy likes, or in the end respects, a domineering, dictatorial, selfish leader. The coach should not expect from his players impossible achievements. The coach should not expect anything from his players that he is not willing to do himself. This should apply both to play and to conduct. Leadership should be by example rather than by precept. This is the lasting kind of leadership and the kind that all parents desire for their children. It will produce the only worthwhile followership.

The coach has a greater opportunity to influence behavior of students than any other school employee or even citizen. Only parents meet their youngsters on the same informal, confidential basis, and some of them do not wield the influence or draw the worship that the coach does. At a school assembly the master of ceremonies, a student, was introducing his coach. He said, "We look at our coach as our friend here in school." Then he stopped, realizing that with other teachers present this might not be a nice thing to say. But it was what he meant, and so he continued, "Yes, that is what I mean. He seems like one of us." No man who cannot measure up to this job with the best of character and ideals is worthy of the title of coach or is safe to trust with young men.

In the actual job of coaching, the players should be considered as part of the family with whom all matters are discussed and explained. Giving the reasons and proofs for plans and procedures makes the players feel that they are an important, human, and intelligent part of the family.

It follows, therefore, that here is the vital element in coaching. It is through the coach-player relationships that the real opportunity for constructive good lies. Since all activity should be directed toward the realization of a good life, the coach shoulders a tremendous responsibility when he accepts the leadership of young men in sport.

CHAPTER II

COACHING METHODS AND PRINCIPLES

IT HAS been stated (Chapter I) that there are no secrets about coaching or playing basketball. However, the difference in the results that are obtained, discounting the difference in the abilities of the players, is usually due to the methods used to impart to the players information about the game. By this I do not mean to infer that all methods should be the same, but merely to observe that all coaches are not equally successful in their choice and use of methods for effecting the learning of skills and for conditioning responses. Methods vary; the laws of learning do not; yet many coaches fail to recognize the importance of these laws. This chapter is devoted to a discussion of methods and principles that have been used successfully in teaching basketball to junior high, senior high, and college boys and, incidentally, to a statement of the laws of learning as they govern these methods and principles.

QUALIFICATIONS OF THE COACH

1. First, every coach should be himself. Many attend coaching schools and read inspirational treatises by other coaches. They become imbued with the personal magnetism of such leaders. As a result they decide to adopt their leaders' tactics, even to the extent of mimicking their mannerisms and policies. This may prove to be a most disastrous procedure. If a coach who adopts another's methods happens to be a prototype of that individual in habits, personality, ability, manner of speech, and so on, there is a good chance that the same methods will work successfully. If, on the other hand, the two are decidedly different, even opposite types,

10

then to attempt mimicry would be a grievous mistake. The effort would be unnatural and artificial and would appear to be insincere. Imagine, for example, a quiet, soft-spoken, retiring individual copying an affable, dynamic, nervous, dramatic personality! Yet each, following his own bent, might be equally successful. The conclusion, then, is that one may use the experiences of another, but he must utilize those experiences in a way that is adapted to his own natural self.

2. Of course, a coach must be a good judge of human nature so that he can direct each player in the way that will develop him to the limit of his capacity. This may entail slightly different tactics for different types of individuals.

3. A coach must be a shrewd analyst of play so that he may direct the movements of his players into paths which lead to success and to the building of a strong team. He must be able to impress his players with his fairness and good judgment so that they will have confidence in his decisions.

4. A coach must be a patient, untiring teacher. His job is far different from that of the classroom teacher, and his attitude toward it should be different. He cannot present his material once and then pass on. His work is a public demonstration. He must repeat and repeat until his players not only give back wholly what he has imparted to them but have added something on their own initiative. Thus if the coach is to fulfill the requirements of his job, it is obvious that all players must become "A" students, or as near top-grade as unceasing effort can bring them. The coach gets no solace out of the statement—or rationalization—that his students do not measure above average. If his students flunk, then he also flunks. He must therefore be thorough, even to the extent of attaining what may appear to be the impossible. If every teacher realized, as does the athletic coach, that few students ever reach the limit of their capacities, then all teachers would strive to inspire their students to constantly greater endeavors.

5. It is very convincing for a coach to be able to demonstrate. This is just another means of helping a player to see and acquire proper playing habits. Generally, ability to demonstrate adds pres-

tige to the coach in the eyes of his players and gives them greater confidence in him. He can often measure the ability and effectiveness of a player by working on the court with or against him. On the other hand, if a coach is not a capable performer, he should not attempt to demonstrate. He will lose prestige by trying to do something at which he is not adept. It is better that he be able to observe, analyze, and describe clearly than that he show poorly.

6. Certainly every coach should have a thorough knowledge and adequate interpretation of the rules of the game, else how can he lead his boys within the law? It is also a part of the game that the players shall know the rules. Coaches are on the whole very lax in discharging this phase of their responsibilities.

7. Finally, every coach, either by his sincerity, his dynamic personality, his stimulating address, his ability to instill confidence, or by his quiet, strong leadership or other characteristics, should be able to inspire his players to their best efforts. Clean speech and temperate habits cannot be emphasized too strongly. However he may accomplish this end, he must always be himself.

SOME LAWS OF LEARNING—METHODS OF PROCEDURE

As a guide to methods of conducting practices, the more important factors—which are important likewise in the learning process—are listed here:

1. Learning by Doing.

We learn by doing. This is by far the most fundamental law of learning. Of course proper guidance is essential in order that the individual may get an insight into the subject. He will not, however, learn to play basketball without playing it. It is important that the coach, particularly the young coach, recognize this fact. He may have a tendency to talk too much, to correct too often, to be too impatient for immediate results. He must give time for learning to take place. He should realize that he did not become an expert in fifteen minutes.

It is also important that the player appreciate this law. If he expects to be able to perform to the limit of his capacity, he must practice, play. He should seek proper guidance to avoid the formation of poor playing habits, but he must work at the job. Nothing worthwhile and of lasting value was ever attained without effort, and the reward is never greater than the price paid. The law of equilibrium seems to hold in the realm of human effort as well as in the physical field.

2. Understanding the Objective.

We learn faster when we have the proper understanding of the objective or goal desired. This suggests that procedures should be carefully, definitely, and clearly explained to the players. They should be given the reasons for such procedures and proofs of their efficacy. This method gives players confidence in what they are doing and assurance that the results will be worthwhile. Future guidance is thus made easier, and progress is more rapid.

Later in this chapter definite methods of imparting techniques to players are discussed. These methods are also discussed in succeeding chapters. However, in spite of the most painstaking efforts, the real objective may not be transmitted. Here is a case in point. At one time defense was being discussed with a player who had been on the squad for three years. He for some reason had never gotten the main idea of defensive play. Yet he was a most attentive and interested player. He was an excellent student and was ambitious to earn a first team position. One night this boy came to my home to talk over his basketball problems. During the course of our conversation on defense, he suddenly brightened and remarked, "This is the first time that I have realized that the object of our defense is to concentrate on the ball." From that moment he began to be a very important member of the team.

3. The Will to Learn.

The player must will to learn. His desire to gain an objective must be so impelling that nothing can prevent him from reaching that objective. A player with the greatest possibilities may never become a valuable member of the team unless he is intent upon reaching the objective. It is the role of the coach to furnish this incentive. A burning desire to be able to play well, a proper understanding of the goal sought, and diligent practice constitute the necessary factors for the realization of the objectives.

A player came to his coach one time with this remark: "Will you please tell me what is wrong with my play? I like this game. I want to play it, and I am going to make your team before I graduate." This boy was a sophomore and without basketball experience. He did practically everything wrong, but he was well coördinated and had a will to succeed. He carried out every suggestion and at the end of his senior year had not only made the first team but was chosen on the all-conference team.

Another player, whose only handicap was size, was a member of a squad of giants one year. These big men were good. But the little fellow made up his mind that he was going to earn a place on the first team. One day early in the season he challenged me with this statement: "You are not going to be able to keep me off that team this year." That boy made good his challenge. He played more than enough to earn his letter.

A guard on a championship team had not contributed much in the way of scoring during the season. Toward the end of the year the opponents would not guard him, but would concentrate five men against four. This handicap made winning games more difficult. This was the sophomore year for this guard. In his senior year he was the seventh high scorer in his conference and the highest scoring guard, in addition to having improved in the other departments of his game. He had the will to learn.

Examples of this kind are legion. (Many might also be recited to the opposite effect, showing the results of a lack of this will to learn.) These, however, are sufficient to show the importance of the will to learn. Without it progress is slow.

4. The Whole versus the Part Method of Learning.

It has been found [1] that, other things being equal, it is easier

[1] Wheeler, Raymond H. *Textbook of Psychology*, pp. 362-63. University of Kansas, Lawrence, Kansas. (Mimeographed.)

to learn memorizable material by studying it as a whole than by breaking it up into parts and learning each part separately. Further, in maze learning, it was found that the progressive part and the direct repetitive methods were superior to the whole method of learning.

This latter applies directly to the problem of basketball coaching. Kimball [2] substantiated this theory in controlled experiments with a basketball squad. The procedure that has been found to be most successful is as follows:

a. Concept of Whole Pattern of Play.—The players are given a conception of the whole pattern of either offense or defense. This is first discussed and demonstrated to the players on the blackboard in its simplest form. It is stated that the variations will be taken up later. The players then practice the general movement slowly and without opposition.

b. Separate Play Situations.—Next the whole picture is broken up into separate play situations. These are demonstrated and discussed to show how they fit into the whole, and then each is practiced.

c. Individual Fundamentals.—The separate play situations are then used to teach individual fundamentals of the game. These are explained in the light of their effectiveness as a necessary part of team play.

In this way the player first gets a concept of the general team movement. He next sees the application of special plays as a part of and variation from the general movement. And finally he sees the significance of individual fundamental techniques which make for the successful execution of the team play.

Certain advantages accrue from this procedure. First, actual play situations are used as fundamental drills. This brings about an incidental learning of plays and team movements while special emphasis is being placed on fundamental skills. Second, no time is lost in learning rote or isolated drills. Each drill is a part of the team movement. Consequently, the same drills are used for all

[2] Kimball, Ed. A *Test of the Whole and Part Methods of Coaching Basketball.* Master's thesis, University of Southern California. 1935.

phases of practice, but at one time the emphasis may be on fundamentals, at another it may be on team play. Third, by this method we have always been able to maintain interest in fundamental drills. This is quite important because unless there is interest in the practice (the will to learn) there will be little or no learning.

From this beginning, more complicated situations are gradually introduced. Then opposition is used, and soon regulation game conditions prevail. It will be noticed in Chapter III, *Program of Practice*, and in subsequent chapters in Parts II and III that this outline of procedure has been followed very closely.

METHOD OF TEACHING FUNDAMENTALS

Some coaches feel that the job of coaching fundamentals is an arduous one and that it is difficult to maintain squad interest. Since fundamentals are the foundation of a sound game, it is important that interest be maintained during the practice and that a thorough job of teaching be performed. The following plan has been used in teaching fundamentals and has been very satisfactory. Never has there been any lack of interest, in spite of the fact that early season work has consisted almost entirely of fundamental drills.

1. Fundamentals are introduced by showing their specific application to play situations that are to be used.

2. The drills used for fundamentals have always been parts of the offensive or defensive system.

3. The element of competition is usually introduced into the drill. This in itself arouses and sustains interest. The coach must see to it that attention to the details of the fundamentals is not neglected.

4. Only the essential points which govern the correct execution of fundamental movements should be mentioned when a fundamental is introduced for the first time. Not more than four main points need be mentioned in connection with a particular fundamental. It will be possible for a player to remember this small

number of facts, and usually he can apply them immediately. To lecture at great length on a fundamental tends only to confuse the player so that he loses even the important points.

If the important points have been chosen intelligently, adherence to them will assure correct execution of fundamentals. As a player becomes adept at using a technique, additional valuable suggestions may be given to him. In Part II all fundamentals have been analyzed so that they may be introduced according to this plan.

5. Over-coaching should be avoided. As mentioned above, there is greater danger in telling too much than too little. Also, the coach should give a player time to absorb the instruction. Do not be too impatient with the progress of the players. When teaching fundamentals it is a good plan to have the squad divided into several groups for practice. This permits each player to get more work and it also gives him an opportunity to work out his interpretation of the instructions independently of the coach. The coach can then spend his time moving from group to group to watch their work. It is often better to have the players come to the coach for help than for the coach to interfere with their practice. The former method indicates that the players are thinking; the latter affords no opportunity to judge.

FUNDAMENTAL SKILLS AS CONDITIONED REFLEXES

Players should not be form-conscious when they are playing. By this is meant, when team drills are under way or when a game or scrimmage is in progress, the player should not be thinking about his fundamentals. Neither should the coach take time during such periods of practice to correct a player in his fundamental skills. If this is done, the player's mind will be centered on his own individual movements, and he will not progress in team play. As a matter of fact even his fundamental movements will suffer by such a mistake in coaching tactics.

Mistakes in fundamentals should be noted, and such observations can be used as a basis for future fundamental drills. This point emphasizes the fact that fundamental skills must be so thoroughly learned that they become conditioned reflexes of which the player is not conscious.

LENGTH OF PRACTICE

The total time for a complete practice will vary with conditions under which each coach works. However, experience has shown that at least one hour is needed for a practice and that never more than two hours should be used. The two hour period gives sufficient time for dressing before and after practice and for the total practice time. This will allow about one hour and thirty minutes for actual practice. If the practice period is well organized, one hour and thirty minutes will afford plenty of time to give sufficient work even to a large squad. If a squad is limited to fifteen players, an hour and thirty minutes is not needed. Squads of thirty players can be handled very efficiently with this amount of practice time.

The length of time for practicing any part of the game will vary according to the type of drill and the ability to maintain interest. All team drills will require more time than drills on fundamentals. Drills on fundamental skills should rarely continue longer than twenty minutes. As a rule, ten to twenty minutes is long enough for such drills. This does not include the time for explanations. Team drills by their very nature require from thirty minutes to one hour. The longer time is required primarily because of the fact that only a part of the squad may participate at one time. In order to give every member of the squad a chance to work for at least fifteen minutes the longer time is necessary.

Unfortunately these statements are based on experience and observation only. No definite information with respect to learning and the length of time necessary for different drills is available. These statements are based on experience in covering the different phases of the game in preparation for games and upon the sustained interest of the players. It is known from experiments in learning memorizable material that several shorter periods of practice are better than a few long periods. Experience seems to indicate that this fact holds true with respect to sports.

REPETITION OF DRILLS

This subject has been partly discussed before. Further facts of importance from the coaching point of view have to do with the problem of repeating fundamental drills during the season. The tendency of many teams is to neglect the fundamentals once the season gets under way.

Observation on this point shows that the teams which neglect their fundamentals as the season progresses become weaker thereby. Shooting practice cannot be neglected. Plenty of shooting practice must be provided each week. Players tend to get careless in other fundamentals, so that in order to keep a team improving throughout the season it is necessary to return to some phase of fundamentals each week.

A travelling team invariably shows the lack of fundamental practice toward the end of a trip, unless the travelling schedule has been arranged so that opportunities for practice have been provided.

CALISTHENICS

There is little excuse for calisthenic drills in basketball. The game is such that the warming-up exercises of shooting, passing, dribbling, running, and jumping provide sufficient muscular movements for proper limbering exercises. The intensity can be regulated as desired. Furthermore, calisthenics are unnecessary because basketball does not make the intense demands on muscles that are made by football and track, for example. Developmental values can be secured from the elements of the game itself.

Rope skipping is the only exercise used that is not primarily an element of basketball. Boys who are weak jumpers and who do not have good coördination for jumping are able to improve in this skill by practicing the boxer's type of rope skipping. They must, in addition, become proficient in the other elements necessary for effective jumping in basketball by working with a ball around a basket and by jumping against another player.

THE USE OF PLAYER ASSISTANTS

The majority of coaches probably learned the most basketball when they began to tell the other fellow how to play. For this reason unusual results have been achieved by using some of the older and more experienced players on the squad to assist in teaching some of the younger members. This method not only helps the younger players but it focuses the attention of the older boys on details of the game in such a way that they themselves profit by their own instruction. This is one way of maintaining the interest of the older players at a high pitch. It has been tried successfully for both fundamental drills and team play.

In following a method of this kind, one precaution must be borne in mind. The coach must be careful not to use as assistants boys whose personalities may tend to cause friction among the players.

THE USE OF PICTURES

Still pictures have been very helpful in pointing out good playing form to players. The advent of moving pictures, however, has provided another very useful means of instruction. Moving pictures have been the means of transmitting information on the effectiveness of plays, the offensive and defensive movements, and even the techniques of fundamental drills in a more satisfactory fashion than any other method that has been used.

For example, a certain type of offense was designed for use against a certain team. For some reason the players were not able to execute the offense effectively against that team. This meant either that the strategy was wrong or that the idea had not been put across to the players. Motion pictures were taken of a game with that team. When the pictures were shown to the squad and the possibilities of the offense were pointed out, they put the offense into practice in the very next game against that team and defeated it with ease.

Educational films on basketball are now being produced so that the style of play of the great teams of the country may be seen and studied by all players and coaches. The play and techniques of the stars may be preserved for future generations to study and to copy.

CHAPTER III

PROGRAM OF PRACTICE

CONDITIONING FACTORS

I T IS not possible to state exactly or dogmatically what shall be included in a practice schedule each day during the season. There are too many variable factors upon which the program for a particular day is contingent. Conditions are not the same from day to day, or from season to season. The ability, the experience, the condition, the attitudes, the individual differences of players vary from year to year, even though the same players are available in successive seasons. The needs of the players change as competition begins and as the season progresses. Certainly the program of practice followed early in the season would differ from that followed after competition starts, in the middle of the season, and at the end of the season.[1] Likewise, if games are played always at the end of the week, the program of practice for the day before the game should be different from that for the middle or for the first part of the week. A winning team receives far different treatment from a losing team, a novice team from a group of veterans, and a phlegmatic, rugged group from a group of high-strung, fragile players.

For these reasons no coach should slavishly or mechanically follow a set routine. He should judge and analyze all these conditions and then, in the light of such a study, he should organize his practices. Naturally there is certain ground to be covered and plans must be made to cover it, but no plan should ever be inflexible. Conditions during the progress of a single practice may alter the

[1] Chandler, William. A *Scientific Study of Free Throwing*. Master's Thesis, University of Wisconsin. 1932.

22

routine as previously laid out for that practice. A coach should not hesitate to make the necessary changes. For example, if interest has lagged during a certain drill, it would be folly to continue the drill. No further learning at that time is possible. Conversely, it may be wise to continue a drill longer than was originally planned because of the value of additional results that may come from continuation at that time.

SEVEN GENERAL PRINCIPLES

It should not be inferred that no advance preparation for practice is to be made. Such preparation is absolutely necessary in order to prevent waste of time. By thoroughly organizing practice in advance, the coach will find that plenty of time is available to do the desired work without ever practicing longer than one or two hours a day. Certain general principles may be stated which will prove to be valuable guides in organizing practice sessions.

1. *The program of practice should be laid out in harmony with the laws of learning,* as presented in Chapter II. It should be remembered in particular that the players learn by doing and that repetition is essential to retention. In planning a schedule of practice, the coach should recognize the fact that perfection will not be attained at one practice and that time should be allowed for necessary repetition.

2. *Provision should be made for using as many of the teaching devices as possible.* Ingenuity in the use of these different teaching devices, as described in Chapter II, not only arouses and sustains the interest of the players but develops insight into the game.

3. *It is wise to lay out in skeleton form the objectives for the whole season.* This is best done immediately at the close of a season. A review of the past season will always give guidance for the following one. A coach who keeps a record of his practice sessions, and who tabulates in detail the results of these efforts in the light of the accomplishments of the players and the team during the season, can make intelligent plans for the next year. For example, if considerable time was spent on the fast break, what were the

results? Were scores produced in proportion to the time spent and method used in this practice? What were the free throw results in comparison with the plan of practice on free throws? How do these results compare with the results of other schemes that have been used? What were the strong points of the team play? What were the weaknesses? How do these relate to the plan of practice for the season? Where is the system weak? Where is it strong?

In addition one must take into consideration schedule conditions and the material for the next year. Does the schedule differ from last season? Are the hard games coming earlier or later? Is an early season trip in prospect? What are the changes in personnel for next year? What is the difference in the material? Is it experienced, made up of veterans, seniors; or is it green, inexperienced, made up of sophomores? Are there plenty of reserves available?

If questions such as these are raised, and if the answers and analyses are thorough and intelligent, much progress will be made toward a successfully conducted season for the next year. The following suggestions were recorded at the end of the 1937 season for the season of 1938:

1. Perfect diagonal offense.
2. Develop 4-man defense with rover.
3. Work out back court game—rushing man with ball at mid-court.
4. Speed up the ball handling.
5. (Weak on held ball tips.) Devise some new system to get possession of ball after held ball—arrange for considerable practice on this point.
6. Raise free throw requirements to 90%.
7. Spend more time on offensive and defensive rebounds—blocking out around the goal.
8. Use fast break drill for warm-up this year.
9. Assign seniors to assist in early season fundamental practice.
10. For early season competition use 3-on-2 drill.

This list of projects does not mean much to the reader without the background upon which it was based. The list is presented as an actual example of the type of procedure that is recommended. The Stanford team to which this outline has reference was a veteran team for 1938. While two regular replacements were necessary, these were practically decided at the end of the season of 1937. The 1937 team was a championship team and had good prospects of repeating for 1938. It can be seen from the outline that the analysis of the past season and estimates for the next season involved essentially three points:

First, it seemed necessary to introduce new strategy for the purpose of anticipating the probable line of attack from opponents. Naturally a championship team is always on the spot. All opponents are after its scalp. Since this was a veteran team, it was logical to expect it to be able to absorb many advanced ideas. As a matter of fact much more was given to it than was originally outlined. However, the trend of thinking is evident in the outline.

Second, the problem of maintaining a high degree of interest was paramount. It was hoped to accomplish this by raising the standard. For instance, the free throw requirement in practice was raised to 90 per cent. This was 10 per cent above the previous year. Strange as it may seem, a majority of the squad attained this goal. The squad average in competition for the season was just under 70 per cent. This was considerably higher than the year before. The use of the veterans to help with fundamentals during the early season was another move in this direction. This bit of strategy worked out exactly as desired. It happened also that the reserves on the squad were largely sophomores. It was desired to transfer the tricks and habits of the senior stars to them. This was another reason for using the seniors to help with fundamentals.

Third, every weakness should be strengthened as much as possible. Recovery of held balls was one weakness of the year before. Considerable time was devoted to held ball practice. An original formation was devised. As a result 90 per cent of held balls were recovered, whereas less than 50 per cent were recovered the year before. Attention was also devoted to rebounds, with the result that 16 per cent of scores for the season were made from rebounds, and opponents were held to the lowest scores in eight years.

4. *Analyze the results of practice immediately after the practice.* The plans for the following practice should be made or altered accordingly. It has been found best to lay out the plan of practice for a week in advance. The results of day to day practice, however, often necessitate changes. These changes are made on the basis indicated above.

5. *Based on a week-end schedule of games, Monday is a poor day for practice, while Tuesday and Wednesday are the best days for a heavy schedule. A very light practice, if any, should be scheduled for Thursday.*[2]

Monday is the best day for lectures and presentation of plans for the week. It is the day to work very lightly those who played on Friday and Saturday. It is the day to give plenty of work to the reserves and to do any experimenting before the plans for heavy workouts on Tuesday and Wednesday are finally made. Thursday is a good day to devote to plenty of basket shooting practice. The practice time can be cut in half with profit.

There is a tendency to work a squad too hard and too much rather than too little. After the squad is organized and competition has started, it would be much better to permit the regulars to practice twice a week only. They would report for chalk talks on Monday. The reserves would be given a hard workout. The first varsity would join the squad for workouts on Tuesday and Wednesday. No one would report on Thursday. This schedule is based on the supposition that games are played on Friday and Saturday. If other arrangements for games are made, then practice plans would be altered accordingly. However, from the standpoint of the least interference with class schedules and class attendance, and for the most satisfactory practice results, Friday and Saturday games are recommended.

The exact plan as presented above has been tried out with the greatest satisfaction. It was found that the highest degree of enthusiasm for practice was maintained throughout the season. Everything necessary was accomplished during the short schedule of

[2] Chandler, William. *Op. cit.*

practice. The condition and health of the whole squad was the best that it had ever been. The same five players were ready for every contest. A normal weight for each player was maintained throughout. The team was stronger at the end of the season than at the beginning. The whole squad was eager to continue for another month or so after the season was over and was disappointed when it was not permitted to enter a tournament.

This is in contrast to other seasons when practice was held every day. There was never a previous season without considerable sickness and injury. It was difficult to maintain the weight of the squad. The players were all glad when the season was over, regardless of whether they had won or lost. Some coaches even hold practice on Sunday, making a seven day schedule. This is absolutely unnecessary, is a reflection on the organizing ability of the coach, and most certainly is contrary to the best interests of the players.

One might hastily conclude that this schedule of practice is all right for a veteran squad, but not for a young and inexperienced squad. Also it might be reasoned that such a procedure is wise for a winning squad, but not for a losing one. Some experience has been gained on these points. The tendency is to work a squad hard after a loss and to feel that a weak team can never get enough work. This had been my own reaction until I deliberately tried other plans.

After the middle of a season, when the team had been losing consistently and when the morale of the whole squad was low, instead of being lengthened and intensified, the practice periods were actually shortened, and one or two practices each week were cancelled. Where additional practices would have increased the inferiority complex of the squad and deepened the gloom, the reduced load and cancelled practice periods acted as a tonic and gave the squad a new lease on life. The enthusiasm of the players returned, they were rested, and they gained confidence. As a result they not only played better but they won their remaining games. No matter what the status of the team is, the plan is sound.

The above plan has proved so satisfactory in every way that it is recommended to every coach. There is more danger in over-coaching than in under-coaching.

6. *Plenty of opportunity for shooting practice should be provided at each session.* This is one phase of the game that must not be neglected. Sometimes the coach becomes so absorbed in working out his strategy for the next opponent that he does not allow any time for shooting practice. It has been found that shooting percentages in games will be affected to the extent that this practice is neglected. At least twenty minutes each day should be devoted to concentrated shooting practice. It has been mentioned that, if practice is held the day before the game, most of the time can be profitably spent in shooting practice of all kinds.

7. *In general, practice may be divided into three periods:* (1) the warm-up, (2) special drills, and (3) team play. The general content of each period is as follows:

(1) Warm-up.

a. Informal work while squad is gathering.

b. Work with individuals on special points to improve their game.

c. Personal conferences with individuals to discuss features of their game, to encourage, to build morale, to discuss personal problems.

d. Shooting practice.

e. Spontaneous group work. Groups may organize of their own accord for some special work such as passing, team play, special foot work, fundamentals generally.

f. Chalk talks are given at this time, before practice gets under way and players perspire.

(2) Special drills.

a. This is the period of organized practice on fundamentals.

b. Mass drills of all kinds—guarding, dribbling, passing, etc.

c. Parts of team organization set apart for special emphasis, *i.e.*, particular movements of the offense or defense that involve the use of only two or three players and not a whole team.

(3) Team play.

a. Continuous passing by teams on offensive system.

b. Play practice.

c. Fast break practice by teams.

d. Offense through defense, five minute periods for each team to see which scores the more points against the other.

e. Held ball practice with and without opposition.

f. Out-of-bounds drills with and without opposition.

g. Free throw with subsequent play against opposition.

h. Offense against defense with quick break.

i. Regular scrimmage.

TIME FOR EACH PERIOD

The amount of time spent on each of these periods will vary a great deal during the season. In general, however, except when a chalk talk is given, about twenty minutes will be used for the warm-up; on days when chalk talks are given, thirty to forty-five minutes will be used. After competition begins, and on the days before a game, most of the practice time may be spent on this first period. Informal shooting practice is very important at this time, and as a rule, the squad should be given relief from organized work.

The special drill period will consume most of the time during the early part of the season when mass fundamentals are being stressed. If the practice time is from one hour and a half to two hours, as much as an hour will be spent on special drills at this time. Such practices will wind up with short periods of team play of different kinds.

As the season progresses, less time will be spent on special drills. As a matter of fact they will be omitted for the most part. It is, of course, wise to repeat periodically during the season fundamental drills on phases of the game in which the players seem to get careless or to need repetitive practice.

The team play period will not consume much time early in the season, but as the job of organizing the team begins, more and more time will be used for team play. During the early periods of practice it is wise to devote the last period of the week to team play. Thus the week's work leads up to this climax. The players will look forward to this period. In a way it will be a means of measuring progress.

At first, team play should consist of continuous passing drills, simple play practice, and fast break practice, all without opposition. The week-end team play can consist of contests at one basket, hunch games, or offense through defense. As a rule, little time can be spent on team defense (man-to-man is always used to teach individual guarding) during the early season. Not more than twenty minutes to half an hour will be used at first in team play, while later in the season team play will consume the major part of the time.

SAMPLES OF PRACTICE

The following examples are given of types of practice during the different periods of the season and different days of the week. These are schedules of actual practice sessions that were held during the 1937—38 season for the Stanford Varsity.

Early Season Practices

October 12

This is the schedule of the second week of practice. Practice was held three times a week for one hour until after the middle of November. The warm-up period is not indicated here.

1. Talk—equipment, diagonal offense, variations.
2. All-purpose drill.
3. Continuous passing, diagonal offense, variations.

October 13

1. Bull pen drills (see Chapter VIII),
   passing.
   guarding.
   dribbling.
2. Warm-up drill.
3. Guarding drill at free throw line.
4. Fast break by teams.

October 14

1. Free throws.
2. Play practice.
3. Scrimmage.

October 20

1. Shooting from spots—follow.
2. Warm-up drill.
3. All-purpose drill.
4. Guarding.
5. Fast break by teams.

November 30

Practice is held daily by this time and lasts from one and one-half to two hours. The first games were on December 6 and 7.

1. All-purpose drill.
2. Held ball practice.
3. Out-of-bounds plays—no opposition.
4. Offensive play practice with and without opposition.

December 1

1. Bull pen passing.
2. Guarding drill.
3. Guard through offense.
4. Scrimmage.

December 2

1. Talk on games. Squad picked for Christmas trip.
2. Screen plays.
3. Work on defense.

December 11

1. Individual work.
2. Four man defense.
3. Offense through defense.
4. Scrimmage.
5. Squad dismissed until after final examinations.

Mid-Season Practices

Monday, February 14

This was the week following a series with the University of Southern California and just preceding a California game.

1. Talk—games of past week-end, plans for California.
2. Worked reserves:

a. Defense against California.
b. Fast break.
c. Ball control.

Tuesday, February 15

1. Variations in offense to be used against California.
2. Offense against defense.
3. Defense against California offense.
4. Fast break.

Wednesday, February 16

1. Talk—California personnel, criticism of attitude, too much elation over University of Southern California victories (Note: Barely nosed out California).
2. Guard—through offense.
3. Cut-back.
4. Rebounds.
5. Fast break.

Thursday, February 17

No practice. Studied moving pictures of last California game.

Friday, February 18

California game. Practice just before a game always consisted of a short warm-up drill or fast break drill or both, informal shooting from the floor (two players to a ball), and free throw practice. Twenty minutes was always used for pre-game practice.

Practice was of this type throughout the rest of the season.

CHAPTER IV

PICKING THE TEAM

The Problem

THE most difficult task in coaching is that of choosing the players who shall make up the team. This problem involves a three-fold responsibility. Not only is it a job of picking the best players, but it is a job of putting the best players in the right places and of getting the right combination of the best players together. It has quite often happened that the five best players have not made the best team, simply because they did not bring together the right assortment of human elements and characteristics to give a smooth, effective, balanced combination. It also happens frequently that the right combination of players is assembled, but the coach has not assigned the players to the right positions. He seems to lack definite standards which give him confidence in his choices. His only test is the trial and error method in actual competition, and this often proves expensive.

There are, of course, many human and intangible factors which defy measurement, but which are important characteristics of players who make up the team. The rating of players according to these qualities may be made only by the observation and judgment of the coach. On the other hand, there are several aids which may be useful, objective measures of a player's ability as an individual and as a member of a team. These not only supplement the judgment of the coach but they give him confidence in his decisions. They also help the players to get a clear picture of their own abilities. When the coach uses such aids, the players tend to accept their status as fair and just. They feel that they are getting a square deal, even on a losing team, and they are given an incentive for greater effort.

RATING DEVICES

Because of the feeling of uncertainty, even helplessness, in making decisions concerning players, the following procedures were adopted after considerable experimentation.

1. Personal Rating Chart.

The first of these is a Personal Rating Chart. This chart is shown in Figure 1. Here are listed items on which the players are checked. These items represent both positive and negative measures of the performance of the players. The positive factors are shown on the left of the chart and the negative factors on the right. These charts may be kept during scrimmages and early season games. Competent recorders, individuals with basketball experience, should be used to record data. Two charts are needed. The positive and negative records are totalled separately and then subtracted to get the net effect of the player during the competition.

Data from these charts give information concerning an individual without reference to his teammates. They help the coach to rate each individual among his fellows. For purposes of such rating, however, each player should compete for the same length of time, and during the period of rating, each group should be given an opportunity to compete against the other.

The data from the charts have proved very helpful in rating players and have been used as an aid in picking the team. They have also been used to analyze faults and weaknesses of players and therefore have helped in individual coaching. The charts have been kept during a competitive season for both teams, and it has been interesting to compare the results of the tabulations on the charts with the outcome of the games. (Mention was made of this point in Chapter I.)

2. Game of "Hunch."

The second rating aid is the game of "hunch" described in Chapter VIII. This is an early season competitive game, by means of which individuals may be rated. The element of team play is

INDIVIDUAL PERFORMANCE CHART
STANFORD BASKETBALL

GAME _____

PLACE _____

PLAYER'S NAME	Shots		Goals		Rebounds		Assists	Intercepted Recoveries	Held Ball Recoveries	Held Ball		Bad Pass	Fumbles	Violations	Fouls	
	Field	Foul	Field	Foul	Defense	Offense				Defense	Offense				Personal	Technical
1.																
2.																
3.																
4.																
5.																
6.																
7.																
8.																
9.																
10.																

Fig 1. A Personal Rating Chart.

35

involved to a certain extent, but individual performance is the predominant factor. In this game in which there are three on a side and all play for the same basket, the players are paired. They play strict man-to-man defense. The competition is so arranged that in the end each player has competed against every other one. The teams are matched so that competition will be as even as possible. The games are for the same length of time (ten minutes is long enough) so that each player has an equal opportunity. The games should be officiated.

The rating is the net result of the points scored by a player against the points scored by his opponent. After the players have gone the rounds, the totals for each player are determined, and the players are rated in the order of these totals.

This contest makes excellent early season competition. The rating device is great for motivation, and the improvement in individual technique is very noticeable.

3. Penny Cup Test.

A third rating device is the reaction time test, which, for want of a better name, has been called the "Penny Cup Test." Mr. W. R. Miles,[1] in his reaction tests on football players, has shown that there is a very high correlation between reaction time, as shown by the test of players on a football charging machine, and football ability. All players for the same position were rated together.

By including the Penny Cup test in a battery of tests used for a group of boys in eight high schools in Oregon, at the beginning of school in the fall, Bob Knox[2] was able to predict 80 per cent of the first team basketball players. He predicted 90 per cent of the players who qualified for the state tournament and predicted the two final teams in the tournament. He predicted 68 per cent of the all-star team in the tournament.

Diagram 1 shows the plan for this test. The contestant starts

[1] Miles, W. R. "Individual and Group Reaction Time in Football Charging." Research Quarterly, American Physical Education Association (October, 1931) 5-14.
[2] Knox, Bob. Prediction of Basketball Ability in Eight Class B High Schools. Master's Thesis, University of Oregon. 1938.

with his toes on the line at point A. He is facing in the direction of the top of the page. The numbers 1, 2, and 3 are three tin cups, each 25 feet from the starting point. Tin cup number 1 is called the blue, number 2 is the red, and number 3 is the white. At a signal "Go," the contestant turns toward the cups. As he turns, a red, white, or blue ball is tossed into the air. The contestant, who has been given a penny, then runs and places the

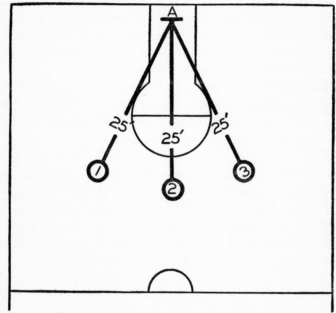

DIAGRAM 1. Plan for Penny Cup Reaction Test

penny in the proper cup as designated by the color of the ball. Time is taken from the signal until the penny is placed in the proper cup. The penny must stay in the cup, and the cup may not be lifted from the floor. Fifteen trials are given each contestant, and the total time for the fifteen trials is his rating. The balls are always tossed into the air in the same order, which is as follows: B, R, W, R, B, W, W, R, B, R, W, B, R, W, B.

In this test one would expect that the small man would perform to best advantage. This did not prove to be true among the varsity basketball players that were examined. The distribution was surprisingly equal throughout the range. The best average time that has been made on the test is 31.3 seconds, the slowest time 51.5 seconds. This is for university players. The best time for a single trial has been 1.6 seconds.

SIX CHARACTERISTICS OF A GOOD PLAYER

It must be remembered that these objective tests are not to be taken as absolute measures of basketball ability. They are aids to the judgment of the coach. They do not measure many of those qualities which make a really great competitor and which can be determined only when the player is seen in action. The coach, however, can materially assist his judgment of players by setting down the criteria which form the basis for his choice of boys for his team. The following are offered as the desired characteristics of a good basketball player. These pegs have been used satisfactorily for several years as a guide in subjectively rating and picking players for a team. They are listed in the order of their importance.

1. Height.

Every coach recognizes the value of height in a basketball player. However, height that is not usable height is of little value. No player should be chosen for a team solely because he is tall. He should be able to move with agility and he should have good reaction time. Height without quickness may be, and often is, a liability to a team. I have never felt that my team was handicapped when playing against an opponent which had one big lumbering behemoth in its ranks. It has been my observation in the many instances when this situation has occurred that the opponents have always played much more effective ball when this big boy has been taken out of the game. He slowed up the rest of the team and was easily "tied up" when he got the ball. It was not possible for him to block shots when the ball was given the proper arch.

Boys over six feet six are seldom effective as basketball players.

As a matter of fact, when a boy reaches this height or goes beyond, I-am always skeptical of his usefulness until he thoroughly proves himself. A boy six feet four is not at all handicapped when playing against one who is taller. Height advantages beyond this point are really negligible. Consequently, the word *useful* should always precede *height* before height is used as a criterion.

2. Coördination.

Hand-foot and eye-hand coördinations are highy essential. There is little place for the awkward, clumsy individual in basketball. Poise, balance, and grace of movement are all evidences of coördination. One must not, however, confuse ignorance of technique, which may be temporary, with lack of coördination, which may be inherent.

3. Reaction.

A basketball player need not be a speedy runner, but he should be nimble and quick. The reaction time of an individual is defined as the lapse of time between the signal for an action and the beginning of the movement.[3] Ability to start quickly, stop instantly, and change direction suddenly are indispensable characteristics of a good basketball player. This is a measure of the reaction time of the individual. The "Penny Cup Test," page 36, in a sense tests reaction time and coördination in movements that are typically basketball movements. It has been found that with practice a player will attain his maximum reaction speed within a short space of time. Therefore it is important to discover early the relative reaction times of players.

These first three characteristics are very important because they are for the most part beyond the control of the coach and beyond the reach of training and practice.

4. Coöperation.

The morale of many a team has been ruined, the success of many teams has been deterred by the refusal of one player to

[3] Miles, W. R. Op. cit.

coöperate. Coöperation here means willingness to put the group above self, to sacrifice personal glory for team success, to submit to a single standard of conduct and training, to be just as willing to follow as to lead, and to become socially agreeable to the group rather than individually rejected. Cliques, snobs, or non-conformists, regardless of ability, do not make for pleasant relations on a squad. Without a happy, friendly relationship among players, the seeds of success do not grow. The old adage, "One bad apple spoils the whole bushel," certainly has its point in connection with a basketball team.

A coach should do everything in his power to produce a good spirit in his squad. Quite often a conference with boys who seem to have slipped will clear up what promised to be a bad situation. Often misunderstandings or misgivings tend to breed bad feeling. These can be corrected by sincere talks. But after a coach goes more than half way to build coöperation within his squad, if certain individuals still do not adjust themselves, everyone will be healthier and happier if such individuals are asked to devote their energies to other endeavors. The best player in the world is no good to a squad unless the proper relations can be established. The coach can do much to develop a coöperative spirit in his boys.

5. Fight.

By this term is meant a willingness to extend one's self, a refusal to admit defeat as long as there is time left to play. Also included in this term is that characteristic which we call competitive ability, the spirit of a player who is the most dangerous when the odds are the greatest and the need is the direst. The player with fight is the one who comes through in the pinch; a player who is a star in practice, but a dub in the game, is not of much value. It is often said that fight is over fifty per cent of any game. My experience has convinced me that this is absolutely true. There is more joy in watching a less capable, but fighting bunch of sophomores than there is in following the play of a sophisticated, seasoned group of seniors. The thing we call college or school spirit is tied up in this word fight. This fight should be spirited but without enmity. It should be enthusiastic but always within the rules and gentlemanly. This characteristic can be instilled in a group by the proper leadership.

6. Judgment.

This factor is placed last in the list of desirable characteristics because it is attained largely through experience in playing. By careful coaching and actual playing experience, the ability to make the correct decisions and the proper moves can be developed during the course of a season within the player who has the other qualities listed above. Therefore, the coach should not be too impatient with the novice. Rather he should estimate and measure carefully a player's other possibilities, lest he cast aside a diamond in the rough.

Of course, all other things being equal, the player with the better judgment as a result of playing experience is the more valuable. However, the sophomore with possibilities is decidedly a better bet for the team than a senior with only experience in his favor. One of the best arguments for retaining a large squad (I always keep thirty on my squad) is that boys with promise for the future have an opportunity to get playing experience during practice sessions. It is also one of the best ways to assure a carry-over of strong teams from season to season, provided of course that the possibilities of development are present. Half of the squad may be used as reserves to scrimmage against the varsity and to mimic the opponents in practice sessions. A regular varsity squad of fifteen players is large enough to have in uniform for games.

PLACING THE MEN IN THEIR POSITIONS

It is seldom possible to choose five players, all of whom have the same characteristics to the same degree. Also, while it is desirable that all players shall be able to play any position, play usually starts with players in certain definite positions. For instance, on offense certain players will be out in front of the defense more than others, while other players will be located around the goal a greater part of the time. On defense certain players, because of size, are more effective around the basket; others are more valuable in positions for fast breaks and for harassing the opponents. Likewise a definite placement of players on out-of-bounds plays, held balls, and along the free throw lanes, when free throws are being tried, is desirable. Because of these facts, and the fact that five tall quarterbacks (the Number One player listed below) are seldom available, the choice of players is listed here in the order of their importance to the team. They should be picked in this order so that the most important jobs will be held by the players best qualified for them. In other words, this is the job of putting the right players in the right places.

1. One Guard.

The player for this position holds the key to the success of the offense. He is the quarterback, the floor general, of the basketball team. He is the play-maker. He may be the outstanding scorer. But above all else, he is the perfect passer, the good dribbler, the player who sees players when they are unguarded. He knows when to make a pass and when not to. He picks out the flaws in the opponent's defense and starts the right plays. In short, he directs the attack. He is intrusted with the ball in all emergencies.

He must be quick and perfectly poised. He must be cool at all times. He must not become excited or confused by the tactics of his opponents. He must have the confidence of his teammates. He may or may not be tall. This player may not play guard on defense. As a matter of fact, he is often the ideal type to harass the opposition by playing in the front line of the defense.

Often this player is found playing forward on a team because he is the best scorer. Because he is in the wrong position, the team does not accomplish the results that would otherwise be possible. Neither does such a player score as much from the forward position as he would from guard. Changes have been made in the placement of players on a team without changing the personnel, with the result that otherwise mediocre performers are turned into champions. The reason, of course, is obvious. Without a play-maker to direct the attack, the ball is not successfully worked into scoring position. The star scorer, if he is also the quarterback, will score more under such circumstances from the guard position than he ever would from some other. Luisetti of Stanford performed all of his phenomenal scoring feats when playing from the guard position. He was listed as a forward because he played that position on defense.

2. Center.

Many coaches feel that their team will be just as strong as their center. To support this contention, they point to the championship teams each year. The centers on these teams are in the majority of cases chosen as the all-conference centers, but it is also true that the quarterback discussed above is always on the all-star team.

The job of picking the center is not as difficult as that of picking the quarterback. It is obvious from the outset whether or not a good center is available. In the first place, he should be tall. A short player might be clever as a "feeder" from this position, but this characteristic is not so important as ability on rebounds. Height is a tremendous asset for rebound work. Since the center is usually under the goal on both offense and defense, height is an absolute necessity. A team without at least two tall players is decidedly handicapped. The small, quick, clever players are valuable, but someone is needed to get the ball for them before they can display their wares.

With height as a prime requisite for the center, the tall player who is most agile, who jumps well, and who rates highest in the other characteristics of a good basketball player should be chosen as center. If two players of equal qualifications are available, and one is slender, nervous, and excitable, while the other is somewhat rugged and phlegmatic, the former should be chosen as center. The latter should be placed as guard.

The nervous, excitable player is in a position where his mistakes will not prove so costly and he can be omitted from most of the passing maneuvers if necessary. In addition, he will occasionally turn in stellar performances. He is likely to come through at the most unexpected times. Experience will usually curb his excitability, and he will eventually become a strong threat on the team.

An important maneuver for a center to perform is to pass accurately to players back of him while he has his back to the goal. It is therefore necessary that considerable time be spent in practice on this point.

A team made up entirely of really great centers would be ideal. This may seem to be a paradoxical statement in view of the importance attached to the quarterback of the team. However, all great centers have the characteristics of a quarterback. In addition, they are always tall. So it might be restated that a team of five tall quarterbacks would be the ideal team.

3. The Forwards.

These players should be at least fair shots and passers. Above everything else, they must be quick. It will be their job to team for the most part with the quarterback of the squad. If they are tall, this is an added asset. If possible, one of the forwards should be tall, six feet in height. He then affords the opportunity for fast break offense, as will be seen in later discussions. It is difficult to make long lead passes to a short player. A tall forward will also support materially the rebound strength of the center. The other forward may be small, but should be exceedingly quick. This quickness will make him a very dangerous defensive player.

4. The Second Guard.

This player, as already stated, should be rugged and not excitable. He may have the slowest reactions of anyone on the team. He is chosen primarily because of his rugged defensive qualities at the backboard. He is a steadying influence on the team. An otherwise high-strung aggregation is kept in hand by the influence of such a player. He is the balance wheel, the salt mixed with the pepper. He is placed at the guard position because he will make few wild moves. He may not see opportunities for plays as quickly as some other players, but neither will he throw the ball away. A mistake by him would be more costly than by another player because there is no one to help him out as is the case with the center described above. This guard, for the most part, will act as the safety man.

Finally, it must be remembered that the ideal is to have five tall quarterbacks. If they are not available, the above descriptions tend to conform to the characteristics of the players found in the usual squad. The placement of the players as nearly as possible according to this pattern will produce the best results.

CHAPTER V

SCOUTING

Definition

BY SCOUTING is meant the observing and analyzing of an opponent's play in relation to the effect that it will have on the play of your own team. It involves not only the study of an opponent when that opponent is playing another team but more particularly when your own team is playing that opponent. A coach must make snap judgments concerning tactics of play during the progress of his own game. These are based on the situation at that particular moment and are far more important than the considered procedures devised a week before the game is to be played. These hurried decisions are just as much a part of scouting as earlier ones and have greater bearing on the outcome of a game than observations that are made a week before.

Therefore, regardless of whether scouting is done in the professional sense or not, every coach should know the vital points to look for when watching two teams play. He should also have a definite procedure to follow in getting this information.

Information Desirable in Scouting

The information may be classed under these headings:

1. Individual Performance.

Most players do some things well, a lot of things in a mediocre fashion, and a few things very poorly or not at all. As a consequence they have a tendency to demonstrate those habits in which they are most proficient and avoid using the movements which they do not do with skill. By careful observation, the playing habits of all contestants may be discerned. Once the strengths and weaknesses of players are known, a team may definitely plan to guard against the strong points and attack the weak points. It pays to play the weaknesses of an opponent. If the scouting has been done thoroughly, a team does not even take a chance when it plays in an unorthodox fashion to take advantage of the weak points in an opponent's game. Some of the typical weaknesses of players and how to play them are listed below.

a. Most players cannot dribble well with both hands. If they are lefthanded they dribble with the left hand, and vice versa. This usually means that, when dribbling around an opponent, they can go only one way. When this weakness is found in a player whose strong play is to dribble around an opponent, the guard, by overshifting, may stop him effectively. For instance, instead of standing directly between him and the goal, the guard should move a step or more toward the side around which the player wishes to dribble.

b. A player may be found to be a good short shot or a good long shot. If he is a good short shot, he should be guarded loosely when far away from the goal and closely when near the goal. A good long shot must be covered every time he gets set for a shot. Many good long shooters must have their feet together just before shooting. This is always a tip to the guard. A player who brings his feet together before shooting is not in a good position to fake or dribble around; so a guard may take more chances in blocking the ball.

c. Some players are altogether righthanded and cannot use their left hands. These players should be guarded on the right side. Fakes or movements to the left do not mean anything and are used to try to pull an opponent out of position. A very outstanding player was of this type. He was stationed at the center pivot spot. He was not a good shot from this position and always wanted to dribble in to the goal by pivoting to his left and dribbling righthanded. By playing from four to six feet from him and over to one side, instead of directly behind him, his opponent was able to stop completely his scoring efforts from this maneuver.

d. Players who are excellent rebound men should always be blocked out from the goal.

e. Many times one finds the individualist. He is a player who will pass the ball only if he must. He will retain the ball in his possession as long as possible and will shoot at every opportunity. Such players may be played incautiously. This is particularly true when unbalanced situations arise, such as two offensive players against one defensive player. When a choice of movement must be made, the guard should play the individualist. If he does pass the ball under such circumstances, it will usually be a bad pass.

f. Some players are weak defensively. They are entirely offensive-minded and are easy to fake out of position. They usually play too straight up, and their general foot work in guarding is weak. As much as possible the attack should be directed at these players.

g. Size should also be noted. Small men are handicapped on defense, hence play should go over their heads. They should be smothered when they have the ball.

h. Speed and coördination should be recorded. Slow players and those poorly coördinated should be rushed when they have the ball. Fast play against them on defense should be the rule.

i. Players who do not protect the ball should be spotted. For example, some players are excellent on defensive rebounds. But when they get the ball, they do not crouch with it but hold it away from their bodies waist high. If these players are "two timed," their rebound effectiveness will be lost, and any possibility of fast break will be stopped.

j. The temperament, poise, and excitability of players should be carefully noted. Excitable or temperamental players may be depended upon to shoot poorly and make mistakes under trying circumstances.

2. Offensive System.

First, the general habits on offense should be noticed. Does the team fast break as a rule or occasionally or not at all? Does the team play a ball control or percentage game, or is it willing to gamble and take chances, shoot from anywhere? Answers to these questions will give a definite idea of the conservativeness of the opponent and will determine the aggressiveness of your own defense against it.

Do the guards enter into the offense in any way other than to handle the ball in front of the defense? Do the guards shoot, or is scoring largely in the hands of the forwards and center? Shot charts should be kept of all games so that this point may be checked.

Next, the pattern of offense used to penetrate the defense should be diagrammed. Is it a continuous movement offense? Is there more than one pattern? Do they play two-out or three-out or both? What types of plays are used? Screen plays? Pivot plays? Weakside plays? Do the plays center around one man? Does the attack go through the defense on the same side always? Are the plays mechanical or are variations and complete freedom of individual judgment permitted? Of all these, the general pattern of movement and organization is the most important factor.

Does the team rebound hard? What is the strongest part of the offensive play?

After these facts, the plays for special situations should be recorded. The most important of these are the out-of-bounds plays. In particular the out-of-bounds plays in the front court at the end line near the basket should be observed. Notes on any movements that will require special defensive emphasis or precautions should be made.

Other situations include the positions and subsequent movements of players on held ball tips, the line-up during free throws, and the center tip formation and play. On held balls do the opponents merely try for possession of the ball, or are scoring plays attempted? Is there a definite formation, or do the players take any position that will give them an advantage over their opponent? To whom do they tip the ball as a rule? Were they successful in getting possession of the ball?

On free throws, where did their best tip-in man line up? Are they good free throwers? Were they successful on tip-in shots? Do they attempt to tip-in or do they bat the ball back to teammates? Where is the most defense needed? What protection do they have on free throws? Is a fast break possible?

On the tip at center what is the line-up? Can your team get the tip? What plays are most likely to succeed? Does the opponent play for possession of the ball only or are scoring plays tried?

A tabulation of information of this type and answers to these and similar questions will give a very good picture of the offense of the opponents. This is the type of analysis that every coach must make.

3. Defensive System.

As a rule there will be less variation in the defense which a team plays than in its offense. A team will play basically either a man-to-man defense or a zone defense. If it plays a man-to-man defense, it will usually be an assigned defense for the purpose of matching the best offense of the opponents with its own best defense. The defense may be of the type that drops back and then picks up the opposing players according to the way the offensive formation develops.

If a zone defense is played, it may be a pure type, where a player is assigned to a particular area and does not move out of that area. Or the defense may be of the team type in which the players are, as a rule, in a certain area, but may move to any part of the court, depending upon offensive situations that may be presented. All these differences should be observed because they will have some effect upon the type of offense that can be used most successfully against them.

Answers to the following questions are also very important. Does the team play a conservative defense, massed about the free throw area? Or is it an aggressive defense? What defensive player should be avoided as much as possible? Does the defense rush in the back court? Will screen plays work? Do the men play close to their men, touching them? Do they try for interceptions? Are they good at blocking out from the goal?

Following this general estimate of the defense, all special defensive formations on the tip-off, on held balls, on out-of-bound plays, and at the free throw line should be carefully diagrammed.

SUGGESTIONS FOR THE SCOUT

For purposes of scouting a basketball team it is best to get a seat high above the playing floor. Such a position gives an unimpeded view of the players and their movements at all times. If the scouting occurs when your own team is playing, it is desirable to have an assistant take a seat high up during the first half.

A shot chart is a valuable record to keep; it affords a good record for the season. During your own games this may be kept by one of the managers. Special books for this purpose may be secured so that a permanent record may be made.

It is best to study the play of a team for at least the first five minutes of a game without taking many notes. This procedure will give an opportunity to form a general picture of the pattern of play of the two teams. After this is done, notes can be jotted down more intelligently.

When your own team is playing, it is a good practice to concentrate on the play of the opponents for the first five minutes of the game. It will usually take your own team some five minutes to hit its stride anyway. You would seldom think of making any changes before five minutes, so that, if you have studied your opponents carefully at the beginning, you will be in a position to make intelligent changes in personnel or strategy if either is necessary.

The scouting notes should be analyzed and summarized as soon as possible after a game while the notes and the game are fresh. The report should be prepared in a form that may be presented to your team not only so that they will have a clear picture of their opponents and their type of play, but also so that your team may have an analysis of the type of offensive and defensive play and strategy that will be most effective against this particular opponent. The report should therefore be presented in the light of the play of your own team. This requires very careful and thoughtful study of the scouting notes. All extraneous material should be omitted, and only those points which are vital to the preparation for the game should be given to the players.

The report may be presented orally or in written form, or both. The practice of working up reports in story form for players to read has been followed most successfully. Then when the players have read the report, profitable discussions may be carried on.

It is not enough to scout a team, to write a report, to have the report read, and to talk about it. The tactics that are to be used against a team should be practiced thoroughly so that playing habits are formed. The best laid plays may fail of execution unless the players have an opportunity to practice them. The procedure is not complete if practice is omitted.

CHAPTER VI

STRATEGICAL SITUATIONS

THREE AXIOMS

THERE are three axioms in basketball play that it would be wise for every team to learn well and to practice continuously.

1. The first is: *Force the opponents to play your game*. The same slogan may be stated in another way: Dominate the play at all times. A team plays its own type of game best. That is the kind of a game it practices most. Its timing, reactions, and habits are all attuned to its own game. Therefore, it is the part of wisdom to play that same kind of a game during a contest.

2. The second slogan is: *Do what your opponent does not want you to do*. This is tantamount to saying that a team should so play that the opponent cannot effectively play its own game. For example, a team that desires to have time to set up its offense before starting to work the ball toward the basket, should be rushed and should not be permitted to get organized. Sometimes slight but strategical changes will entirely upset the usual poise and smooth working of an opposing team.

3. The third axiom sounds like a Boy Scout slogan: *Be prepared to meet any emergency*. Most teams think and practice in terms of their own little narrow field of offense and defense, on the theory that it is not good coaching to load a team with too much offense and defense. This, however, is merely inviting disaster. The well-organized team of outstanding players is best attacked by surprise strategies. If that team is not prepared to meet such emergencies, it may be routed and will be forced on the defensive. It will not be able to dominate the play. The opponent has been

surprised by your doing the thing that was not wanted, was not looked for. The hope of the weak team lies in gambling on such strategies. In this way it will find out if its opponent is really as strong and as great as predicted.

The foregoing is an argument for training a team in the broad general principles of the game. Too many teams are equipped with a very restricted style of play. The average team can be developed into one of the greatest of competitors and a most dangerous contender by adherence to the above axioms.

TEN TYPES OF TACTICS

On the following pages ten types of tactics, strategies, are listed and discussed to show how these three axioms may be and have been applied in actual games. Each one of these examples represents actual experiences that have turned out successfully and that the author believes to be sound practice. They are possible because most teams are not versatile, but are quite mechanical in their play.

1. *Rush a slow or mechanical team.* A slow-moving team does not like to be hurried. It is like a pondering checker player, who studies every possible move before going into action. The slow team is like a patient worker. It plays a conservative game and abhors taking chances. Upset this equilibrium, and all its technique and smoothness collapses. Therefore, it is wise strategy to force the slow team. Experience has shown that it is difficult for a slow, methodical, mechanical team to play fast, or to hurry. When it is forced to play fast, the slow team becomes erratic, excited, and inefficient. Since most coaches are conservative and are distrustful of the initiative of young players, they treat their players as pawns on the chess board and almost literally move them about by hand. It is true that fewer mistakes result from this type of a game, but it is also true that the team playing this type of a game falls to pieces when properly attacked.

Examples of the above strategy are legion, but three recent examples are sufficient to substantiate the facts. Two very prominent teams, favorites to place high in the first basketball competition in the Olympics, fell by the wayside, and both were defeated by teams that were proved by the record of the season's play to be inferior. One of the teams had won twenty-four straight games, only to be humbled by a greatly inferior team, inferior so far as individual personnel was concerned. Other reasons may, of course, be offered for the defeat, but primarily the inferior team won by dominating the play and by not permitting the better team to set up its highly organized mechanical offense. In situations of this kind, where a team has amassed a great record, the tendency for opponents is to try to hold such a team to a close game. They hope they may get a break and win. They do not realize that such reasoning is their own defeat. By trying to hold another team, they play into their opponents' hands. They mass their defense about the goal and permit their opponents to dominate the play, to play their own slow game, and inevitably to win. The team that goes out, not to hold, but to win, and to do it by forcing the play, always has the better chance to win, regardless of the comparative strengths of the two teams.

The second team, Stanford, lost its chance for Olympic fame because it failed to rush its opponent, Oregon State, which was a slow-playing team. The loser was recognized generally as having the better personnel, but it permitted its opponent to nurse the ball in a slow, methodical, crowd-exasperating fashion and consequently it lost. Here again other reasons might be advanced for the defeat—for instance, the sterling play of the opponent—but primarily the defeat was due to failure to apply the proper strategy.

The third example has to do with a conversation concerning styles of play and their effect on teams. It is well known that the teams on the western slopes of the Rockies stress the offensive type of game. They probably neglect defense. But nevertheless they play a pleasingly aggressive, rushing game. Certain western teams had been in the habit of playing these Rocky Mountain teams during the pre-conference competition. Two of the coaches, both in the same conference of the western schools, were discussing their pre-conference schedule. The team of one was playing the Rocky Mountain school, while the other's was not. The coach had definitely cancelled such competition from his schedule because, he said, these teams played such a wild game that his players were completely disorganized. Their play became so ragged that it took them two weeks after such games to settle down. This was equal to saying, "Don't have your team rush my team because such tactics disturb our set, methodical, mechanical play. We do not like to play fast or to take chances." But, unfortunately for this coach, he had tipped off his opponent and colleague to a strategy which has been used most successfully ever since against him.

2. *Use screen plays on a close-guarding team.* Some players are taught almost literally to hang onto their opponents. While this is ineffective guarding when the speed and quickness of the players is the same, nevertheless it works when the offense is slower and not as shifty as the defense. In such cases it is usually necessary for one teammate to aid another so that he may escape his opponent to receive the ball for a shot at the basket. To accomplish this end, screen plays are used. Screen plays, if properly executed, cause defensive players to shift men. Such shifts usually leave one of the offensive players in a scoring position. It should be remembered that screen plays will work against a man-to-man, a zone, or a team defense under close-guarding conditions.

3. *Pull key defensive men away from the basket when a man-to-man defense is used.* The fact that defensive men can be lured away from the basket is one of the outstanding weaknesses of a man-to-man defense. The only salvation of the defense in this case is to hope that the offense is not versatile enough to take advantage of it. As a rule, the best rebound players on a team will be so assigned that they will play around the goal. A versatile team will maneuver so that the players who are good goal tenders do most of their playing out near the center line of the court. A study of Diagram 11, described in Chapter XVII, will demonstrate how this may be done.

4. *Tease a nervous team.* A young, inexperienced team is often nervous and impatient. If such a team does not get its fingers on

the ball regularly, it tends to get panicky. If an offensive team will play "keep-away" with such a team for a short time, its defense will tend to disintegrate in its frantic efforts to get the ball. Stunts like this often turn a close game into a rout.

5. *Play keep-away with a threat in the last few minutes of a game.* When many teams play keep-away, they weaken their attack, they are subject to rushing tactics, and they become the objects of booing. If the keep-away tactics are a part of the regular offensive movements, so that there is always a threat of a score, then few can detect that a stall game is being attempted. The guard-through movement, as shown and discussed on page 199, is typical of this kind of keep-away tactics. The fact that someone out in front of the defense is passing and then breaking for the basket always gives a threat of scoring and in addition opens up passing lanes. If the defense becomes too aggressive, opportunities for scoring may be capitalized.

6. *Play fast against a team that is not in condition.* When it is found that an opposing team is not in good physical condition, it should not be permitted to drag the game along. Even though the game becomes ragged for a time and no appreciable results are noticed immediately, the speed will eventually take its toll. The accuracy of the opponents in shooting will soon be destroyed, and their reaction time will be considerably slowed. In the end speed will often defeat an otherwise superior team.

7. *Mass the defense about the free throw area on a poor long shot team.* The massed defense increases the difficulty of working the ball in close to the basket for a short shot. It practically forces a team to take long shots, and these usually spell its downfall. In using such tactics, a defensive team should not be deceived by a few random long shots which may score goals. These shots are only used to draw out the defense and will not continue to succeed.

A very good example of such strategy occurred in a Stanford-U.C.L.A. game a number of years ago. Frank Lubin, who played guard in college, seldom if ever took long shots. In the final game with U.C.L.A. that year, the Stanford defense was instructed to

mass about the free throw line and let Lubin shoot if he chose.
Evidently Coach Works of U.C.L.A. had anticipated such tactics.
The first two times that U.C.L.A. brought the ball into offensive
territory, Lubin shot long, without hesitation. Incidentally he
scored on both shots. It appeared that the Stanford strategy was
all wrong. However, Lubin did not take another long shot during
the game, and by effectively stopping the deadly short shots of
the U.C.L.A. team, Stanford squeezed out a victory at the end.

Of course, the converse of this strategy should be used against
a good long shooting team, *i.e.*, always cover the man with the
ball when he is set to shoot.

8. *Put four men through on a team which plays a zone defense
or a team which always leaves two men out.* This strategy, of
course, demands accurate ball handling by a team. It puts four
offensive men against three defensive players and will produce a
score in the majority of attempts. There should be no fear of a
fast break. The best place to stop a fast break is at your own
goal, before the play gets under way. In other words, tie up the
player who rebounds the ball. To use any other method destroys
your own offensive threat and thus weakens the scoring ability of
your own team. If the defense plays three out and two back, then
the job of scoring is made much easier. Often only three offensive
players will need to go through the defense.

9. *Two-time a star at every opportunity.* This job is made much
easier if there happens to be one weak cog in the opponent's
line-up. Certainly, if a choice must be made between stopping a
star and letting a weaker player go unguarded for a moment, the
star should always be stopped.

10. *Play to the peculiarities and weaknesses of an opponent.*
Many of these will be discussed in subsequent chapters, and only
enumeration of the principal points will be made here.

If a player seldom shoots or is a poor long shot, let him go when
he has the ball. This will permit five players to guard four and
will greatly confuse the offense of the opponents. Do not worry
if he happens to take a shot once in awhile or score a goal or two
during the game.

If a player can dribble in only one direction, overshift in that direction, even though the defensive position is not one that would be ordinarily considered fundamental.

If a player can shoot in only one way, plan for that one shot, even at the risk of permitting other shots.

If a player is a ball "hog," remember that in a pinch he will keep the ball. Play him accordingly, regardless of other considerations.

If a player is slow and a poor ball handler, charge him when he has the ball. The first six baskets in one particular Stanford game were scored by such tactics. The ball was stolen from the opponent.

If a player is excitable and lacks confidence, yell at him, rush him, and he will become confused. Often he will throw the ball to you.

If a player has a tendency to overrush on defense, use stops and fakes against him.

These are a few of the many peculiarities and weaknesses that are found in players. The methods of attack require, in many cases, a certain amount of daring. If, however, advantage is not taken of these opportunities, a weakness in a player is inconsequential. A team must be willing to take chances. A weak team has no other choice. A strong team becomes even stronger when it takes them.

Finally, as has been emphasized throughout, if a plan of attack is to be carried out successfully, it must be practiced.

CHAPTER VII

TRAINING AND CONDITIONING; EQUIPMENT

TRAINING AND CONDITIONING

Definitions

TRAINING and conditioning, as used here, refer to those practices which best prepare the player for efficient performance and healthful living. Efficient performance is attained through a carefully planned program of progressive practice which will perfect coördination, eliminate unnecessary moves, accomplish results at the expense of a minimum of energy, and condition the muscle structure and the circulation to withstand without harm the intensive demands made upon them.

By healthful living is meant the adjustment of habits of eating, sleeping, protection against exposure, exercise, drinking, and of social and mental intercourse, to conform to the increased energy consumption of the body caused by the heightened level of activity.

No Need for Pre-Session Calisthenics

Some basketball coaches plan to have their training program start even before the students register for school. They lay out a comprehensive system of calisthenics for their candidates to follow. Except as a plan of exercise that may be useful when the individual leads a more sedentary existence, there is little need for this emphasis—overemphasis—on the sport. As was stated in Chapter II, there is little need for calisthenics in basketball, and certainly they are not necessary weeks and months before actual practice begins.

Procedure for Best Method of Conditioning

The early practice for a season should be organized so that the intensity of work is increased gradually. There is little excuse for a basketball player's having sore muscles or sore or blistered feet. The coach should feel responsible when these occur. If the type and amount of work is gauged correctly, then the player should reach perfect condition without suffering any ill effects whatever.

Specifically, players should not at first use drills which require too much squatting. The fundamental position is all-important, but strenuous practice at first will develop extremely sore quadraceps muscles. Drills which require quick stops and pivots should not be used intensively at first. These will cause sore feet because a great deal of friction on the feet comes from this exercise. For the same reason early season scrimmage should be avoided or should be of very short duration. Drills not exceeding ten minutes, if they are not intense, are sufficient for the first week. If the players are not pressed, but rather are held in check, discomforts of the kinds just described, can usually be avoided. Passing and shooting drills, which require mostly straightaway running, fit into this first week of practice.

After the first week, the intensity of the pace may be gradually increased until the players are able to play a full game without excessive fatigue. Once the players reach this point in their training, it is not difficult to maintain excellent condition. The practice of reaching playing condition as rapidly as possible is preferable to that of continually increasing the pace until almost midseason. Once the team is in good condition and well organized, practice sessions may be lightened and practice need be held only twice a week for the regulars. If as many as two games per week are played, the games themselves provide sufficient strenuous activity for the regular team.

Many coaches are afraid that their teams will go stale if they push the players to top season form too early. Staleness is really a mental condition. It consists of a loss of interest caused by too much emotional tension and too much practice. The plan of lighter and fewer practices, as outlined above, together with constant emphasis on and practice of the idea of fun when playing, will remove any possibility of staleness. As a result of the foregoing system, the problem of curbing the enthusiasm of the squad has always been a greater one than that of instilling interest.

With respect to habits of healthful living, it may be said in general that one should live during a period of competition in the same manner as one should when not competing. In other words, if it is healthful to get sufficient sleep, good food (in the right proportion), to guard against sickness, and to abstain from intoxicants and from smoking during a training season, it is just as healthful to follow a similar regimen when not engaged in strenuous competition. Regularity and temperance at all times, in all habits, are very good principles to follow.

The Proper Diet

Since food for athletes is always a subject of much discussion, this part of the training regimen is discussed in detail here.

The problem of diets is always a difficult one. It is difficult because of the many cults, theories, phobias, and individual eccentricities with respect to diets. However, in general a balance between the amount of carbohydrates, proteins, and fats should be maintained. This should be done regardless of the activity of the individual.[1] According to Dr. Walter H. Brown, head of the Division of Hygiene, Stanford University, who supervises all training table diets at the University, this balance in calories should contain 10-12% protein, 32-40% fat, and 50-58% carbohydrate.[2]

Fortunately, the problem of maintaining a proper diet with young athletes is not a difficult one. They are healthy, vigorous,

[1] Sherman, H. C. *Food and Health*. New York: The Macmillan Company. 1934.
[2] Brown, Walter H. *Constructive Hygiene Syllabus*. School of Hygiene and Physical Education, Stanford University. (Mimeographed.) 1937.

and always hungry. They are eager to do the thing that will help them best to gain their end, namely, a place on the team. So, with the proper guidance, they will follow enthusiastically.

The feeding of the Stanford basketball player during training has consisted of the following basic diet. He could have other food, but in order to provide a nutritional balance he must have included in his daily diet the foods listed below: [3]

> 1 quart of milk.
> 2 servings of fruit—one fresh.
> rye, corn, or wholewheat bread.
> 3 vegetables—one must be served raw, as in a salad; one should be leafy; and one a root.
> potatoes.
> butter—three pats.
> eggs—two; alone or in some food.
> meat (beef or lamb recommended) or fish once daily.
> wholewheat cereal once daily.

The food should be cooked simply. Rich pastries, fried food, or highly seasoned food should be avoided. The normal diet should contain an adequate amount of the bulky, residue-containing foods to insure natural movements of the bowels.[4]

The quantity of food that an individual needs is dependent, in general, upon the weight of the individual and upon his activity. Below are listed different levels of activity. Opposite these are listed the number of calories per pound of weight of the individual that are needed to maintain that level of activity [5]:

Sleeping .... .43 calories per pound per hour
Sitting (in class, study,
    eating, etc.) .... .67   "   "   "   "   "
Light exercise (slow walking,
    archery, etc.) .... 1.10   "   "   "   "   "

[3] Sherman, H. C. *Chemistry of Food and Nutrition.* New York: The Macmillan Company. 1937.

[4] Sansum, W. D. *The Normal Diet.* St. Louis, Missouri: C. V. Mosby Company. 1928.

[5] Storey, T. A. *Principles of Hygiene.* Stanford University: Stanford University Press. 1930.

Active exercise (golf, danc-
ing, tennis, field hockey,
baseball, riding, etc.) .... 1.95 calories per pound per hour
Severe exercise (basketball,
football, swimming, box-
ing, etc.) .... 3.00   "   "   "   "   "

By tabulating the amount of time spent in each of the activity
levels in twenty-four hours, one may calculate the energy consumption of the body in calories for a day. Carbohydrates and proteins
yield approximately 1,800 calories per pound. In fats there are
approximately 4,000 calories per pound. From these figures the
amount of food necessary to maintain the proper level may be
determined.

It has been our experience that we have had very few digestive
upsets since our training table diets have been carefully super-
vised. One precaution has been necessary when travelling. The
players are much less active on the train than when they are going
through their regular daily routine of practice. Their appetites,
however, seem to be even more voracious, if that is possible. It
has been necessary, therefore, on long trips to reduce the quantity
of food to as much as one-half, while at the same time the balance
is maintained. It is well to remember that there is greater danger
in over-eating than there is in under-eating, the howls of the young
athlete to the contrary notwithstanding. A lean, healthy grey-
hound runs faster than a fat, sluggish one.

Pre-Game Meals

There are two prevalent practices with respect to pre-game
meals. Some coaches follow the practice of having their teams eat
a heavy meal at three o'clock in the afternoon when the game is
to be played at eight o'clock at night. This disturbs the regular
meal time habits of the player. The other practice is to have the
team eat a very light meal at five-thirty, preceding the eight o'clock
game. This does not disturb the regular routine because the usual

meal time is around six o'clock. This latter plan is, therefore, much to be preferred.

At this five-thirty, pre-game meal the maximum amount of food that should be eaten is a dish of canned peaches or pears with syrup, two pieces of toast with preserves, some very weak tea, and two poached eggs. A predominance of sugar (quick energy) will be noticed in this diet. Many players will not eat the eggs. This meal in particular should be eaten under the most pleasant and happy conditions. An attempt should be made to remove the nervous tension usually present just prior to a game. Digestion cannot take place properly when the digester is undergoing emotional strain. Therefore, game talk should be taboo.

Desired Mental State before Games

This free, relaxed condition of players not only stimulates the digestive fluids but furnishes the right mental attitude for the game itself. A team that is too tense never plays well. Here we are concerned with the mental hygiene of the player. The following experience is an actual instance of an emotional situation before a game.

The Stanford team was eating its pre-game meal before the first championship game in 1936 against the University of Washington. It was a sophomore team. This game meant a great deal to it. A Stanford team had not been in a championship series since 1921. Here was history in the making. For the first time during the season the players ate their pre-game meal in silence and looked down their noses. It was evident that they were thinking too seriously of the game. Every attempt to relieve the situation seemed forced and unnatural and fell flat. Something heroic had to be done to save the situation.

Dinty Moore, captain and guard, and Howell Turner, forward, were usually late to such meals (the squad always slept in the afternoon before a game). This time the meal was half over when they arrived, arm in arm. As they passed behind the chair of Hank Luisetti, who was more than serious on this occasion—he was visibly jumpy—they stopped, hesitated for a moment, and then chanted in unison, "I'll see you tomorrow night after the game, Eleanor." Someone had overheard Hank talking over the phone to a girl friend.

This was the needed relief. Dinty always seemed to be able to supply it at the right time. The color gradually crept up Hank's neck to the base of his hair. He betrayed his guilt and for a moment was so embarrassed he could not speak. Everyone began to roar with laughter. The pressure was off. This spirit carried through the game, and Stanford pulled one of the most surprising and overwhelming upsets in Pacific Coast championship history. Stanford won the game 63 to 30. Luisetti had scored 32 points in 32 minutes.

Drinking and Smoking Habits

Drinking and smoking have no place in a program for healthful living or successful playing. The words of Dr. David Starr Jordan, first president of Stanford University, state the case very clearly:

Many years ago I formulated my views on smoking as "Three counts against tobacco": First, nicotine, the essential content of tobacco, is a deadly poison, acting—in small quantities—as a nerve irritant under the guise of a sedative. Any drug, however, which affects the nerves tends to put them out of order, thus deranging the most delicate of all machinery. Second, nicotine retards the development of the growing boy and weakens virility. Third, the tobacco habit begets a lack of consideration for the rights of others, pollutes the air, and causes much discomfort to those not hardened to it. Furthermore, to be hardened is not a sign of strength, but rather an indication of loss of sensitiveness on the part of nerves which should be delicately alert. The advice given by Professor George F. Swain of Harvard to his graduates in Civil Engineering, "Let your competitors smoke," seems to me good sense.

In the matter of alcohol, my theory has been as rigid as my practice. Accepting the validity of conventional temperance arguments drawn from physiology and the need of social sanitation, I press the case still farther. The sole purpose of alcoholic drinks is to force the nervous system to lie, and thus to vitiate its power of recording the truth. Men use alcohol, weak or strong, to feel warm when they are really cold, to "feel good" without warrant, to feel emancipated from the restraints and reserves which constitute the essence of character building. Alcohol is a depressant, not a stimulant, appearing as such only because it affects the highest nerve operations first.

Its influence impinges alike on the three chief mental functions, sensation, reason, motion. It leaves its subject uncertain as to what he sees or feels, hazy as to cause and effect, and unsteady as to resultant action. No man of high purpose can afford to endanger the validity of these nerve processes which register his contact with reality.[6]

Coach as Leader and Example in Training Habits

In this phase of training, as well as in all others, the coach must act as both an example and a leader. The excuse that the coach is not competing and therefore has no reason to follow the same training rules has a very weak and hollow sound. If these training practices are healthful and therefore desirable, then they are just as valuable for the coach as they are for the player. If a coach is to retain the respect of his players and is to be an influential leader, then he must not expect them to do anything that he is not willing to practice himself.

Protection against Exposure

There are several protective measures which should command the attention of the coach. Players are sometimes very careless about exposure after exercise. Three precautions may be taken in this connection. Each player should be provided with practice sweat clothes. Gray cotton, fleece-lined, long pants and shirts are very satisfactory. They will wear for several years and may be laundered. Each player should have his own, and for sanitary reasons no exchanging of equipment, without first having it washed, should be permitted. These sweat suits should be put on after

[6] Jordan, David Starr. *The Days of a Man*, Vol. I, pp. 47-48. New York: World Book Company. 1922.

exercise to prevent too rapid cooling of the body. Individual face towels should be provided. No two players should be permitted to wipe on the same towel. Pieces of worn out turkish towels cut into squares furnish excellent face towels. After showers the players should be cautioned to dry thoroughly. Particular attention should be given to the hair and to the feet. Most students do not wear hats; so the hair should be dry before they go outside. The fungus growth, which is "Athletes foot," likes a moist environment; so the feet, especially between the toes, should be carefully dried. Likewise, walking around on cold damp gymnasium floors with bare feet is not a wise practice.

By constant supervision the coach can develop in his squad intelligent habits with respect to protective measures of this kind. There are of course many other similar and worthwhile habits that should be encouraged. The attempt here has been simply to call attention to this phase of a coach's responsibility and to mention a few of the more important precautions.

The Bugaboo of Fatigue

The problem of fatigue caused by the strenuousness of basketball has been very much in the public eye. Attention has been drawn to this problem largely because of recent rule changes, i.e., the 3-second rule, 10-second rule, and elimination of the center jump. If there is grave danger of over-exertion, certainly this should be a concern of the coach. No coach should ever do anything that would jeopardize the health of a boy. Certainly no sport should be sanctioned if it is too strenuous for the players.

Fortunately several studies of the fatigue caused by the game are available. None of these gives any credence to the fears of the public with respect to over-exertion. At Rockford, Illinois, five doctors followed the high school team throughout its season of play during 1937–38. They examined the boys regularly every week to determine, if possible, any ill effects of basketball, from a physiological point of view, that might be revealed. They studied pulse rate, blood pressure, respiration; they took cardiographs and made several other observations. They found that the reactions of the boys at all times were within the normal physiological limits that would be expected after exercise of this type. They found no ill effects resulting from participation in the game. This team was the championship high school team of Illinois.[7]

A study of the recovery time of athletes after playing tennis, swimming definite distances in prescribed times, after playing basketball, and after running a 440-yard dash indicated that, on the basis of the time for the recovery of the pulse rate and blood pressure, the 440-yard dash was considerably more strenuous than playing a full game of basketball.[8] And yet in a single afternoon a track man may run a couple of 440-yard events and possibly a 220 or a half mile. Very few, if any, question this practice. In the light of the above, certainly the strenuousness of basketball should not be questioned.

Dr. Naismith, in 1924, made rather extensive studies of high school boys during the Kansas State Basketball Tournament. His study was based on urinalyses. In general he found no deleterious effect of basketball, even through the exciting stages of a tournament.[9]

EQUIPMENT

PROTECTION OF THE FEET

Equipment is discussed here primarily as it pertains to training and to protection of the players. Shoes are the most important item of equipment. A basketball player is just as valuable as his feet are sound. Because of the fact that he plays on a hardwood floor; goes at a terrific pace; makes lightning starts, stops, and turns; and is continually jumping, the feet of the player are subjected to more wear and tear than they are in any other sport. It is therefore most important that he have perfect-fitting, comfortable

[7] Porter, H. V. *Proceedings of the National Association of Basketball Coaches.* 1938.

[8] Bunn, J. W. *Proceedings of the National Association of Basketball Coaches.* 1938.

[9] Naismith, J. N. *Basketball Guide.* American Sports Publishing Company. 1925.

shoes. The toes should not extend to the end of the shoe. About a half-inch of play is desirable. This protects the toes from rubbing and crowding on sudden stops. The rest of the shoe should be snug, but not tight. A good arch support and a snug fit about the arch is desirable. The inside of the heel of the shoe should be well cushioned to absorb the jar. The shoe should extend above the ankle and should fit tight about it.

Leather uppers are recommended because they can be made form-fitting much more satisfactorily than can the canvas ones. A leather upper is not recommended unless the shoe is of a type that can be rebuilt at a nominal cost, because the extra expense of the leather shoe will not warrant its use. The author has used a type of leather shoe which meets these specifications, and as a result, after five years, every pair of shoes was still in use.

For further protection of the feet a light pair of cotton socks should be worn next to the skin. Over these should be a heavy pair of wool socks. Two pairs of socks tend to relieve some of the rubbing and to lessen consequent danger of blisters. The cotton socks next to the skin are further protection against athlete's foot. It has been found that this fungus thrives on animal tissue, and the cotton sock separates the wool sock from the foot.

Sweat Suits and Game Uniforms

The value of sweat suits has been stressed already. These will be needed for games also, but here the matter of appearance is important; so, in addition to protection, aesthetics are brought into the picture. It is well to consider the attachment of hoods to the game sweat suits. These are particularly valuable for keeping the neck and head warm when going from the dressing rooms to the court and back and while sitting on the sidelines during the games.

In choosing materials for game uniforms and sweat suits, three points should be considered. First, *comfort*. Rough and scratchy materials should not be chosen. They irritate the skin and cause real discomfort. Second, *appearance*. Basketball players are very close to the spectators so that neatness or lack of it is very notice-able. Uniforms should be made to fit. Pleasing, harmonious color schemes should be used, as well as colors that will contrast with opponents' uniforms. Brightness and richness of appearance are desirable. The dress, of course, does not make the player, but it certainly sets him off in a pleasing fashion. Third, *durability*. Here is a real problem for the coach. When one realizes that it is a simple feat to spend as much as twenty-five dollars per player for equipment, he should expect to receive long wear from the equip-ment. Certainly sweat suits should be expected to last from four to eight years. Game suits should last from two to four years. Therefore, unless one has a very generous budget, one should choose one's materials with this factor in mind. It does not pay to buy cheap equipment, but neither is it economy to buy expensive material that is not durable. There are many shiny materials on the market that look exceptionally well, but the fabric breaks so easily that even before a season is over the suits are worn out. Color-fast materials should always be secured.

There is such a difference in tastes and there are so many good quality products on the market that no attempt is made here to do more than state general principles.

Many coaches emphasize the importance of long hose for basket-ball. The importance of such equipment is vastly exaggerated. Long hose are an additional expense and are too often uncom-fortable. The advantage is doubtful even from the point of view of identifying teammates.

Likewise, as fancy dictates, knee guards may or may not be used. Abrasions seem to occur as often with knee guards as with-out them. They are very uncomfortable to many players and inter-fere with their freedom of movement.

BASKET BALLS

One hears considerable comment on the different types of balls and their durability. Since the ball is an expensive item, it is a very important consideration. However, it has been found by a thorough test under playing conditions that almost any of the standard makes of balls is satisfactory.[10] It has not proved profitable to buy the cheaper grade of balls. The materials are of poorer quality, and consequently the ball does not hold its uniform shape, the general stretch is greater, and the period of actual usefulness is reduced. Occasionally defective materials appear, but such exceptions do not represent the general quality of the grade A balls.

The new, molded ball is a valuable development. As its design is improved, it will be universally used. It will prove more economical and will hold its shape. The use of wax on the ball acts the same as a wax job on the finish of an automobile. Dirt is kept out of the grain of the leather. The color is maintained for a longer period. The same grip or feel of a new ball can be kept throughout the useful life of the ball. As the ball tends to lose its grip, it should be cleaned and rewaxed. A damp (not wet) towel usually suffices to clean the ball. A light application of saddle soap may be used for cleaning, but if an application of wax is maintained, the soap is not necessary and is not recommended.

Game Equipment

In connection with the games themselves, a water and towel cart should be provided for each team. A square cart with five compartments is a very valuable part of the game equipment. A wet and a dry towel, as well as individual paper drinking cups, should be provided for each player. Sections of oranges are also refreshing to players during time-out periods. If all of these are kept in the carts, they may easily be brought to the teams during time-out periods. Towels are thus kept off the dirty floor, and each player has his own equipment. This is much more hygienic than the common water bucket and towel method. Every coach should read the recent survey that was made of sanitary practices in the high schools of the State of Illinois.[11]

[10] Bunn, J. W. *Op. Cit.*
[11] Jackson, C. O. "Practical Sanitation in High School Athletics." *Illinois High School Athlete*, IX, No. 4 (December, 1936); No. 5 (January-February, 1937); No. 6 (March, 1937); and No. 7 (April, 1937).

CHAPTER VIII

PRACTICE DRILLS

THE problem of suitable and effective drills for practicing techniques in basketball is always a difficult one to solve. If drills are too complicated, they require too much of the players' time to learn the drills. This leaves little or no time to practice the technique for which the drill was intended. It has been found that drills which are used only as drills are seldom remembered for long. They represent rote learning, and time is lost "re-learning" the drill each time it is used. Since practice is always against time, those things should be done which will accomplish the most in the shortest time.

For these reasons we have set down five rules as guides in choosing or planning drills:

1. *The drill should be as simple as possible if it is to be used as a drill only.* If a drill has no connection with the team play movement, but applies only to the practice of some individual technique, little time should be wasted in learning a complicated movement which has no future use. The coach who feels that he does not have enough time to get everything done will probably find some of the reason here. Efficient planning and organizing of the practice by the coach will usually produce capable, efficient players.

2. *A drill is more useful if it can be adapted to the teaching and practice of a great number of techniques.* It will be observed that one of the drills described below is called for this very reason an "all-purpose" drill. This reduces the total number of drills. It should be stressed, however, that usually only one phase of the drill will be emphasized at a time. For example, if shooting technique is the point to be stressed in a particular practice,

73

attention should be focussed on this one thing to the exclusion of all others. They are incidental to the main issue for the moment.

3. *The drill should, if possible, be made into a game and should be informal at all times.* It is felt that the most good will be obtained for the greatest number if practice and playing are made to be a lot of fun. Everyone should enjoy himself. This is good mental hygiene in practice. Since health is our main objective, we must not lose sight of it in our desire to win. Some will say that the joy will come after the winning. This may be true, but to me the real test comes when we find that a group has fun even when it loses.

Boys like to play and they do not like laborious, tedious drill. If the drills can be practiced, then, in the spirit of a game, two ends are accomplished—a happy, healthful boy and a perfected technique. I really think that adherence to this philosophy accounts for the fact that my boys never seem to have enough of the game. After a most gruelling season they are always back on the court during the spring quarter—just to play.

4. *The drill, if possible, should be taken from a part of the offensive or defensive system that is to be used.* By this plan several things are accomplished. The offensive or defensive movement is being learned as an incidental part or by-product of the drill. The player sees the application of the particular technique to the type of game that his team will play. The practice has sound qualities, in that the ultimate aim or goal—the reason for the particular technique—is kept before the player in an incidental manner.

5. *As few drills as possible should be used.* It is not considered here that little special stunts that may be used with an individual to get across an idea, to demonstrate a special movement, or to correct a particular fault, are to be thought of as drills. Similarly the special practices that are suggested following many of the explanations of fundamental techniques are not considered as drills. Drills, as the term is used here, are practice formations that make up the backbone of our organization of practice.

Following are the drills that have been used day after day and year after year. These are not taken at random from a list of drills that may have been used at one time or another, or that are merely suggested. They are the drills that form the backbone of practice. They are changed at times, yes, but when a change is made or a new drill is introduced, it replaces something that was used before. The number of drills, therefore, is kept at about the number that appears here. These drills are the result of many years of study of our game in order to find what was needed to perfect it and then what was the best way to accomplish that end. It should be observed that comments are made after the drills to indicate at what times during the year they are used and for what purposes.

Bull Pen Pass

One of the best drills for teaching faking, deceptive use of the eyes, all kinds of passes, and individual guarding tactics is one that we have called "bull pen." The drill is used every day early in the season. It also serves as a good drill for the reserves just before a game, during the time that the starting five are practicing free throws.

A circle is formed by at least six players and not more than eight. This circle is the bull pen. One player is chosen to get into the pen to start the game. He is the "bull." A ball is given to the players forming the circle. They pass the ball back and forth from one to the other. However, no player may pass to another on his immediate right or left. If he inadvertently makes such a pass, he must take the place of the bull in the pen (Diagram 2).

It is the job of the guard (bull), who is inside the circle, to touch the ball. When he touches it, the player who last touched it before him must take his place in the circle. The guard may use any tactics that he chooses. However, if he is making guarding errors, his opponents are sure to take advantage of them. For instance, if he assumes the wrong stance (the wrestler's stance instead of the boxer's), they will bounce the ball between his legs.

The circle may be made large or small. If the guard cannot

seem to get the ball and tires, the circle is made smaller, and the passing becomes much snappier and cleverer. If a fresh player, or a particularly good guard, gets into the pen, the players will gradually enlarge the circle in order to give him a real work-out and to make his task the more difficult.

It is surprising to see how much fun the players get out of this game. It has the element of teasing in it. Then the players may

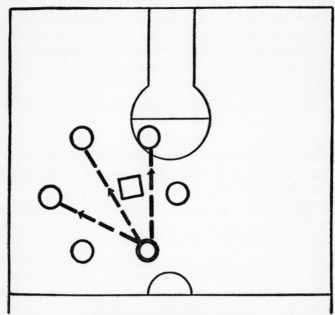

DIAGRAM 2. Bull Pen Pass Game

work to get a certain player in the pen by continually passing him the ball until he is caught. As the passing develops, a player may be put in the pen for making a bad pass. This now requires someone to form judgments on the passes. There has been a noticeable improvement in passing since this drill was adopted, and it made the guards very shifty.

WARM-UP DRILL

"Warm-up" is a drill which the author used for several years when the team first came on the court before a game. It was also used as a part of the daily drill early in the season and intermittently throughout the season.

This drill has the element of timing in it. The players are in motion when they receive the ball and shoot. The receiver must judge when to dart for the basket. The passer must judge when to pass the ball, how hard to throw, how much lead to give the receiver. Good practice in every one of our short passes and the hook pass is obtained from the drill which simulates actual playing conditions, but without opposition. It gives practice in cutting across the court to meet the ball, in rebounding from the backboard, in changing direction, in pivoting, in stopping, in faking, in shooting (both left and right handed), and in getting back into the court after a shot to receive the ball. The movement in the drill is also a part of our regular offense; so, incidentally, the players are getting practice in a phase of their team play.

The players line up on one side of the court just inside the side line. They are in single file and all facing toward the goal. The front player in the line should not be closer than thirty feet to the end line. (Diagram 3.)

To open the drill, the player at the head of the line starts to dribble toward the end line and then cuts across to the free throw line. When he is inside the free throw circle, he stops and pivots. The second player in the line darts for the basket as player Number 1 pivots. Player Number 1 passes to player Number 2, who shoots a one hand shot for goal. Player Number 1 follows in to the goal to recover the ball. He passes it to player Number 2 who, after shooting, gets back into position on the court to receive the pass. Number 1 now goes to the other side of the court to continue the drill from there when his turn comes again. Player Number 2 then passes to player Number 3, who by the same route that was followed by player Number 1, has come to the free throw circle to receive the pass. Number 2 then falls in behind

Number 1. Player Number 3 passes to player Number 4, who has followed in the footsteps of player Number 2, and the drill continues as long as desired.

Since the players work in pairs, they should arrange themselves in the line as their turn approaches so that all get practice in both passing and shooting, as well as in the other elements involved. Diagram 3 shows the movement in this drill.

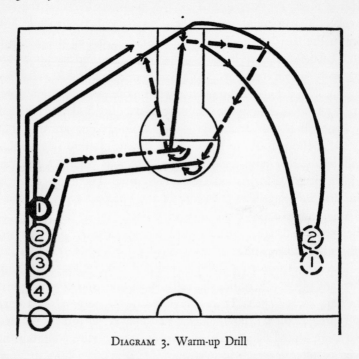

DIAGRAM 3. Warm-up Drill

It can readily be seen that various passes can be used. Many variations are introduced in the drill from time to time during the season. The drill is so simple that it can be learned in a few minutes. It was given to a group of boys twelve to fourteen years of age. Only two of the group had ever played basketball, but they learned the drill in less than five minutes.

The play element that always seems to creep into this drill is the effort to make as many consecutive good passes and goals as possible. The boy who misses is kidded, and the boy who makes a good recovery of a poor pass and then scores is cheered.

Continuous Passing Drill

In order to start a squad toward learning the general features of a pattern of offense as early as possible, a continuous passing drill is used. Work is started on this movement during the first week of practice and is continued throughout the season. This drill is the basis of an offensive movement. It has all the elements of a balanced offense in it. To this drill plays and variations are gradually added until it comprises a complete offense for the season. The details of the offense will be discussed in the chapter on team offense; only the simple passing drill is described here.

The drill is used at first as a vehicle for passing practice. The fact that the players are learning the system of team offense that will be used is quite incidental. Nevertheless, this fact gives an added incentive for enthusiastic and spirited practice, because in the drill the players see a reason for the different types of passes. I have come to the court may times and found the players of their own initiative formed into teams of five and working diligently on this drill.

The drill is somewhat complicated and requires longer to learn than any of the others, but since it is the foundation of our offense, the time is well spent. It was taught to this same group of twelve to fourteen year old boys, (mentioned above), in fifteen minutes. No team would adopt this drill unless it were also adopting the type of offense which is involved. The drill may, however, suggest a means of developing a similar drill which fits the needs of another team.

The squad is divided into groups of five. As many groups can practice at one time as there are half courts to practice on. The movement of the players is shown by Diagram 4. In order that all players may get practice in all positions, the movement should be reversed after the players become familiar with the movement in one direction.

Players in positions **Z** and **X** should be on the inner third of the court at all times. They should be at least six feet away from the center line. Players in positions **T** and **R** on either side of the court should, as a rule, start back of the free throw line extended —that is, between the free throw line and the nearer end line. They should be six feet away from the side line. They must be

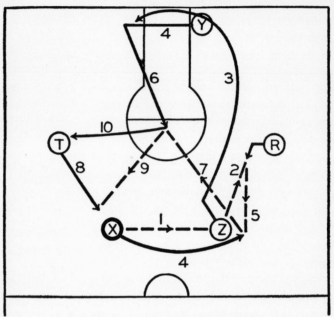

DIAGRAM 4. Continuous Passing Drill

careful not to crowd in toward the center. The player in position **Y** may be on either side of the free throw lane and anywhere along the free throw lane.

The movement, as indicated in Diagram 4, the timing sequences, the particular footwork, and the passes are as follows:

Z and **X** may pass the ball back and forth between them, imagining that there is an opponent against them and that they are jockeying for an opening. They may even criss-cross back and forth, exchanging positions as they handle the ball. They may floor bounce, push pass, or one hand underhand pass. While this is happening, T and R should maneuver up and back along the side line. When Z has the ball, R should come out to meet it. R's first move is to step laterally toward the center of the court, and then dart out to meet the ball. Z then starts the drill by passing the ball to R. Z may use a bounce pass, a roll pass, a push pass, or a two hand underhand pass. These give an idea of the variations, which depend upon the circumstances. As Z passes, he darts past R, between R and the center of the court. R fakes a pass to Z. Z continues to a position along the free throw lane on the opposite side of the court from R.

As Z passed R, X came over to take Z's place. Also as Z passed R, Y retreated to the side of the free throw lane opposite to R. R now passes the ball to X. T now starts out to the position originally occupied by X.

As X receives the ball, Y darts to and beyond the free throw line, where he receives the ball from X. Y should so time his movement that he does not stop until after he receives the ball. R now retreats to his original position.

Y fakes, as long as he is allowed, in the free throw area and then passes to T. After passing to T, he moves over to the position originally occupied by T. The movement is now ready to begin again.

If there is not sufficient space for the whole squad to work at once, the groups can alternate. Usually three minutes of continuous passing is enough for one time.

It is probably better to have the players start this drill with a push pass. Then, as they begin to learn the movement, the passes may be varied to fit hypothetical situations of play. Likewise variations in the movement and additions to it may be introduced gradually. Also opposition will be added as the players become conditioned to the drill. Finally it develops into a drill for practicing offensive movements of all kinds against a defense in one half of the court. The numbers indicate the sequence of movements.

HUNCH

How the name of "hunch" ever became attached to this drill is beyond me. But hunch it is, and so far as I know, it has always been hunch, although this is, I believe, a purely local name.

The game of hunch is played with not more than three on a side and may be played with two on a side. Four on a side are too many. One team starts with the ball and passes it around among themselves in an attempt to score. Their opponents try to prevent them from scoring. If the ball is recovered by the team defending the goal, this team then attempts to score at the same goal. If one team shoots, the other team may rebound the ball and score. The score counts for the team caging the basket. After a score has been made, the team scored upon is given the ball beyond the free throw circle, from which point that team must put the ball in play by a pass; and then the game proceeds as before. The game continues until one team scores twenty-one goals.

This game is particularly valuable in the practice of rebounding. It teaches aggressiveness and gives passing practice in competitive situations. It is also very good in developing team play on both offense and defense. We use it early in the season, before our systems of offense and defense have been developed, in order to give our players scrimmage competition. As a rule, we play strictly a man-to-man defense so as to check on the individual guarding technique of each player.

During the time that this drill is used as a part of our organized practice, a score is kept for each individual, showing how many goals he scores against each of his opponents, and how many goals are scored against him. The players are rotated so that a different opponent is drawn each time. The teams are balanced as nearly as possible.

These scrimmages are always officiated; otherwise more harm than good may come from them. Ten minutes is long enough for each group to play during the early part of the season because, under the conditions outlined, the competition is always intense.

A very good estimate of a player's ability can be made as a result of this drill.

We never use this drill after we get into our system of team offense and defense. However, the players like the drill very much and play it informally throughout the season. There are two dangers in it which must be controlled or they will be a detriment to the players. There is a tendency to dribble too much and to foul indiscriminately.

Fast Break Drill

The fast break drill has been so named because it was designed to give practice, primarily, in the final movement and ball handling incident to our fast break. It is also used to practice the principle of cutting to the center of the court when in possession of the ball along the side line. The pivot and follow-up after a pass are also valuable parts of the drill. At times a guard is used in the free throw lane to teach deceptiveness. This drill is good for use as a warm-up drill before a game. It has not been used very much, as a rule, until quick break practice is begun later in the season. At this point it becomes a regular part of practice several times during each week.

Three lines are formed as shown in Diagram 5, one in the center of the court and one along either side line. The ball starts with the center line. As soon as the player at the front of the center line receives the ball, the players at the front of the line on each side start for the basket. The ball is thrown to one of them immediately. This player dribbles the ball and cuts to the outer half of the free throw circle. Here he stops, fakes a pass to the player on the other side of the court and pivots back. After the player in the center line has passed the ball to a player on the side, he cuts around to the outside of this player and breaks for the basket. As the player in the free throw circle pivots, the next man in the center line breaks down the center of the court and toward the basket. He receives the ball from the pivoter. After

receiving the ball, he immediately passes it to either of the players
on either side of him. As he passes the ball, he advances to a
point just inside the free throw line and receives a return pass.
He immediately passes to the player from whom he did not receive
the ball. This player shoots, and the other two are in position to
rebound. The player who pivoted stands on the free throw line
for a pass out. It is evident that after this routine is learned many

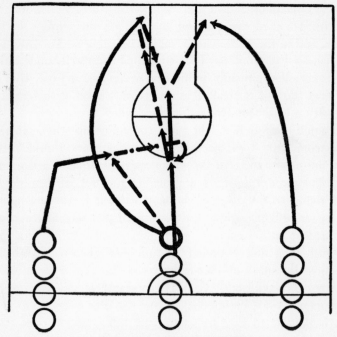

DIAGRAM 5. Fast Break Drill

variations of passing around the basket may be introduced. This
practice, particularly with a guard, or an imaginary one, in the free
throw lane, will help to develop some very clever ball handling.

No particular sequence has been used for rotating the players
from one line to another. It has been found to be less confusing
and much simpler merely to instruct them to get into one line
or the other on their own initiative and to alternate from one line

to another. In this way, practice at every position is obtained.
More players will, of course, be needed in the center line.

ALL-PURPOSE DRILL

The "All-Purpose" drill is named after one of Pop Warner's
golf clubs. Pop at one time manufactured his own wood clubs.
He put the shafts in the center of the head as in a croquet
mallet. One shorthandled club with a very heavy head was his
favorite. He used this club off the tee, on the fairway, in the
rough, and in the traps, with equally satisfactory results. One day,
when he was playing out of a sand trap with this club, one of his
foursome asked him why in the world he used a wood club in
the trap. To this query Pop replied, "Oh, this is my all-purpose
club. It's a good club to use for everything."

The following drill has so many good uses that, remembering
Pop's comment, it has been named the "all-purpose drill." It is
good for the practice of dribbling, approaching and attempting
to dribble around a guard, stopping, faking a pass, pivoting to
both right and left, trailing, driving by a guard, several kinds of
passes, screening, guarding, and shooting. It happens that we have
side baskets on our court; so we terminate each drill with a shot
for goal. The drill does not form a part of our offensive or
defensive system, and therefore is very simple to learn. It is
excellent for mass work. We use it constantly in our early season
fundamental work, but do not use it much after mid-season.

It is possible to have six all-purpose drills going at once on a
full length court. The squad is divided into six groups, but only
four players in each group can participate at one time. These
groups form six lines along one side line. The lines are equal
distances apart as shown in Diagram 6. The general set-up and
movement of this drill may be seen in this diagram.

Each group is given a ball. Two players in each group are
stationed as guards in tandem across the court in front of their
groups. The guards should divide the distance across the court
into equal thirds, so that the distance from the first guard to the

player with the ball is equal to the distance between the guards,
and this distance in turn is equal to the distance between the
second guard and the other side of the court.

For the best supervision, all groups should work simultaneously.
The players with the ball get ready to dribble, with one knee
down on the floor, the head back, and the ball extended at arm's

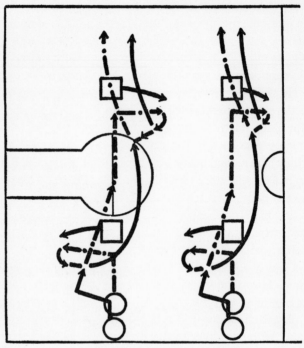

DIAGRAM 6. All-Purpose Drill

length in front and on the floor. The signal can be given, "On
your mark—Get set—Go." All start dribbling toward their first
guard. As they approach him, they all cut to their left. The guard
moves over to prevent the dribbler from going around. At first
the guard should play a passive game. As the players become adept
at the drill and at the various techniques of the drill, then more
competition and opposition may be offered. The dribbler stops

and fakes a pass forward. He then pivots. The next man in the line is directed to trail about ten to fifteen feet directly back of the dribbler at all times. As the dribbler pivots, this trailer darts by him and receives the ball. The trailer now becomes the dribbler and approaches the second guard. The first guard has finished his job, so goes to the back of the line of his group. The first dribbler now becomes the trailer. As the second guard is approached, all dribblers cut to the right (the dribbler's right). The guard moves over to prevent the dribbler from going around. The dribbler stops, fakes, and pivots back. The trailer now comes through for the ball. As the ball is passed to him, the pivoter, after passing the ball, continues with the dribbler to keep between him and the guard. He thus acts as a screen and the trailer may continue in toward the side goal and shoot.

At the finish of the shot, whoever recovers the ball throws a catcher's peg pass back to the player across the court in the front of the line. The second guard now goes to the end of the line, and the two players who were handling the ball (the offensive players) become the two guards for the next drill. The next drill is begun by the commands as before. This organized method of starting each drill permits an opportunity for offering suggestions, if necessary, before the start each time.

It is a very good plan to designate players to give the commands each time. This develops leadership and gets the players over any self-consciousness that they may have. Talkative players are confident players. Talkativeness is a valuable asset for every player to acquire. Better results with this drill will be obtained if the players start slowly and gradually work toward speed and snappiness.

Individual Guarding Drill

Offensive fundamentals and team play are always stressed first because they are the more difficult to learn and to perfect. When work on defense begins, the individual guarding drill is an excellent mass drill for teaching most of the phases of individual guarding technique against competitive situations.

We have six baskets on our court that can be used for this work; so the squad is divided into six groups. This group idea has proved to be a very valuable teaching device for much of our fundamental work. The coach can give an explanation of the drill to the whole squad. Then, when the squad breaks up into groups, the coach moves from one to another. While he is watching, demonstrating, or making suggestions to one group, the others are busy. In this way fewer players are kept idle at one time. There

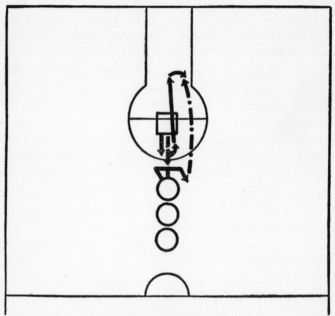

DIAGRAM 7. Guarding Drill

is less chance of over-coaching, which is the greatest fault of most coaches. The opportunity of doing a technique with freedom is offered every player. This last encourages players to think for themselves and for their group and to work out their own difficulties, a process which is one of the best aids to learning.

The player who is to guard takes the ball and stands on the free throw line. The rest of the players stand in file outside the free throw circle and directly in front of the basket. When the guard is ready to play, he tosses the ball to the player at the front of the line and proceeds to guard him. By having the guard start the play in this manner, the proper timing is given to the drill.

The player with the ball may tease the guard as much as he wishes in order to get the guard off balance or out of position if possible. The offensive player may shoot from his position or may attempt to dribble around the guard for a set-up shot. In any case the ball is in play until a goal is made, or until the guard recovers the ball or it goes out of bounds or a foul or violation is committed.

After completion of the play the offensive player becomes the guard, and the guard goes to the end of the line. The players should change around in the line somewhat so that they do not play against the same player all the time. Each guard may take two or three trials before he goes to the end of the line.

While this drill is designed primarily for defensive work, it is evident that some good offensive practice is also derived. Diagram 7 shows this drill in its simplest form. The guard passes to the player on the circle. This player fakes and then attempts to dribble around. The guard drops straight back to set a new guarding position and then advances toward the ball.

Ten Goals Net

Whenever shooting is neglected during practice, the effects of such neglect are always reflected in the shooting percentages of the game. The tendency on the part of the coach is to become too absorbed in developing offensive and defensive strategy against his opponent. Practicing the strategy to be used against your opponent is important, but never should anything interfere with adequate goal shooting practice each week of the season.

Shooting drills tend to stimulate interest in this phase of the practice. Competitive drills, after the technique of shooting has been learned, tend to improve shooting in game situations.

The game of "ten goals net" gives practice of this kind. In addition, it gives practice in versatility of shooting. To be able to score from only one spot on the floor is the same as helping to make the defensive play of the opponents easier. This game encourages practice in shooting from either side and from the center of the court. This drill is used after team-play practice gets under way and on the day before a game, when most of the time is spent in shooting.

The game is best played by two players competing against each other. More may participate in the same group, but a larger group tends to slow up the drill too much. One ball is used. The players start at one corner. If one player scores and the other misses, then one goal is counted for the one who scores. They next move out to a spot which is on a line that makes an angle of about 45 degrees with the backboard and at a point about 25 feet from the basket. Now if the player who missed the first time scores on this shot, while his opponent misses, his goal will cancel the goal made by his opponent on the first shot. Thus the net score is now zero. The game then is to get a net of ten goals.

The third spot is at the outer edge of the free throw circle and directly in front of the basket. The fourth is the same as the second but on the opposite side of the court. The fifth spot is in the corner opposite the first spot. The shots are rotated from one spot to another in order until one player secures a net of ten goals.

This drill affords good practice in medium-long floor shots and is a means of preventing too much shooting from one spot on the floor, without at the same time necessitating too much supervision from the coach. While this game is quite simple, it has a real challenge in it. The players like it so well that they get out early in order to start their competition. It has the particular advantage of being a very informal drill. The improvement in shooting and the confidence that players acquire as a result of this drill have been definitely measurable.

GAME OF TWENTY-ONE

The game of "twenty-one" is another shooting game, but is different from the game of "ten goals net." It generally affords practice in medium-long shooting from one spot on the floor. The apparent fault of this drill can be corrected easily by changing the spot from which the players shoot after each round. The game is more competitive than "ten goals net" because the winner is determined by the team which first scores twenty-one points. This fact increases the intensity of the competition. It also speeds up the shooting. The opposing contestants do not take turns, but each group shoots as fast as it desires. The drill also gives good practice in follow shooting.

We have used the game to conclude early season practice drills, and later, groups of players play it informally throughout the season.

There are many ways of playing the game. Two sides are needed. One or more players on each side may be used. The sides may or may not be equal in number. The opposing groups may or may not shoot for the same goal. We have found that on the whole more complications arise and greater interest is aroused when both groups shoot for the same goal. Any spot on the floor may be chosen from which to shoot. Each group should use relatively the same spot.

Generally the game is scored by counting two points for a goal made from the chosen spot on the floor. If the goal is missed, the player who shot can score one point for his side if he is able to recover the ball before it touches the floor and then shoot a goal from where he recovers the ball. The side first scoring twenty-one points wins.

THREE ON TWO

"Three on two" is an offense and defense drill. We have used it primarily as a means of teaching the shifting and sliding movement in our team defense. The principles involved are certainly necessary at any time when two defensive players are confronted with the job of guarding three offensive men. These principles and the technique of two guards covering three offensive players are explained under guarding situations on page 183, Chapter XV.

The purpose here is to show a means of practicing these techniques.

If one desires to give two players continued practice in guarding three players, then it is only necessary to have the three offensive players pass the ball about until they score or lose possession of the ball. This procedure is followed when practice on a situation of this kind first begins. A rather interesting game has been made of this type of practice.

The two defensive players continue on defense until the offense misses its try for a goal or until the ball has been recovered by one of the defensive players. When either of these events occur, one of the defensive players becomes an offensive player, and the offensive player who missed his try for goal or who last touched the ball before it was recovered by a guard becomes a defensive player. This change of position takes place each time the defense recovers the ball or a goal is missed. In this way the competitive element is introduced and the fun of a game is added. It seldom fails to give every player plenty of work on both defense and offense.

Two on One

The same procedure is used to make a game out of two offensive players against one guard as was described for the game of "three on two." In this drill, when an offensive player misses a goal or loses the ball to the guard, he becomes the guard, and the guard becomes the offensive player.

Offense through Defense, Out-of-Bounds Drills, Held Ball Drills, Free Throw Drills

In these drills, two teams are lined up against each other. The plays or movements used for scoring in these situations are practiced. In order to give each team practice on both offense and defense, and to give each team an opportunity to test its ability against the other, a game is made out of this practice. Each team is given ten trials. A trial consists of continued possession of the ball until a goal is made or until it has been recovered by the defense.

After one team has had ten trials, that team goes on defense, and the defensive team plays on the offense and is given ten trials. The team scoring the most goals is the winner. The incentive offered by this drill keeps both teams on their toes on both offense and defense. Instead of conducting these drills on a trial basis, a time limit may be introduced. Five minutes is enough for each period.

PART II

INDIVIDUAL TECHNIQUES

CHAPTER IX

THE FUNDAMENTAL BASES OF ALL PLAY

ALL of our successful individual techniques in basketball are predicated on two basic principles. The first has to do with body balance or control. All of our essential movements and maneuvers depend for their successful execution on body balance. This is true in all sports. We have made a very careful study of body balance as it pertains to basketball. We have kept in mind the effectiveness and efficiency of all the necessary movements. It is desirable to maintain a pose from which one can move quickly in any direction and at the same time be ready to change direction just as quickly, from which one can jump vertically or reach out horizontally to best advantage and without interference, and from which one cannot easily be dislodged by the common incidental contacts that occur in basketball.

As a result of observing players under all conditions of play (dribbling, shooting, guarding, stopping, passing, pivoting, jumping, protecting the ball, etc.), of observing soldiers in marching drills, and of observing the movements of animals (particularly cats and tigers), and of studying the laws of equilibrium, it seemed wise and possible to adopt one position from which to initiate all movements. This is a fortunate development because it simplifies the learning of techniques when all start from exactly the same position. It saves time from the standpoint of eliminating many practice drills and teaching devices. This one position we have called the "fundamental position." It is the safety position in basketball, and it is the first thing that we teach to all of our players.

THE TECHNIQUE OF THE FUNDAMENTAL POSITION

POSITION OF FEET

Because of the fact that most players tend to assume a position more nearly vertical than horizontal, in order to get normal results the extreme fundamental position should be taught. The feet should be spread so that they are just wider apart than the width of the hips. One foot should be slightly in advance of the other. Under conditions of stopping and pivoting, the particular foot to advance will be discussed. The forward foot should be pointed in the direction that the player is facing, while the rear foot is turned so that the heel is nearer than the toe to the median line of the body. The toe of the rear foot should be slightly to the rear of the heel of the forward foot. This position of the feet gives good lateral balance and thus eliminates a striding stance and prevents a tendency to fall forward when stopping. The turning of the rear foot relieves a certain muscle tenseness in the leg due to the lateral spread.

THE CROUCH

For purposes of putting the body in a stable state of equilibrium, and at the same time of making it possible to move quickly and with a minimum of effort, a deep knee bend is used. The extreme position is to sit on the heel of the rear foot. The tendency of players is to throw the weight of the body almost wholly on the forward foot. By "sitting on the heel," the center of gravity of the body is held almost half way between the two feet and thus the weight of the body is equally distributed on both.

POSITION OF BALL

In situations where the ball is being handled, the shoulder should be over the forward knee, and the arm should be to the outside of this knee. The ball should be held so that it is between

Fig. 2.   Hank Luisetti in the fundamental position.

the legs, just to the side of and in front of the forward foot and practically touching the floor, if not actually on the floor.

POSITION OF CHIN

To finish the picture, the chin should be out away from the chest as far as possible. That is, the head is back much in the fashion of a rabbit sitting in its burrow, but alertly on guard. When the head is held back in this fashion, it is possible to see to either side and to the rear without the interference of the shoulders. With the chin held in against the chest, which is a common fault, the shoulders act as blinders and cut off all vision except straight ahead in much the same fashion that blinders on a "scarey" horse prevent him from seeing too much. A basketball player should see as much as he can all the time. He should be alert, a little "scarey," so that he is not surprised by his opponents and so that he sees all possible opportunities for plays to his teammates.

Figure 2 shows a player in the fundamental position. Each of the above points may be carefully studied in this figure.

With the player in this position the ball is well protected from attack by the opponents, and the player is well poised for any eventuality. As a matter of fact, he resembles a porcupine to a certain extent. His pointed elbows, sharp tailbones, square shoulders, and rugged hips are all painful projections for any opponent who ventures too close and is too aggressive. Yet he is alert and ready to react most quickly to any atttack.

This, then, is the fundamental position from which a player, no matter how tall or how short, starts his shot, starts his dribble, passes; and which he assumes when stopping, after rebounding, when preventing a held ball, when taking a ball away from an opponent, when being guarded closely or from the rear, after recovering the ball in a scramble of players. In guarding, the same general position is maintained, except that the crouch is not quite so extreme and the trunk is not inclined so far forward—and, of course, the player does not have the ball but is fighting for it.

DRILLS

Aside from actual play situations, only one drill is used for teaching the technique of the fundamental position. The players may be lined up, arm's distance apart, along one of the side lines of the court. At a signal of "Go," all players start across the court. At signal "Stop," every player assumes the fundamental position. It is best for beginners to walk at first, and then, as the technique is learned, the movements may be accelerated. Since in all our stops the two count rhythm is used, the player will find it easier to assume the fundamental position with the least amount of jar to the body if he will hop or skip into the position. At the same time the knees and trunk should bend in an elastic movement. This will remove practically all of the strain and tension in stopping and will be found to be a successful means of placing equal weight on both feet.

The value and effectiveness of this position can best be shown by citing the following examples of actual situations where a decided advantage is to be gained by the use of the fundamental position and where trouble arises when the position is violated.

RECOVERING THE BALL FROM THE OPPONENT'S BASKET

The extreme fundamental position is most useful for protecting the ball, for preventing a held ball, for avoiding the end lines, and for getting out of a group after recovering the ball from the opponent's basket. In this last situation, when the player recovers the ball with his arms stretched high above his head, he should bring the ball down against his chest as quickly as possible. This causes the elbows to extend beyond the sides of the body and affords considerable protection from attack by the opponents. He should alight with the feet spread as in the fundamental position. Immediately upon reaching the floor, he should bend over the ball and take it to the floor forcefully as he assumes the extreme fundamental position. At the same time, he should start moving toward the side lines in an attempt to get into an open

Fig. 3. Jack Calderwood in first step in recovering the ball from the backboard. Ball is caught at highest point of jump. Player has legs spread to make room for himself.

Fig. 4. Second step in rebounding. Phil Zonne has brought the ball to his chest. The elbows are extended to the side for protection.

FIG. 5. Third step in rebounding. Phil Zonne has reached the floor and is crouched over the ball.

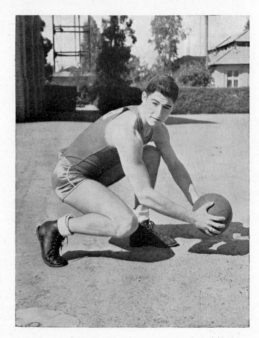

FIG. 6. Fourth step in rebounding. The ball is forced to the floor. The player is shown in the extreme fundamental position.

part of the floor so that the ball may be passed to a teammate without interference.

If the opponents are aggressively rebounding for the ball and the above procedure is not followed, a held ball and even loss of possession of the ball by having it stolen by an opponent or by carrying it out of bounds may result.

Sometimes, after a player assumes the fundamental position, the opponents crowd from both sides in an attempt to get the ball or to cause a held ball. The player with the ball will always be warned of this situation by reason of feeling his opponents with his protectors (the elbows, shoulders, hips, buttocks). If he has made room for himself by his low squatting position, he can successfully escape by quickly drawing his feet together and pivoting out toward the center of the court.

Figures 3, 4, 5, and 6 show the progressive steps in correct rebounding. In Fig. 3, the player is shown as he gains possession of the ball. Note that he is directly under the ball and that possession is gained at the height of his jump and reach. Figure 4 shows the ball after it has been brought to the chest. The elbows protrude from the sides of the body. This position gives excellent protection for the ball. The expression of the player's face indicates that he has brought the ball to this position forcefully. Figure 5 shows the player as he alights. He is not yet in the full fundamental position. The body is bent over the ball, and a crouch stance has been assumed. The ball, however, is still at the chest so that if any opponent has a hand on the ball, the greatest force may be exerted to take it to the full fundamental position where complete protection is assured. Figure 6 shows the final and fundamental position, which completes the maneuver. The player is now ready to move out away from the goal and end line.

RECOVERING THE BALL FROM OWN BASKET

Often a player is not in a position so to control the ball after it rebounds from his own basket as to make a successful tip shot. But usually in this situation it is possible to gain possession of the ball either directly or by first tipping it so that it can be caught. In such a situation, if the player will assume a fundamental position with the ball, he may fake as if to dribble away from the basket, or as if to pivot away from the basket in order to pass to a teammate, and then he may jump into the air for a one hand shot. As a matter of fact, such a maneuver, largely because it is not common practice, is more effective in scoring than are repeated attempts to tip the ball into the basket.

Preventing a Held Ball

The situation often arises that a player receives the ball and at the same instant an opponent charges for it. The safest maneuver always is to take the ball to the floor quickly (assume the fundamental position) and then to move away from the opponent. If the opponent advances from in front toward the player with the ball, the first move is to step toward (not away from, as is the usual movement) the opponent. The ball is taken to the floor; thus the shoulder and elbows will protect the ball. Then the player may retreat or pivot away from his opponent. Protection comes first, flight second. This further prevents any possibility of a second opponent making a surprise attack. It is a mark of unskilled technique for a player to have sole possession of a ball and then to permit an opponent to cause a held ball under any circumstances.

Stealing the Ball from an Opponent

An opportunity frequently occurs during a game to grab the ball when it is in the possession of an opponent or to catch a ball at the same time that it is caught by an opponent. When this happens, the common habit seems to be to pull and tug at the ball with all your might in bulldog fashion. As a result, about all that ever takes place is that you swing your opponent around in the air, if you are the stronger, and the official calls a held ball. Nothing has been gained, and energy has been lost.

If instead of pulling away from the opponent, you move toward him, you can without any doubt get possession of the ball. As you grab the ball, bring your shoulder down over the ball. Next, step toward the opponent so that one foot is placed between his feet. If he stands with his left foot advanced, then place your left foot between his feet. This will cause less interference and will give better leverage and freedom of movement. As the step is taken, a quick straightening of your arms toward the floor with the shoulders held stationary will snatch the ball out of the opponent's hands. By holding the shoulders stationary, you will prevent the opponent from following after the ball, for his downward movement is blocked by your shoulders. If he has a strong grip on the ball (which is not usually the case under actual playing conditions), a quick rotation of the ball as you straighten your arms will twist it out of his hands.

This technique may be taught effectively by dividing the squad into pairs. Each pair is given a ball, or as many groups are formed as there are balls. Then one player of the pair takes the ball and holds it in front of him. The other player steps in as outlined above and takes the ball away from him. Then they reverse their positions so that all get practice. After each player becomes familiar with the movement, a little resistance may be offered by the player who has the ball at the start. It will be most difficult for the players to form the habit of moving toward their opponents until the ball has been pushed to the floor. The tendency is always to pull away with the tenacity of a bulldog.

Figures 7, 8, and 9 show the steps in stealing the ball from an opponent. Figure 7 shows the first contact with the ball. Figure 8 shows the player stepping toward his opponent as he forces the ball to the floor. Figure 9 shows the player who has stolen the ball after he has pivoted away from his opponent.

One might be quick to say that this is a held ball situation. However, officials should not be too quick and eager to call held balls in such cases. The action happens quickly, and players who by clever maneuvering gain possession of the ball should not be penalized. Held ball should not be called except when the conditions for a held ball are thoroughly apparent. In this case a held

ball should be called only when the players are holding the ball
so firmly that neither can gain sole possession of it or put it into
play.

POINTS TO STRESS IN TEACHING THE FUNDAMENTAL POSITION

In teaching the fundamental position, stress primarily, and in
the following order:

1. The position of the feet.
2. Sitting on the rear heel—the crouch.
3. Holding the head up.
4. Position of the ball.

BALL CONTROL

The second basic principle upon which all of our techniques
of handling the ball are dependent is ball control. Simply stated,
it refers to the method of holding the ball in the hands in readiness to start a pass or a shot. After careful analysis of the movements of the wrists, it was found that the greatest freedom of
movement was attained when the hands were placed on the ball
in one certain position. From a study of the kinesiology of the
wrists, we find that, as the hands are held in front of the body
with the palms facing each other, they may be moved up and
down, toward or away from each other, as well as rotated, all by
a movement from the wrists. Also the hands, by a movement of
the forearm, may be rotated into a prone or supine position. Thus
it may be seen that the greatest variety of movement is possible
in the wrist joints.

It is desirable to utilize these movements in handling the ball,
first, in order that there may be complete relaxation, and second,
because these movements are necessary in well coördinated shots
and passes. For this reason, one uniform method of gripping or
handling the ball is taught for all situations. This again simplifies
the techniques that the player must learn in handling the ball

FIG. 7. First step in stealing the ball. Player in lower position has the advantage.

FIG. 8. Second step. Player has continued toward his opponent until ball is forced from him and is on the floor.

FIG. 9. Third step. Player in white jersey is pivoting away from opponent after gaining possession of the ball.

Fig. 10.   Hands in correct position on the ball.

and eliminates the likelihood of poor or delayed ball handling because of the necessity of changing the position of the hands on the ball for the start of different maneuvers.

HOLDING THE BALL

1. *The ball should be centered in the hands.* This is to say, if the ball were mounted on a shaft which is an axis of the ball, this shaft would pass through the hand between the knuckles of the middle and ring fingers. This position is such that the palms of the hands as they are placed on the ball will face each other directly. The fingers should not be spread apart abnormally or to the extent that there is conscious tension in the muscles controlling this lateral movement. Relaxation of the muscles of the forearms, hands, and fingers is necessary in order to maintain accurate control of the ball. The example of the exaggerated jerk of the knee when the muscles of the trunk, arms, and face are forcefully tensed illustrates the lack of muscular control under situations of extreme muscular contraction.

2. *Likewise, the thumbs should lie along the side of the forefingers in the same manner as when the hand is hanging freely at the side.* In handling the ball under all situations, the thumbs are used only as supports for the ball to prevent it from slipping back toward the body through the hands as the ball is pushed away from the body in a pass or a shot. To spread the thumbs away from the forefingers so that in the extreme position they are practically at right angles with the forefingers causes a muscular tension in the forearm which must be overcome for accurate ball control. The difference in tension in the two positions may be demonstrated by holding the ball first with the thumbs placed at right angles to the forefingers and practically touching each other and then, after sensing the amount of forearm tension present, moving them back to their natural relaxed position along the forefingers. Any advantage gained by this abnormal method of placing the thumbs on the ball is certain to be lost in the increased tension that must be overcome to secure accurate ball control.

3. *The ball should be held loosely in the hands to aid further in relaxation and accurate control.* To grip the ball tightly means muscular tension which, as already demonstrated in the case of the knee jerk, causes uncoördinated neuro-muscular control. As a consequence, the ball tends actually to jump from the hands on a pass or a shot and too often without accurate direction and with too much speed. Figure 10 shows a player holding the ball correctly.

TECHNIQUES TO AVOID

You will observe that no mention is made here of holding the ball in the fingers so that daylight may be seen between the ball and the hands.[1] This has been deliberately avoided. It is of course recognized that our tactile sense is most pronounced in the last phalanx of our fingers. It is with this part of the fingers that we give direction to the ball in passes and shots. These are the last to touch the ball as it leaves the hands. But to emphasize that only these parts should touch the ball is to violate the principle of relaxation, because such a position of the hands with respect to the ball cannot be attained without unnecessary muscular tension. As a matter of fact if one handles a dirty ball under relaxed conditions for a short time, one will find the dirt markings will show on practically all parts of the fingers, thumbs, and palms except the centers which are too concave or depressed to touch the ball at any time. I observed this to be true on the hands of the players who have been taught the finger tip technique. It follows, therefore, that not only is such procedure bad technique, but it is also practically impossible of attainment.

The common method of holding the ball so that the hands are on top of it and the palms are facing downward is conducive to many bad passes. The tendency is to pass the ball too low or to lob it too high. Such a position of the hands on the ball also limits the variety of movements of the wrists that is possible when the

[1] Allen, Forest C. *My Basketball Bible*, p. 185. Kansas City, Missouri: Smith-Grieves Company. 1924.

palms face each other. A little experimentation with the two methods will demonstrate these facts.

PRACTICE METHODS

The novice with no previously formed habits of holding the ball will learn the correct technique in one short practice. It will, however, require concentrated conscious effort on the part of a player who has learned a different habit pattern to change successfully to this technique. At least, this has been my experience in working with young boys from ten to fourteen years of age who have had little or no basketball experience and then with college freshmen who come to me from schools in many sections of the United States and who have been taught a wide variety of handling methods. Other methods of holding the ball either handicap or prevent certain types of passes (particularly the push pass), and cause so many bad passes that every player who has been trained by me, no matter what his previous experiences or techniques have been, is taught the method of holding the ball as described above. It must be remembered that accurate ball control is the most important part of successful basketball.

A very simple way for a large squad to practice the technique of holding the ball is to form as many groups as there are balls. Each group will form a circle approximately ten feet in diameter. The ball is then passed across the circle from one player to another. Each time that the ball is caught the hands should be adjusted to the correct position on the ball as it is brought back toward the body in the movements preparatory to making a pass. Since no running or other movement is involved in this practice, full attention may be concentrated on the technique of holding the ball. Even when the ball is caught with the hands in the proper position, a slight adjustment will tend to relieve the muscular tension incident to stopping the force of the ball when it is caught.

If sufficient balls are available, or for special individual instruction, two players may pass the ball back and forth between them.

Another plan of practice that we sometimes use is for one player to bounce the ball against a solid wall and catch it. Each time the ball is caught, there is sufficient delay to adjust the hands properly on the ball. As the habit becomes a conditioned reflex, the catching, adjusting, and passing or shooting will seem to be simultaneous movements.

POINTS TO STRESS IN HOLDING THE BALL

The important points of this technique to stress at the beginning are:

1. Hands centered at the ends of an axis of the ball with the palms facing each other directly.

2. Thumbs lying on the ball and naturally spaced from the forefingers.

3. Work for as complete relaxation of the muscles of the forearms, hands, and fingers as possible.

CHAPTER X

METHODS OF PASSING

T HE next step in learning basketball techniques is to put the principles of the fundamental position and ball control into practice. In all explanations which follow, it is assumed that body balance and ball control, as already described, are the bases upon which all other techniques are built. They apply first, but because they have been fully considered in Chapter IX, no repetitions will be made. In many explanations these two principles may not even be mentioned.

Passing Most Important Fundamental

Of all the many techniques in basketball which are to be explained here, passing is by far the most important. It even eclipses shooting in importance. While the purpose of the game is to score —to out-score your opponents—it nevertheless follows that there are many more passes during a game than there are shots. A successful sequence of accurate passes is necessary to make a shot possible. A number of years of tabulating shot charts of hundreds of games has disclosed the fact that the team which is able to pass the ball so that it is maneuvered in close to the basket for a shot is the team that wins over ninety-five per cent of the time.[1] Thus, a pass poorly executed and badly timed will often cause a missed shot, if it does not eliminate the possibility of the shot altogether. No matter what kind of a pass is to be used, there are twelve important rules or axioms which every player should not only know

[1] Works, Pierce. *Methods of Analyzing Offensive Efficiency.* National Association of Basketball Coaches, Bulletin No. 5. March, 1935.

but should also adopt as inviolable habits of play. It should further be emphasized here that, in spite of the contrary opinion of many coaches,[2] every player should learn to pass and shoot equally well with either hand.

Twelve Passing Axioms

1. *Always be well balanced or poised before passing.* In other words, assume the fundamental position as the ball is received. If the body is under perfect control, full attention may be given to the pass so that there is not the likelihood of making a bad pass because of imperfect balance.

2. *Always hold the ball correctly before passing.* Players who hold their hands on top of the ball, for instance, have difficulty in making a push pass. As a matter of fact, it is impossible to make a correct push pass under these circumstances. The ball is likely to be directed too low to be received with ease, or it is lobbed too much. Putting the thumbs behind the ball, that is, at right angles to the forefingers, results in passing with too much force.

3. *See the player to whom the ball is passed.*[3] The word "see" is used instead of "look at" because one of the common faults of players is to telegraph to their opponents their intentions of passing, by looking fixedly at the player to whom they are about to pass the ball. Some players form the habit of looking in one direction and passing in another. This is little better than looking directly at the player and in a short time becomes just as much of a "give away."

Players should form the habit of seeing all nine players at all times if possible. In other words, develop a wide vision. This can be done with practice. Once the habit is formed, seldom will a player miss an opportunity for a pass. Even less frequently will his opponents intercept his passes. It is best for a player to look directly into the eyes of his guard. This will remove any possibility of in-

[2] Lindley, Frank. "Basketball Theory, System, and Style." *Athletic Journal,* XVII (January, 1937) 16.

[3] Ruby, J. Craig. *How to Coach and Play Basketball,* Ch. 9. Champaign, Illinois: Bailey and Hines Publishers. 1926.

forming him or any other opponent as to the direction of the pass before it is made.

4. *Fake in a vertical plane to prevent a guard from blocking a pass.* When the ball is moved back and forth horizontally in front of a guard, practically no movement on his part is necessary to block the ball. Most guards will hold their arms and hands at the level of the ball, so are in a strong position to trap it as long as it remains at the same level.

It is quite difficult, if not impossible, to follow the ball—to keep the hand in front of the ball—when it is moved up and down in front of the guard. Thus, by watching the guard's hands as they move up and down in an effort to follow the ball, it is comparatively simple to pass over or under them. Even the novice will have little difficulty in fooling a seasoned player by this method.

5. *It is better to pass the ball with too little force than too much.* Passes should be made quickly but not too forcefully. It is a good rule that, if the ball must be thrown like a baseball to get to its receiver and to prevent interception, that situation is not one in which the ball should be passed. Some players have the habit of throwing the ball so hard that it knocks their teammates off balance when they catch it. I have seen otherwise excellent players have this bad habit of passing the ball too hard. Usually it is due to their inability to relax before passing, and this is caused by their excitement at seeing a teammate free in a good scoring position. The defense does not even need to attempt to block the pass, because it will either be fumbled, missed entirely, or if it is caught, there will be plenty of time to guard the receiver while he is recovering his balance or attempting to relax so that he may control a subsequent pass or a shot.

I can never forget the loss of an important ball game caused by this particular fault on the part of the best player on my team. He threw the ball so fast to a teammate standing unguarded under the goal that this player, upon receiving the ball, was so tense when he attempted to score that the ball shot out of his hands like an arrow from a bow and went over the top of the backboard. We were one point behind at the time. The game was over less than ten seconds later. Proper execution of the pass when there was really plenty of time would have made it possible for the teammate to relax before shooting and without doubt to score the basket that would have won the game.

6. *The ball should be thrown to the spot where the receiver can most easily and surely catch it.* The rule of teaching players to pass waist high, belt high, elbow high, to the belly button, at the belt buckle, really seems ridiculous when the many passing situations are studied. For example, a player is going toward the basket at great speed and it is possible to "feed" the ball to him for a shot. It is usually wiser to lay the ball about head high or even higher so that he need not slacken his pace but can take the ball in stride and go up into the air for his set-up shot. Again, a player is being closely guarded from the rear as he stands along the free throw lane. In this case it is better to throw the ball, or even roll it, so that the receiver must stoop to get it and also step away from his opponent at the same time. This is the one spot that, under the circumstance just described, is the most difficult for the opponent to guard. A tall player is guarded by a short player. It is advantageous to utilize the difference in height and throw the ball high above the head of the short guard. There are many other equally important examples but these will suffice to show the value of adapting the pass to the particular situation.

7. *The player who passes the ball is primarily responsible for the successful execution of the pass.* It is the duty of the player with the ball to decide whether or not his teammate is in a position to receive the ball. The passer is not relieved of the responsibility for an intercepted pass simply because a teammate called for the ball. The player with the ball is in the best position to make the judgments in all situations. This rule is not intended as a means of convicting a player, but rather as a means of teaching correct procedure. Too often a teammate calls for the ball when he thinks he is unguarded, whereas actually he is either in a poor position or else does not see that he is covered.

8. *Flat passes should be avoided.* This means the ball should not be passed parallel to the end lines. There are two places where

there is a tendency to do this. Players are standing on either side of the goal. The ball is passed across the free throw lane from one to the other. The possibilities for interception here are legion. The guard will be between the two players. His position alone makes it very difficult to pass the ball across the lane. Either the receiver should move out into the lane and in front of the basket, or another teammate should move into this position so that the ball is first passed out away from the goal and then to the other side where an opening will be left for a teammate. This movement is commonly called "passing around the horn." If this movement is followed, the guard must change his position to guard the ball or else a shot for goal is possible. When the players are standing on either side of the goal, the guard need not move at all to cover the situation perfectly.

The other situation which results in a flat pass occurs when a player on one side of the court, but out in front of the defense, passes the ball over the defense or close in front of it to a player on the other side of the court. Here again, there are too many chances for interception. The same "round the horn" technique should be used here. The two guards out in front of the defense have a tendency to make flat passes. These are very risky because an interception is almost sure to mean a field goal for the opponents. It is better for these guards to stagger their positions (in some situations it is necessary for one guard to go around directly behind his teammate) and to stand within at least fifteen feet of each other.

9. *The receiver should come to meet the ball.* There is little danger of interception if the receiver comes to meet the ball and does not stop until after he has the ball in his possession. In this situation he is usually moving away from the basket (see exception below) and is in a position between the ball and his opponent. A player is considered to be coming to meet the ball if he is moving across toward the side of the court where the ball is, even though he may be moving toward the basket, and in this sense away from the passer.

10. *The receiver should watch the ball until it is caught.* People

are much like horses in that they follow their noses. If a player turns his head to start a shot, a dribble, a pivot, or another pass before he has actually received the ball, the tendency is for his hands to move with his head. Too often this movement is just enough to cause a fumble. How often have you seen a player fumble the ball as he started to make a set-up shot, all because he began his movement up toward the basket before he had actually caught the ball!

11. *Generally speaking, follow the ball after passing it.* The ball may or may not be returned to the passer. However, two things are accomplished by following it. First, the passer may get into the open for a return pass if he is successful in escaping from his guard. At least he causes the defense to move and in this way opens up the possibility of producing an unguarded spot for one of his teammates. Second, if the receiver of the pass fumbles the ball, the passer by following his pass places himself in an excellent position to recover the ball.

12. *Generally speaking, the ball may be thrown over an opponent's head if the opponent is closer to the passer than to the receiver or if the receiver has enough space between himself and the goal so that he may catch the ball on the run either before or after it hits the floor.* This rule applies particularly to long passes and in connection with quick breaks. Often a forward pass situation arises so that the receiver has an opportunity to run away from his guard and receive the ball over his shoulder. Fast break offense can develop into so much wild passing that this rule affords an excellent means of judging when and when not to heave the ball down the court. In the case of the hook pass, the guard should always be rushing the passer, not just closer to him than to the receiver.

These basic principles of passing are so vital to successful offensive play that they determine very largely most offensive team movement. As a matter of fact, a team which is well trained in these fundamentals needs no other offense to be successful in its play.

Short Passes

For purposes of discussion, passes may be divided into two classes. The first consists of those types which are used for short, quick passes. The push pass, two hand underhand pass, one hand underhand pass, and the bounce pass (all kinds) are in this group. These passes should not be used when the ball must travel over twenty feet to reach a receiver. For most players the ball would travel much too slowly when thrown greater distances by any of the above methods.

The Push Pass

The push pass is without doubt used more than any other. The technique of the push pass is the most difficult to master of all the short passes. The coördination of the arm and wrist movement is the important movement to learn. Preliminary to passing, the player brings the ball back against the chest. The fingers should point out away from the body. The elbows should fall slightly away from the sides for the least amount of tension. The elbows in this position act as protection for the ball. In the movement of pushing the ball out away from the body prior to releasing it, the fingers are turned so that they point up in almost a vertical direction. There is then a counter motion of the hands and forearms. As the forearms begin their extension away from the body, the hands begin their movement (by the flexion of the wrists) back toward the body. The ball is released by a final quick extension (snap) of the forearms just before full extension is reached, while at the same time the wrist joint becomes fixed with the fingers pointing vertically. Because the small or accessory group of muscles of the hands, fingers, and forearms, together with the triceps of the arm, are used in this movement, quickness is possible. For the same reason, long passes of this type are not possible for the average player because these muscles are not strong enough to pass the ball fast for any great distance. It is assumed of course that a good fundamental position is maintained and that the ball is held according to our previous instructions. It will be necessary to raise the trunk to a more nearly vertical position than is required when protecting the ball in the extreme safety position. Figure 11 shows a player poised to pass, while Fig. 12 shows the position of the arms and hands just as the ball has been released. The true push pass does not put any spin on the ball. All of the technique just described (except the actual movement) may be closely studied from these two figures.

Simple Drills.

The really important point to learn, then, is the coördinated movement of the hands and forearms. In order to get the "feel" of this movement and to establish a habit pattern, a player may bounce the ball against a wall and catch it, or bounce it on the floor and catch it, or two or more players may pass it back and forth between them. The technique of the push shot in this respect is the same; it should be learned perfectly.

The Two Hand Underhand Pass

It is necessary to assume the extreme fundamental position in many situations. Many times, for reasons of safety, it is not possible to straighten up at all before passing the ball. In such cases the two hand underhand pass is used. It is even necessary sometimes to lift the pivot foot and almost complete a full step as the pass is made in order to get safely out of a closely guarded position.

Preparatory to being passed, the ball is brought back to the inside of the pivot foot. It is kept close to the floor for protection. As this movement takes place the weight is shifted to the pivot foot. The fingers are pointing vertically toward the floor. The arms are almost fully extended. A slight bend at the elbow will tend to prevent stiffness. In passing the ball, the arms are started forward and the weight is shifted to the front foot. Just as the arms pass the front foot, the ball is released by a quick forward movement of the wrist joint. This snap of the wrists will tend to put reverse spin on the ball. However, for ease in catching, it is better practice

FIG. 11. Player poised to make a push pass.

FIG. 12. Position of arms and hands at moment ball has been released in push pass.

FIG. 13. H. B. Lee poised to make two hand underhand pass.

FIG. 14. Player has stepped with pivot foot and passed ball just before pivot foot touches floor. This is a follow-up of Fig. 13.

FIG. 15. Luisetti demonstrating the one hand underhand pass.

to put little or no spin on the ball. If the player raises the pivot foot before passing the ball, then the ball is really not released until just before the pivot foot touches the floor. In this case the ball will be released with the arms out in front of the pivot foot and at the instant just indicated. Figure 13 shows the player poised to pass the ball. Figure 14 shows the same player just as he passes the ball. It will be noticed that he has raised his pivot foot (the right foot in this case) from the floor. The ball has left his hands before his pivot foot has touched the floor again. This is a maneuver that every player should learn.

THE ONE HAND UNDERHAND PASS

In the explanation of all techniques where one hand is used to handle the ball, it is understood that players should learn the technique with both the right and the left hand.

The one hand underhand pass is a natural development from the two hand underhand pass. It is a quicker pass and can be used while the player is moving. It should be noted that one hand passes (as well as shots) can be executed while the player is in striding motion. Two hand passes, on the contrary, for perfect coördination and the incident successful execution, require that the player be set. The reason, of course, is the difference in maintaining balance in the two types of passes. This point will become clear as the explanation of the one hand passes is developed.

There are really two types of one hand underhand passes. One is used when faking is needed or when the arm of a guard needs to be blocked. As the ball is received, the player is usually not in the extreme safety position. He desires to pass to a teammate who is on one side or the other or who is passing him, but going in the opposite direction. The pass is made by shifting the ball to the palm of the hand (right hand if passing to left and left hand if passing to right), raising the other arm as a protecting guard, and then swinging the ball across in front of the body and under the free arm. The ball goes off of the ends of the fingers by a quick movement of the wrist so that the hand moves upward. The palm of the hand is turned up throughout. This pass is always a very short pass of ten feet or less. Figure 15 shows a player in position execute a one hand underhand pass.

The other type of one hand underhand pass has identically the same use and movements as the two hand pass except that the ball is carried on the palm of one hand which permits a longer back swing. It is released from the ends of the fingers as just described. This pass may be used for considerably longer passes, as the leverage of the arm may be brought to play in its execution.

The Bounce Passes—Two Hand

The two hand bounce pass is a variation of the push pass. The technique is exactly the same as for the push pass, except that the ball is pushed to the floor before it is caught by the receiver. The bounce pass is used to get the ball past an opponent who is in a position to block a straight push pass. The pass is usually made after the guard's arms are drawn up as a result of a faked movement. This pass can be used to best advantage when the guard is more than three feet away from the passer.

For successful execution the ball should hit the floor directly under the outstretched hand of the guard. Since this is the lowest point of the pass, it will be necessary for the guard to reach the lowest in order to block the ball. One precaution, however, must be emphatically voiced here. In using bounce passes do not ever bounce the ball closer than three feet to the receiver. To do so will mean a sure fumble because the ball will hardly have time to rise from the floor high enough to be caught easily.

If any spin is put on the ball, it should be reverse (back) spin. When a ball with back spin strikes the floor, all spinning is stopped, the angle of bounce will be nearer ninety degrees than the angle at which the ball struck the floor, and the speed of the ball will be retarded. All these facts aid the receiver in catching the ball. A ball with forward spin bounces at a more acute angle, has increased speed and faster spin. These facts hinder the receiver in catching the ball because the ball will tend to twist out of his hands, and he must be quicker in catching and must stoop lower. For these reasons, forward spin should not be put on a ball in a bounce pass.[4]

For accuracy in this pass it is quite essential that the passer crouch well and follow through with his arms in the direction of the pass. It is obvious that this pass can be used for short passing only.

ONE HAND BOUNCE PASS

The one hand bounce pass is used under two extreme situations: one, when the guard is rushing or closely guarding the passer, and the other, when he is closely guarding the receiver who is in motion. The technique for the pass in each of these situations is slightly different.

In using the bounce pass when the passer is guarded closely, the passer steps either to the left or right, depending upon the direction he plans to pass. This movement enables him to get the ball out of the reach of the guard. As the step is taken, the ball is held out at arms length to the side to which the passer has stepped. It is then shifted to one hand. With the hand behind it, the ball is thrown to the floor out of reach of the guard. The ball should hit the floor directly to the side of and back of the guard. It should leave the hand over the tips of the fingers and should be thrown with a quick wrist movement which may be likened to the movement in slapping with the palm of the hand. The palm of the hand at the release of the ball will face the direction of the pass. Figure 16 shows the passer after he has stepped to the side and has the ball in position to start the pass. This pass, as a rule, is a comparatively short pass with an approximate maximum of ten feet.

The technique of the second type of one hand bounce pass differs in just one essential point from that of the first type—the passer is unguarded. The receiver in the typical situation where

[4] Barry, J. M. *Basketball, Individual and Team*, p. 36. Iowa City, Iowa: Clio Press. 1929.

this pass is effective is running toward the goal and is barely ahead (no more than a half step) of his opponent who is between him and the passer. A direct push pass or one hand pass will be intercepted or deflected by the guard if thrown so that it can be caught by the receiver. If it is thrown directly but out of reach of the guard, it cannot be reached by the receiver. The times are legion when such a pass has been tried. I have yet to see one time when it has been successful. A bounce pass, and a particular type of bounce pass, is the only possible means of completing such a play. It is a clever way to get the ball to a receiver and makes possible a shot for goal, which under all other circumstances would be out of the question.

This pass is a one hand pass. The passer strides toward the receiver in the same manner as a pitcher in the act of delivering the baseball to the batter. The ball is brought up over the shoulder beside the ear and is shifted to one hand. The hand is back of the ball as the arm starts forward and down to bounce the ball. As the ball is released, the forearm and hand are rotated so that the hand cuts under the ball. This gives a back and side spin to the ball. The quicker and snappier the rotary movement, the faster the spin that will be given to the ball. The faster the spin, the more successful the pass. The movement used in this pass is the same movement that a baseball pitcher uses in throwing a curve ball.

The ball should strike the floor just in front of but out of reach of the opponent who is guarding the receiver. When the ball bounces, if it has received sufficient back and side spin, it will come back toward the receiver and will tend to bounce as high as three feet from the floor. The receiver may catch it without even slackening his pace or changing his stride. This technique may sound somewhat difficult of execution, but it can be mastered with comparatively little practice. It has been the means of scoring for our team several needed goals which could not have been made in any other way. The pass may be thrown successfully for a distance of from fifteen to twenty feet.

This pass may be practiced by setting up the situation that has just been described. Place the passer at the outer edge of the free

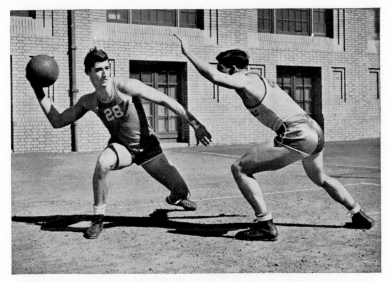

FIG. 16.   Passer has stepped to side to make one hand bounce pass.

FIG. 17.   Use of the one hand bounce pass to feed a closely guarded player running to the basket.

Fig. 18. Player poised to throw catcher's peg pass.

throw circle. Place two players out near the side lines. The receiver is nearer the end line and one half of a step ahead of his guard. At the signal "Go," both run toward the basket. The ball is passed so that the receiver takes one step after catching the ball before he goes into the air for his shot. Figure 17 shows the players in position at the time the ball is being released.

There are many other variations of short passes. It has been our intention here to discuss only those that are the most fundamental and those that are particularly useful in game situations that occur repeatedly.

LONG PASSES

The second class of passes consists of those which are used for long passes. There are two passes of this type. Both are one hand passes. They are particularly suited to long passing because they have greater leverage and because the whole body is employed in their execution. These factors naturally furnish greater power to the passing movement. Also, they lengthen the time required to get the pass away, as compared to the short, snappy passes of the first group. The two passes may be designated as the "catcher's peg pass" and the "hook pass."

CATCHER'S PEG PASS

The catcher's peg pass is exactly what its name signifies. It is thrown in exactly the same manner as a catcher throws the ball to second base. The time required to release the ball in this pass is much less than in the hook pass. The catcher's peg pass is the ideal pass to use in feeding the ball to a player who has gotten ahead of his guard on a quick break down the court. The use of this pass assumes that the passer is unguarded, at least that he is not guarded closely. As a matter of fact, if the guard is fairly close when the ball is shifted to the throwing hand, the other arm can be used to block off the guard. The ball can be thrown on a direct line if no opponent is between the passer and receiver, or it may be arched to get it over the head of an opponent so that the receiver may catch the ball high above his head. Because of the great distance between passer and receiver in this pass and because the receiver is usually in rapid motion, the element of timing is very important.

Preparatory to throwing the catcher's peg pass, the player brings the ball up over the shoulder and beside the ear. As it is brought to this position, it is shifted to one hand. The hand is behind and under the ball. The elbow will be slightly below the level of the shoulder. The pass is made by a quick, forceful movement forward of the whole arm. As the ball is released, the arm is fully extended. The ball should leave the hand by going off the tips of the fingers. The palm of the hand at the finish is snapped downward.

As the ball is brought over the shoulder preparatory to passing, the weight is shifted to one foot. For instance, if the pass is to be thrown with the right arm, the ball will be over the right shoulder, and the weight will be on the right foot. As the pass is made, the passer pushes off of his right foot and steps forward with his left foot. He literally throws from the toes so that the force of the whole body may be put into the passing action.

The most important part of this whole movement is the releasing of the ball from the tips of the fingers. This prevents the ball from curving to one side and assures a direct path to the receiver. The surface of the ball is so great that releasing the ball over the side of the forefinger, for instance, will cause it to curve far out of line and thus spoil an excellent opportunity to score. Figure 18 shows a player in the act of throwing the catcher's peg pass. The relative position of the various parts of the body may be checked from this figure.

In order to get the timing of this pass with relation to the movement of the receiver, the following drill has been used to good advantage:

The passer stands at the edge of the free throw circle at one end of the court. The receivers line up along the side line and at the center of the court. One at a time they dart to the goal farthest from the passer. The ball is thrown so that the receiver catches it over his head and either takes a step and a jump before shooting or dribbles once or twice before going up for his shot. The players in this formation may rotate so that all get practice in passing and receiving. As the players become adept at this pass, a guard may be placed between the passer and receiver to introduce the element of arching the ball to get it over the guard.

Practice in the catcher's peg pass is also gained as a part of the "all-purpose drill" which is described on page 85.

Hook Pass

The hook pass, which is the other type of pass in this class, may be used for either long or short passes. It may be either a short arm pass which is thrown quickly from a position on the floor, or a long arm pass which is thrown after the passer jumps from the floor. These terms will be made clear as the passes are explained. As the long arm hook pass is the one most commonly used, it will be described in detail.

1. Uses for the Hook Pass.

This pass is used only when the passer is rushed, closely guarded, or cornered so that there is likelihood of a held ball being called for withholding the ball from play or of any other kind of a pass being intercepted. In other words, if a pass is to be made, it is necessary to get the ball over the heads of opponents. It should be remembered that, because the hook pass is slow of execution, if a catcher's peg pass or any other pass can be used, it is to be preferred.

The following are situations in which the hook pass is particularly useful and necessary:

1. When a defensive player recovers the ball from the backboard. If his opponents block his progress and try for a held ball or interception, his most effective means of getting the ball to a teammate is the hook pass.

2. When a player is crowded into a corner or along the side, end line, or center line, and is in danger of either going out of bounds

or permitting a held ball to be called. Here his safest and surest
escape is by use of the hook pass. He can jump across the boundary
line and make his pass before touching the floor and thus avoid
his opponents.

3. When a player is rushed in the front court, the very nature
of the hook pass permits him to feed the ball to an unguarded
teammate inside the defense.

4. When a closely guarded player is dribbling fast along the side
of the court toward his goal and sees a teammate dart under the
goal unguarded. The one sure way to get the ball to this teammate
without the loss of time and the chance of having the pass blocked
is to use the hook pass.

The hook pass is so necessary for aggressive play in these cases
that it is hard to understand how coaches can underestimate its
value and even refuse to teach it to their players.[5] They often say
that it is too difficult to learn and therefore entails too much risk
for a young player. It has been my experience that the young,
plastic player learns new habit patterns with greater ease than the
college player. The college player comes to the coach with definitely set habits which, in spite of psychologists' opinions to the
contrary, are difficult to change.[6] Nevertheless, we use the hook
pass and learn the technique for both the left and right hand.

2. Technique of the Hook Pass—Foot Movement.

Whether the player is in motion or is standing still, the hook
pass should start from a low crouching position. If the player is to
pass with his right hand (the technique is reversed for the left
hand) his first move is to step with his left foot in the direction
opposite to that in which he plans to pass the ball. The left foot
crosses over the right. Another conception of the movement is for
the passer to step at right angles to the direction in which he has
been moving and his body is facing.

[5] Lindley, Frank. "Basketball Theory, System, and Style," *Athletic Journal*
Vol. XVII (January, 1937), page 16.
[6] Wheeler, R. H. A *Textbook of Psychology*, Vol. II, p. 374. Lawrence,
Kansas: University of Kansas. (Mimeographed.) 1928.

This movement, which is contrary to the methods used by some coaches,[7] is taught for four reasons:

First, the cross step, particularly for the player in motion, is a means by which he gains body control preparatory to making his pass. By this quick change in direction, he tends also to dislodge his guard.

Second, the cross step delays the actual pass long enough to deceive the guard. If the guard has guessed the intention of the passer, his tendency is to jump too soon to block the pass. As a consequence, the cross step spoils the guard's timing. He reaches the height of his jump before the passer has even left the floor. Thus, even though a short player is being guarded by a very tall guard, the pass cannot be blocked.

Third, the cross step not only permits the passer to retreat from the guard, but it places his body sideways between the guard and the ball. This affords the greatest possible amount of protection. The left hip is presented to the guard.

Fourth, the left foot is always used when the player is passing with the right hand to permit the freest body movement and thus the most efficient muscular coördination. Since the hook pass is used to get the ball up over the heads of opponents, the movement which will permit the greatest height is desirable. It is evident to everyone that he can reach higher with the right hand if he stands on the left foot and lifts the right foot from the floor. One of the reasons for this is that the broad muscle of the back, the latissimus dorsi muscle, is attached to the hip bone and also to the humerus of the arm. When the right foot remains on the floor, the freedom of the arm in stretching is limited; but when the right foot is lifted from the floor, then greater freedom and stretch of the right arm is possible because the latissimus dorsi muscle is relaxed, no longer fixed, when the hip bone is permitted to rise.[8] There is also the compensatory curving of the spine with the incident coordination, relaxation, and contraction of the back muscles con-

[7] Meanwell, W. E. *Basketball for Men*, p. 61. Madison, Wisconsin: Democrat Printing Company. 1922.

[8] Garrish, F. H. *A Text-book of Anatomy*, p. 261. Philadelphia: Lea Brothers and Company. 1899.

cerned.[9] Space need not be devoted here, however, to a discussion of this rather complicated matter of reciprocating reactions.

Since, when a player is hook passing with the right hand, the right foot is lifted from the floor first (the take-off is from the left foot), these points apply directly to the hook pass technique. Therefore, the importance of stressing this particular foot work can be seen. It may be that those who oppose the use of the hook pass have attempted to use another technique which sets up the muscular conflict referred to above.

3. The Jump and Rotation.

This cross step is followed immediately by a spring from the left foot. Since the cross step has permitted the passer to retreat from the guard, this jump should be a high jump (vertical) and not a broad jump. The cross step helps the player to get momentum for this jump. Consequently the cross step should not be too long, should be taken quickly, and the foot should be set down on the floor forcefully in order to produce as much spring as possible.

As the passer jumps into the air, he twists his body around so that at the finish of the pass he is facing in the direction of the pass. This twisting need not be forced. The swing of the arms in passing the ball will tend to turn the body in this direction. The twist therefore is incident to the swing of the arms in passing.

4. Recovery after Pass.

As the player returns to the floor, his feet should be spread laterally. He should permit at least a half knee bend. His hands should rest on his knees. This position at the finish of the pass will permit the passer to follow up the pass without any lost motion or any unnecessary steps. From this position of recovery after the pass, if the guard persists in covering the passer instead of turning to get position with respect to the ball, it is possible for the passer to fake going in one direction to throw his guard off balance and then quickly dart in the opposite direction to follow

[9] Martin, E. G. *The Human Body*, p. 131. New York: Henry Holt and Company. 1926.

up the play.[10] The hands on the knees can be used effectively to push off quickly in any direction.

If the player does not return to the floor in this position, the result is that he will usually take several steps in the direction away from the pass. As a consequence he loses entirely any chance that he may have to get quickly back into the play. Since basketball is more of a game of quick starts and stops than a game of speed in running, these points that may seem to the novice to be quite trifling are really of major importance. They make the difference between a team that cannot be beaten and a team that is easy to stop.

5. Handling the Ball.

The handling of the ball is the next phase of the pass to consider. As the cross step is taken, the ball is carried in both hands across in front of the body and back in the direction of the step. The ball is held in both hands until the passer jumps from the floor. This is done in order not to lose control of the ball until the pass is actually under way. For instance, if the guard, instead of continuing to rush the passer, drops back away from him, the passer may withhold the pass and recover to the position he was in before he started the cross step.

As the passer jumps from the floor, the ball is shifted to the right hand. The left arm is held at shoulder height to act as a buffer to the guard. The ball, for the best control of it, is actually held in the cup made by the hand and forearm. Many players can "wrap" their arm and hand around the ball in this fashion with sufficient strength of grip to be able to swing the arm forcefully around in any position without dropping the ball.

As the passer reaches the highest point of his jump, the arm is swung up above the shoulder so that the ball goes above and back of the head. The ball is carried back of the head in order to overcome the common fault of swinging the arm around to the side. Such a movement would destroy the advantage gained by reason

[10] Allen, Forest C. *Better Basketball*, pp. 136-37. New York: McGraw-Hill Book Company. 1937.

of the jump for height. It would further remove the protection afforded by the fact that the body of the passer was placed between the ball and the opponent. If the arm is swung sideways, the rotation of the body, as already described, would tend to throw the ball directly at the guard.

The ball may be released at any point along the arc of its swing. If the guard has jumped too soon to block the pass (this is usually the case) so that the passer is above him when he makes his pass, then the ball should be released after the arm has passed the vertical point on its downward swing. If the guard has jumped with the passer and is at the same height as he, then the ball should be released just before the arm reaches the vertical position. Finally, if the guard is much taller than the passer, is above him at the time of the pass and is really smothering his movements, then the ball should be released as the arm reaches the horizontal point in its upward swing.

6. Focus of Attention.

These points in connection with releasing the ball suggest the final part of the hook pass, the position of the eyes of the passer. At all times in the movement, the passer should watch both his guard and his teammates. As he takes the cross step, his chin should be over his left shoulder. (A pass with the right hand is still being described.) If the guard retreats, he sees that it is not necessary to go through with the pass. He is no longer crowded. As he goes into the air to make the pass, he must see, first, the position of the hands of his guard and, second, the receiver of the pass. The first point needs the most emphasis because too often the opponent is ignored. The pass can never be blocked if the passer watches the hands of the guard. He can arch his pass just enough to clear the finger tips of the guard.

It must be remembered that this pass can be thrown very hard. The whole body is swung into it, and care must be taken to pass the ball so that it may be easily handled by the receiver. This is particularly true if the receiver is close and if it is not necessary to arch the ball much to get it over the guard.

FIG. 19. Calderwood, All - Conference guard, demonstrates the four steps in the hook pass. The cross step.

FIG. 20. Take-off for the hook pass.

FIG. 21. Release of ball
and body twist.

FIG. 22. The recovery.

7. Summary of the Hook Pass.

The most important points to stress in teaching the technique of this pass are presented below in order:

1. The cross step.
2. The high jump.
3. The twist.
4. The recovery.
5. The handling of ball and arm swing.
6. The head position for looking.

When practice is begun on the hook pass, just one point at a time should be stressed. Little attention should be given to other points until proficiency has been gained in the point under consideration. Gradually the whole technique is built up. I have found that the most rapid progress is made if the order indicated above is followed. Practice at first should be without opposition. The players may form in a circle and in passing always step away from the center. Figures 19, 20, 21, and 22 show the various stages of the hook pass.

A special drill for practicing the hook pass may be used after the players have learned the general technique. The squad is divided into groups of three. Two of the three are offensive players and one is a guard. The guard always covers the player who is making the hook pass. It is the job of the passer to pick the right moment to pass. The guard may do all the faking that he chooses. After the pass, the passer follows through for a return pass. It is the job of the guard to prevent this maneuver if possible. The three players rotate in their jobs so that each receives practice in passing.

CHAPTER XI

METHODS OF SHOOTING

I F ONE is to coach an aggressive, gambling type of game, one will encourage his players to take chances on shots at the goal. This policy will entail many types of shots. It has been my observation from a number of years of studying the shooting percentage of teams that the team which used many different types of shots and which took shooting chances had just as good a percentage as the very conservative team. It is not, therefore, the kind of a shot, but rather the trained shooting ability that counts. If the shooter is well poised and coördinated, he can with practice score equally well with any shot.

An analysis, however, shows that all shots have their foundation in one of three types of shots. In other words, the fundamental movements and technique of all shots may be traced to three basic shots. These are the two hand push shot, two hand underhand shot, and the one hand push shot.

The technique of these three shots will be discussed in detail, and then the many variations of them will be enumerated, together with the circumstances under which they are useful.

THE TWO HAND PUSH SHOT

As indicated in the description of the push pass on page 115, much of the technique, particularly the coördination of the wrists, hands, and arms in releasing the ball in the push pass, is repeated in the push shot. If the "wrist snap" has been learned for the push pass, then it will be very easy to apply the same movement in the push shot.

The push shot is used as the "set" shot from anywhere on the court. But in order to use this shot successfully for long shooting, one must have strong wrists, fingers, and forearms. For this reason very young players and others of medium strength will find difficulty in shooting accurately with push shots from distances greater than twenty-five feet from the basket. This accounts for the development of shooting forms which are half-way between a push shot and an underhand shot. Practically all such shots have weaknesses. For this reason it is not wise for players to shoot the push shot from a distance which is greater than their shooting strength. When it is necessary to shoot from greater distances, the two hand underhand, or free throw shot should be used, thus bringing the full arm swing into play. This gives a much wider shooting range to most players. The push shot is used as the principal floor shot because it requires that the guard be very close (closer than three feet) to block it. At the same time, the player is always in a position to dribble quickly around his guard instead of taking a shot in case the guard over-rushes in an attempt to block the ball.

Technique of Push Shot

The technique of the push shot presupposes that the feet are in the fundamental position and that a plumb line from the center of gravity would fall between the feet. The knees are about one-quarter bent. The trunk is practically vertical. The knee bend and the trunk position are usually a recovery from the extreme fundamental position which is assumed in stopping or receiving the ball preparatory to poising for the shot.

1. Trunk Position.

The vertical trunk position is necessary for several reasons. If the trunk is inclined forward, the player will not be able to get the proper arch on the ball. Instead of the arms moving in a more vertical direction, they will tend to move in a more horizontal direction as the shot is made. This will permit a guard to stay farther away from the shooter and still block the ball or interfere with the accuracy of the shot. The arch of the shot is important from the standpoint of shooting percentages. By the trigonometric law of sines it can be shown that as the arch of the ball increases, the effective opening of the basket increases. Therefore, conversely, the less arch that is given to the ball, the greater must be the accuracy of the shot because the effective opening of the basket is smaller.

Furthermore, if the trunk is inclined forward, the freedom of movement of the arms will be restricted. This freedom of movement is necessary if the arms are to move in the direction described above. When the trunk is inclined forward, the latissimus dorsi or broad muscle of the back, which is attached to both the hip bone and the humerus, is extended. If the arms are raised vertically, further extension occurs; in order to avoid this, the player develops the habit of shooting straight out from his chest.

By a simple demonstration one may test to his own satisfaction this condition of hindrance and freedom of motion of the arms with an inclined and with a vertical trunk. Stand in a position for shooting. Incline the trunk forward, then raise the arms vertically, or at least hold them in line with the angle of the trunk. Observe the feeling of muscular tenseness in the back and about the shoulders. Now raise the trunk to a vertical position while at the same time holding the arms fixed at the shoulder joint. The relaxation of the back muscle and the freedom about the shoulder are apparent immediately. This alone should convince any player of the wisdom and practical advantage of the vertical trunk position.

2. Ball Held under Chin.

Preparatory to making the shot, the player should bring the ball back under his chin. This statement is meant literally. If the ball is brought this close to the body, the guard will have to weaken his defensive position in order to block it. In the act of shooting, the ball will often just graze the point of the chin. The chin must be out away from the chest, and the eyes must be on the basket.

3. Position and Movement of Arms and Wrists.

At this point in the shot the fingers will be directed upward. The arms will be away from the sides. The forearm, for greater freedom, will make an angle of about forty-five degrees with the horizontal.

As the ball is brought under the chin, the vertical movement of the arms is started. As the arms move upward, the hands, by the movement of the wrists, go back toward the face. Just as this flexion of the wrists is complete, the wrist joint is held fixed, and by a quick extension of the forearms and fingers the ball is released. While this explanation is here given by steps, the coördinated movement of the arms and hands in actually releasing the ball is lightning fast. Only the fastest speed of the moving picture camera can catch this movement sufficiently to enable one to analyze it.

The ball is actually released as it passes the level of the eyes and just before the forearms are fully extended. The arms follow through after the shot is made. This follow, however, should not be emphasized to the extent that there is a "drag" in the shooting movement rather than a snap. The player will usually bring his whole body to a fully extended position at the finish of the shot. He may even jump from the floor as he shoots. This is sometimes necessary in order to get sufficient power in the shot. The player should not, however, finish the shot with all the weight on the forward foot. The shot is started from a crouched position. It is assumed, of course, that the ball is held as described on page 105.

4. Flight of Ball.

The ball is always so directed that it is moving in a vertical plane which would cut the basket through its diameter. It is aimed so as just to clear the nearest edge of the rim. Even though the ball hits the front edge, its chances for skidding through the basket are excellent, whereas, if the ball is over-shot so that it hits the back edge, the chances of missing the goal are greater. The ball is never directed to hit the backboard before entering the basket. Direct hits from all positions are the aim. This concentrates all push shots on just one objective.

If the arms in making the shot move in a more or less vertical direction, the ball receives the right amount of arch and will enter the basket from a more or less vertical direction, so that practically the whole eighteen-inch diameter of the basket is available as a target. Figure 23 shows a player poised for a push shot. He is at the point of starting the movement toward the basket, prior to releasing the ball.

COACHING SUGGESTIONS

In teaching the technique of the push shot to a squad, the following three points should be emphasized. This emphasis will prevent confusion in the mind of the player and will keep the important elements before him. He can remember these points without difficulty. They are vital to correct execution. If they are mastered, the other points, which are incidental to these three, will be learned automatically.

1. Keep the trunk vertical.
2. Start the shot with the ball under the chin.
3. Release the ball with a forearm and finger snap while the hands are held with the wrist joint fixed.

PRACTICE DRILLS

There are many simple drills that can be used to emphasize different phases of the techniques and to help players attain coordination in shooting.

To demonstrate and stress the vertical trunk position and holding the ball under the chin, have the players form a circle around the basket. They should not be farther than a step away from under the center of the rim. It will be necessary to hold the trunk vertical and to keep the ball against the body in order to get the ball over the rim so that it may enter from above. In shooting, the players can experiment with just getting the ball over the nearest edge of

Fig. 23.   Player poised for push shot.

the rim. Such a drill should not be continued for a long period and probably will not need to be repeated as a squad drill.

To help the players get the feel of the rather difficult arm and wrist coördination in shooting, as well as the sense of body rhythm with this movement, have them hop slowly on one foot and go through the movement of shooting with each hop without releasing the ball. For example, as the player leaves the floor in his hop, the ball is thrust up from under the chin, and the arms are quickly extended as if to shoot. As the player returns to the floor, the arms are lowered, and the ball is brought back in a circular motion to its position under the chin. The movement is repeated on the next hop. After six or seven such hops the player may release the ball. It is surprising how this will help players to sense their coördination or lack of it. This drill should not be attempted at a distance of more than fifteen feet from the basket.

To help a player with his wrist and arm movement in shooting and to emphasize the fact that the shot is actually a forearm and finger movement, have him shoot while sitting on a chair. The chair should be within ten feet of the basket.

When players first start practicing the push shot, it is all right for them to stand in order to study their shot before actually making it. Later, however, it is better to have them move to meet the ball in order to get poised before shooting. This will give them practice in shooting under conditions similar to game conditions.

It is valuable to have a little opposition during shooting practice in order to make the players conscious of the arch they give the ball and of the presence of a guard. This opposition may be provided by dividing the squad into groups of two or more players and having one member of each group guard the player who is trying to make the shot. After a player shoots, he should always follow his shot for a possible rebound. Incidentally the player who shoots is almost always the logical one to get the rebound. He is in the best position to judge the place of the rebound. After getting the ball, he rolls it back to the next shooter. Rolling the ball gives him enough time to get back to guard the next shooter. It also necessitates the movement of the shooter to get the ball. The guard should not get so close as to prevent the shot, but close enough to make the shooter conscious of his presence and to cause him to keep his trunk vertical, the ball close under his chin, and to give the proper arch to the ball.

In addition to these drills, the game of "twenty-one" and "ten goals net," described in Chapter VIII, are excellent for shooting practice for the push shot.

THE TWO HAND UNDERHAND OR THE FREE THROW SHOT

The two hand underhand, or free throw shot is without doubt the most accurate floor shot. It is the most mechanical, and therefore there are fewer variables involved in its execution. Consequently, there are fewer chances for errors. Since it is made with a full arm swing, greater power may be applied, so that there is less chance of error due to lack of force or to "pressing" because of lack of force. Because of this fact, young players will find this shot easier for them. They are not likely to form bad habits of execution as they so often do in the use of the push shot. The two hand underhand shot is without doubt the best shot for most players of all ages to use when they shoot from a distance of more than thirty-five feet from the goal. The free throw should be mastered by all players. It is a good shot to use at all times when the shooter is not closely guarded. It should always be used for free throws. A variation of it is taught by some coaches with the very evident plan of drawing fouls on pivot shots close to the basket.

There is one drawback to its use as the only floor shot in basketball. It is too easily blocked. Since the shot starts from between the thighs, a guard may be stationed some ten feet away from the shooter and still block the shot. If this shot were used exclusively, all dribble threats would be lost, there would seldom be any over rushing by the guard, and at the same time many otherwise good opportunities for shots would be missed. Many teams, however, use it for extremely long shots, and a few use it as their principal floor shot. Never should the cramped shot which is half-way between a push shot and a free throw shot be permitted. It has been demonstrated too often that the shooting efficiency of most players is reduced thereby. What scoring they are able to do is done in spite of their handicap of poor form.

Technique of Free Throw Shot

The technique will be given for the shot as used in a free throw situation. The feet are spread as in the fundamental position. The front foot (usually the left foot) is just behind the free throw line. The player is directly in front of the basket. He stands erect with shoulders back and his weight equally distributed on both feet. The ball is held in front of and against his body. His arms are fully extended. The ball is held, as described on page 105, with the palms facing each other and centered as on an axis. The eyes are focused on the front edge of the rim. The player should be as completely relaxed as possible.

1. Movement in Shooting.

The preliminary movement in shooting is a swing of the ball out in front of the body, with the shoulder as a pivot. Neither the arms nor the ball should reach the height of the shoulders in this preliminary swing. This preliminary movement is for the purpose of relieving any tenseness in the arms, wrists, or shoulders. Some players are so tense that the muscles of their arms may be observed to stand out like taut cords. This should be relieved before the start of the shot, or control of the ball will be lost when it is released. Tenseness may be overcome by bouncing the ball on the floor a few times, by spinning it in the hands, by shaking the hands and ball, or by flexing the wrists a few times.

The arms should now be permitted to drop back against the body. As this occurs the knees should be spread and bent slightly so that the ball comes back between the thighs. The back of the hands may even touch the thighs. The arms and hands are fully extended. There is no flexion of the wrist at this point. The instant that the ball is dropped between the thighs, the upward swing of the arms in making the shot should be started.

The ball should be released just before the arms reach the level of the shoulders. The release is made by a quick upward movement of the hands and a flexion or "snap" of the wrists. This snap causes the ball to leave the fingers with a back spin. The top of the ball is rotating back toward the shooter. This wrist snap is the one important judgment factor in the whole shot. It is the one thing that must be studied carefully so that the same force may be given to the ball each time in order to "groove" the shot. This will also determine the proper arch for the ball. All the other movements are wholly mechanical. The arm movements should be as free as and similar to the swing of the arm in walking.

As the ball is released the arms should continue their swing in order that the whole movement will be smooth and relaxed. They should finish in a position above the head. As the ball is released, the elbows will bend as a result of the sudden snap.

2. Body Balance.

During the whole of this procedure, the weight of the body is kept equally distributed on both feet. It is considered much more important to be perfectly balanced than to lean as far forward as possible and to fall over the foul line as the ball hits the rim or enters the basket. This is taught by some coaches, even to the extent of having players raise one foot off the floor.[1] The author has seen so many shots declared illegal because the player crossed the free throw line too soon that he does not permit such tactics. Also the act of leaning forward in making the shot tenses the player's back muscles, prevents complete freedom of arm movement, and interferes with the proper arch of the ball. The ball should leave the hands at a very acute angle with the vertical so that it is two or three feet above the basket as it starts down. The ball should enter the basket at about the same angle at which it leaves the

[1] Allen, Forest C. Better Basketball, p. 157. New York: McGraw-Hill Book Company. 1937.
————. My Basketball Bible, p. 188. Kansas City, Missouri: Smith-Grieves Company. 1924.

fingers. The shot should be aimed to just clear the front edge of the rim. If it is well above the rim and just inside the front edge, there is little chance of a missed shot. The back spin will pull the ball through if it hits on the front edge, but will cause the ball to rebound out of the basket if the back edge is hit.

COACHING SUGGESTIONS

The important points to emphasize in teaching the free throw shot are:

1. The trunk should be vertical throughout the shot.

2. The arms should be fully extended and swinging free until the ball is released.

3. The ball should be released with a quick snap of the wrists as the arms approach the level of the shoulders.

If these three major points are emphasized first, the others must of necessity follow and they may be easily picked up later.

PRACTICE METHODS

The greatest amount of practice in free throwing should be devoted to grooving the shot. Many coaches argue that practice should be conducted under pressure, under game conditions. But since the main job is to learn how much force to give the ball, the most favorable conditions for learning should exist during practice. Emotional stress is certainly not the most favorable condition for learning.

It is found that the practice of shooting until a certain number of goals are scored produces the best results. At the beginning of the season an objective has been set for everyone to reach and maintain. This objective has been as high as 90 per cent, or 45 out of 50, and as low as 70 per cent, or 35 out of 50.

Each day every player shoots until he scores, say, 35 goals. His aim is to get consistently 35 or more out of 50. It is surprising that practically the whole squad will reach such an objective in a short time. No player should score less than 70 per cent of his free throws in practice. We have tried the plan of raising each year the objective to be reached. Each year it is reached by practically every member of the squad, but few go beyond it. They seem to be satisfied when they reach their aim. In 1937 the objective for the Stanford Varsity was placed at 90 per cent, or 45 out of 50. Even this high standard was reached by a surprising number of our players.

Early in the season, time is devoted each day to the technique of the free throw shot. Not more than three players should shoot at one goal. If there are not sufficient goals for the whole squad, then part of the squad may practice other shots and techniques at one goal while the remainder, divided into groups of threes, may work on free throws at the other goals.

It is a practical plan for each player to throw ten consecutive shots before another player is given a chance and to step away from the free throw line after each throw. This gives each man sufficient practice to get the feel of the shot and at the same time does not keep the other players idle too long. The two players who are waiting their turns should practice rebounding, pivoting, darting to the side, and passing out after each free throw.

If a record is kept of each player's progress in free throwing, he may see just how well he is doing and where he stands with respect to the rest of the team.

As the season progresses, little time will be available for mass practice in free throwing. The players must get this practice as they gather on the court and while they are waiting to take their turn or after they have finished their practice at team drills.

It is a wise plan to have the players work part of the time on free throws after they have finished their other practice. This teaches them to correct for fatigue effects. Since, after team drills begin, only a limited number of players can be used at one time, all do not finish at once; so part of the squad can always work on free throws and other techniques. Thus the whole squad can be kept busy throughout the practice.

Free throwing is so slow that little time is taken for it during regular practice. Some practice is desired during scrimmages, but if

Fig. 24. Preparation position for free throw.

Fig. 25. End of preliminary movement in free throw.

Fig. 26. Finish of free throw movement showing follow through after release of ball.

FIG. 27. The one hand shot at instant ball is released.

free throws are awarded just for the sake of shooting, such practice seems to lose its value, and for this reason it is not recommended.

A free throw practice drill, such as is described on page 92, is used for purposes of team organization after missed free throws. There is little value, however, in this drill for actual free throwing.

An excellent drill for testing to see if players have "grooved" their free throw shots is to have practice in shooting with the eyes closed. If the shot is well learned, eight out of ten shots will be scored consistently. The procedure is for the player to get ready to shoot. Just before starting the shot he closes his eyes and holds them closed until the shot is made or missed.

Figures 24, 25, and 26 show a player in three stages of the free throw shot. Figure 24 shows the preparatory position. Figure 25 shows the end of the preliminary or practice swing. Figure 26 shows the follow through of the arms and the body balance after the ball has been released.

ONE HAND PUSH SHOT

The one hand shot was originally used for set-up shots. It was considered bad form to shoot with one hand when away from the basket. Now, however, with defensive play developed to perfection, one hand shooting of all kinds from all over the offensive end of the court has become quite common. Some teams, particularly those in the East, still follow the more conservative practice of reserving the one hand shot for shots close in around the basket.

The one hand shot is used primarily for two reasons. First, the technique is used in order to get the player as close to the basket as possible before he shoots. Statistics collected over a period of years have shown that the closer to the basket one gets before shooting, the more accurate will be the shot.[2] It is also true that the defense becomes more concentrated and intense close to the basket. Contact is much more likely to occur near the basket. Holding often occurs, but because of the close contact play, offi-

---

[2] Works, Pierce. *Methods of Analyzing Offensive Efficiency*. National Association of Basketball Coaches, Bulletin No. 5. March, 1935.

cials frequently fail to detect it. If the one hand shot is correctly used, holding will be made evident to the official.

Second, the one hand shot is used away from the basket when a two hand shot would be blocked. Some players use it when they find that they are off line with their two hand shots or when some little thing seems to be wrong with their timing or coördination. It is practically always used when a player is shooting on the run because, as in the case of the hook pass, better coördination of body movements is attained.

The technique of the one hand shot will be discussed here for shots close to the basket. Application of this technique will then be made to shots under other conditions.

TECHNIQUE OF THE ONE HAND SHOT, THE TAKE-OFF

The player should start his jump when he is not more than five feet away from the goal. Height is desired in order to get close to the basket. By taking off when close in, a high jump rather than a broad jump results. Just before jumping the player should crouch. This stops the forward progress and permits the gather for the high jump. It is much the same as the practice of the high jumper just before his take off. It also gives the player time to shift his feet so that he can take off with the proper one; it lets the ball "float" long enough to prevent fumbling and assures legal foot movement.

If the player is shooting with the right hand, he will jump from the left foot. Likewise, if he shoots with the left hand, he jumps from the right foot. Except when the player is running parallel to the end line, he will shoot with the left hand when on the left side of the basket. When the player is running parallel to the end line, this technique is reversed in order to permit him to bank the ball against the backboard, a process which always produces more accurate shooting. All players should learn to shoot accurately with either hand.

1. Handling the Ball.

As the player jumps from the floor, he carries the ball in both hands to prevent fumbling. If an opponent is holding an arm, a firm grip on the ball with both hands will help the player to pull free from his opponent without losing possession of the ball, and at the same time will cause the illegal play of the opponent to be more easily detected by the official.

The ball is held close to the body throughout the shot. This is done, first, to prevent blocking by the opponent. Many shots are blocked by opponents because, as the shooter jumps from the floor, he reaches out away from the body with the ball; therefore, this point cannot be too strongly emphasized. Second, the ball is kept close to the body so that all effort and coördination can be directed vertically for the purpose of gaining height.

2. Back of Hand toward Face.

As the ball passes the height of the shoulders, it is shifted to one hand (the proper one for making the shot). Holding the ball in the fingers should not be emphasized as this produces too much tension. The ball is pushed up by and close to the side of the face and directly above the shoulder in order that the player may reach to his greatest height. Care should be taken not to get the ball behind the shoulder, as this would cause the player to throw the ball against the backboard, a fact which perhaps would result in a missed shot. In order to extend the arm vertically above the shoulder with perfect coördination and relaxation, it is necessary to hold the ball so that the back of the hand is toward the body. One need only try to reach vertically above his shoulders with the palm of his hand toward the face to feel the tension and lack of muscular coördination in his forearm. Demonstration of this point suffices to convince the most skeptical players of its importance.

3. Release of Ball.

The ball is released by a quick extension of the forearm and a backward flexion and fixing of the wrist. This movement is similar to that used in the push shot, except that the ball is carried on one hand. In order that the full height of the jump may be utilized, the shot should not be made until after the player has reached the highest point of his jump. This will also divorce the force of the jump from the shot so that the ball may be laid lightly against the backboard. Further, it will prevent a hurried shot with attendant inaccuracies. This point is violated by players more often than is any other phase of the technique. Probably the reason is that they feel their opponent is coming fast behind them and they wish to avoid contact.

4. Playing the Backboard.

The ball should always be laid lightly against the backboard. There is a rather large surface of the board that one may hit and still be certain of scoring a goal. The best place at which to aim is a spot just above the rim and just outside the nearest edge. One should therefore focus on this spot on the backboard rather than on the basket. Playing the backboard corrects many mistakes in shooting this shot. Hence, in order to play the backboard, players are always taught to cut to one side or the other when coming in to the basket from directly in front. Experience has shown that a shot is seldom missed if this practice is followed.

5. Spin Not Emphasized.

It will be noticed that no mention has been made of giving spin to the ball. Absence of spin is the reason why the shot is called a one hand push shot rather than a one hand English shot. As a matter of fact, it is better not to encourage spinning the ball on this shot.[3] In theory, the spin may be considered a desirable feature of the shot, but in practice it has proved to be a detriment. Particularly is this true when the players are young and inexperienced.

[3] Allen, Forest C. *Better Basketball*, p. 161. New York: McGraw-Hill Book Company. 1937.

Variations in One Hand Shots Away from Goal

Some of the instructions for this shot are altered when the shot is made from a distance. For example, the backboard is not used for most floor shots. Shots may be made from out in front of the basket. Players will jump into the air as they make the shot only when they are on the run. When shooting from set locations the same body position is assumed as for the two hand push shot.

When a closely guarded player is going away from the basket or cutting across the center toward a corner, a one hand hook shot is used as a variation of the one hand push shot. The technique is exactly the same as that described for the hook pass. This technique is also used in pivot shots when the player starts with his back to the goal.

Figure 27 shows Luisetti making a one hand push shot. The ball is just leaving the fingers.

Major Points to Emphasize

So many phases of this shot must be taught that the most important elements are listed here for emphasis. If these are stressed, the player may be expected to grasp them quickly; if all points in connection with the shot are covered, the players will be kept in a state of confusion, so that they get practically none of the technique. If these few points are followed, most of the others will of necessity be adopted.

1. Keep the ball close to the body throughout the shot. Do not reach away from the body with the ball. The back of the hand should be toward the face when shooting.

2. High jump rather than broad jump. Get up as close to the basket as possible.

3. Shoot after the high point of the jump has been reached.

Drills

In order to learn the hand and forearm movement in the shot, the players may group around close to the basket and practice this technique to the exclusion of everything else. They should practice with either hand until they become ambidextrous in their one hand shots.

Next the foot work may be introduced. A player stands in front of the basket. He steps to one side and takes off for his shot. He catches the ball as it comes through the net, steps to the opposite side, and jumps to shoot with the opposite hand. After he repeats this performance ten times, another player takes his place. Players who have trouble learning this shot may get off by themselves and use these two drills.

The next step is to introduce running in to make the shot. The warm-up drill and the fast break drill as described on pages 77 and 83 are used for this purpose. The regular offense play practice is also a means of getting practice in this and other shots.

Of course, one player or two or three together may get practice in the one hand shot by taking a ball and dribbling in to the basket. The drill suggested on page 135 for practicing the push shot may be used. The player, after receiving the ball from his teammate, will fake and then dribble in to the basket for a one hand shot instead of shooting a two hand shot from a distance.

Much practice in this shot will be gained when playing "hunch," "three on two," or "two on one."

CHAPTER XII

METHODS OF STOPPING AND
TURNING—PIVOTING

THE two count stop is really the only stop that is consistent with good body balance. This type of stop agrees with the fundamental position which was described in Chapter IX. It fits perfectly the carefully worked out technique of "to the rear—march" used in military tactics. Even players who are taught the one count or jump stop, almost invariably and inadvertently fall into the two count stop simply because the jump stop is unnatural and quite difficult to execute.[1] Careful observation of players thoroughly drilled in the one count stop has proved this point beyond contradiction. This, then, takes away any alleged advantage in being able to pivot on either foot.

Players who use the one stop technique, but who actually stop in two counts and pivot by lifting the pivot foot are committing a violation. Officials are lax in dealing with such illegal maneuvers. As a result, defensive players are put at a decided disadvantage. This is one point on which officiating needs to improve.

The two count stop gives greater protection to the ball as will be shown. It also permits the player making the stop to approach his opponent much more closely and with perfect safety. Getting close to the opponent affords excellent opportunities for getting around him. Also getting close teases the opponent and encourages

[1] Meanwell, W. E. *Basketball for Men*. Madison, Wisconsin: Democrat Printing Company. 1922. P. 86.
Veenker, George F. *Basketball for Coaches and Players*, New York: A. S. Barnes and Company. 1929. P. 54.
Lambert, Ward L. *Practical Basketball*. Chicago: Athletic Journal Publishing Company. 1932. P. 20.

him to attack the ball, with the result that it is quite easy to draw him out of position.

For these reasons the two count stop is the only logical stop to use. It is the only one that will be presented here.

WHEN TO USE A STOP AND PIVOT

The stop and pivot are used effectively under many situations:

1. *A good slogan to adopt is "When in doubt, stop, pivot, and pass back."* The tendency of players is to pass and move toward their goal. This is particularly true when a fast break is attempted. Unless the way is absolutely clear to "drive" in to the goal, this policy is more often wrong than right. It ends in a bad pass or an interception by the opponents. Because the possibilities and strategy of the play following a pivot are not visioned by the players and because of the temptation to try to get through to the goal without hesitation, the value and effectiveness of the pivot are seldom realized. For these reasons teams should be made pivot conscious by repeating to them the above slogan.

2. *The stop and pivot are used to change quickly the direction of the play.* The value of this point may be seen when the players of both teams are madly rushing for the goal. The defensive players are just slightly behind, but are close enough in pursuit to give trouble, and they are trying hard to get between their opponents and the goal. A quick stop and pivot by the player with the ball will cause the opponents to rush on by. As the ball is passed back, the opponents rush out to meet it and then, by another quick pass back in toward the goal, the opponents are caught moving counter to the ball.

A like situation results when a player, who is being chased so closely as he dribbles to the goal that his shot may be blocked, stops, pivots, and passes back to a teammate who is following. This teammate has not been pressed; he is therefore more relaxed and in a much better position to shoot for the goal. In this case the player who pivots may himself shoot after he has displaced his opponent. Thus the use of the pivot to change quickly the direction of play is effective strategy.

3. *In all cases when the forward progress of the offense is blocked, the stop, pivot, and pass back should be used.* In addition to the situation described above, need for this technique occurs when an attempt to go around an opponent is blocked. This usually happens out in front of the defense or along the side line.

4. *The stop and pivot are used to displace an opponent.* This applies to the player without the ball as well as to the player with the ball. The player without the ball, in an effort to free himself from an opponent, uses the stunt of feinting or even starting in one direction and then quickly reversing so that he may receive a pass. The player with the ball may dribble from the center to the side, or vice versa, in an attempt to get around his guard. By so doing, he opens up lanes for a subsequent attack. Then by stopping, pivoting, and passing back, he makes it possible for a teammate to dart through the opening. Also, since the player with the ball may come very near his opponent in this type of stop, the opponent is often displaced by reason of charging the ball.

5. *The stop and pivot are used to protect the ball from an opponent.* Since the stop is made so that a leg is always between the ball and the guard, there never is any opportunity for that guard to get the ball. This is the big advantage of the two count stop.

6. *The pivot and movement following the pass back are used to screen an opponent from a teammate who has come up to get the ball.* After a player has pulled his opponent to the side of the court by a dribble and has pivoted and passed back to a following teammate, he may continue his pivot and run between his teammate and the opponent whom he has displaced. In this way he sets up a screen for his teammate. In football parlance, he becomes a personal interferer for his teammate. This movement is perfectly legal as long as the player who forms the screen does not move into his opponent. (See Diagram 6, the All-Purpose Drill, for this type of screen maneuver.)

The execution of this type of screen shades into blocking and charging much less than the type of pivot used from the jump or one count stop.[2] Here the pivoter uses his leg as a flail in an attempt to encircle his opponent. In doing this, the rump and thigh bang into the opponent. Often he is knocked back several feet or even knocked down. This, of course, is decidedly illegal.

TECHNIQUE OF STOP AND PIVOT

In this description of the stop and pivot it is assumed that the opponent is in his logical position between the player with the ball and the goal.

One should always approach an opponent in such a way as to cause him to move laterally on the court. This tactic opens up more play possibilities than if the opponent can either stand in position or back straight toward the goal. This same point was emphasized under rules for passing on page 112.

If one receives the ball and at the same instant is attacked by an opponent, he should turn to the side. If he is dribbling the ball when he approaches an opponent, he should turn to the side.

1. Stop with Body between Ball and Opponent.

If the player's progress is blocked, he will of course stop. A good body balance is most easily maintained by the use of a skipping movement in stopping. If the player with the ball is to the right of the goal when he stops, he should stop with his left foot forward and in the extreme fundamental position. (The right foot is forward if the player with the ball is on the left side of the basket.) This will place his left leg between the opponent and the ball. If the opponent charges the ball, he will run into a thigh, a shoulder, a rump, or an elbow, instead of getting the ball. The charging of this opponent in no way affects the balance of the player who has the ball. It will help him to pivot and it may be quite damaging to the opponent if he happens to run too hard

[2] Barry, Justin M. *Basketball, Individual and Team Play.* Iowa City, Iowa: Clio Press, 1929. Ch. 6, p. 49.

Fig. 28. Stop and pivot, first position. Correct stop with leg between guard and the ball.

Fig. 29. Stop and pivot, second position. The pivot away from the guard.

onto one of the projections mentioned above. These protecting points may be likened to the quills of a porcupine. They are the "animal's" protective mechanism.

2. Value of Foot Position in Stopping.

In stopping, the toe of the forward foot should be pointed in the direction the player was travelling. This also is for protection. The tendency to turn the side of the foot toward the direction the player was travelling is the cause of many sprained ankles. The correct position of the foot gives the player a more aggressive and threatening stand. He will usually be facing diagonally across the court. In this position he can still pass forward. This possibility prevents the guard from becoming too careless in his tactics. If the player stops with the forward foot sideways, he is facing to the rear. From this position he cannot see the front court, nor is he situated to fake passes in the direction of the basket. Consequently the guard can take liberties that are not possible under the correct conditions. Figure 28 shows a player stopping correctly. The guard is also shown in order to give an idea of the protection possible and the closeness of the player with the ball to his opponent.

3. Movement when Pivoting.

In pivoting, the player *steps* with his forward foot. (Many players get the idea that merely reversing on the balls of the feet is pivoting. This is not pivoting, and it is one of the reasons why so many players fail to escape from attack after they have stopped.) His movement is back and away from his guard. He turns so that his body is always between the ball and the guard. Figure 29 shows the result of this movement. The position in Fig. 29 follows that in Fig. 28. An alert guard will take advantage of any other movement to gain a held ball or even to steal the ball. The pivoter should not raise up as he turns. To raise up, leaves the ball unprotected and does not move it through a great enough distance during the pivot. Since the ball is near, if not touching, the floor and is just inside the forward foot at the moment the player stops, it should be carried along the floor during the pivot. This causes the ball to travel at least six feet in the pivot and helps to displace sufficiently an opponent who follows after the ball, thereby making a subsequent play effective. Also, by keeping the ball along the floor and maintaining a low crouch throughout the pivot, the player is protected by all his projecting spines.

These are the advantages of this type of pivot over the pivot from the jump stop. The only means of protection from the jump stop is distance, since no part of the body is between the ball and the opponent. The player who uses the jump stop must always stop at least three feet away from his opponent; otherwise an alert guard can tie up or steal the ball every time. The ball moves about a foot on the pivot, and at the most, not more than half as far as on the pivot from the two count stop. Consequently, there is not much chance to displace an opponent.

PRECAUTIONS FOR THE PIVOTER

The pivoter should be cautioned about taking steps that are too long. He will throw himself off balance with long strides and he may be successfully guarded from the rear. Some teams "two-time" a player who pivots; that is, an opponent comes up from the rear and surprises the pivoter as he turns. Some players also fall into the careless habit of taking for granted that a teammate is behind them and pass the ball blindly. This leads to interceptions. To avoid interceptions and attacks from the rear, the pivoter should first turn his head in the direction that he pivots. Second, an elbow and shoulder should always precede the ball. Thus, if he is guarded by more than one player, these moves will give him sufficient warning so that he can protect the ball. He can then keep both his body and the ball thrashing back and forth until he can fight into the clear in order to pass the ball to safety. It may be found that players who have trouble keeping their balance after pivoting, yet who are not taking long strides, are failing to turn the heel of the rear foot turned toward the median line of the body.

Coaching Suggestions

The important points to stress in teaching the stop and pivot are:

1. Stop with one leg between opponent and ball. This permits player to get right against opponent and to tease him with the ball.

2. Step so that body is always between opponent and the ball.

3. Keep ball along floor throughout stop and pivot.

4. Turn head before pivoting.

Most of the other points will come into play as a natural consequence of stressing these movements first. The player can easily keep these in mind without confusion.

Drills

The drill on page 100, which was used in teaching the fundamental position, can be used to advantage in teaching the stop and pivot. This technique is really just an advanced stage and an application of the fundamental position. In order to relax, the players should step several times or continue to pivot several times after they stop.

The drill that is used more than any other to teach the pivot is the All-purpose drill described on page 85.

The Fast Break drill (page 83) is also used.

The Warm-up drill (page 77) has a pivot in its movement which may also be used.

CHAPTER XIII

METHODS OF DRIBBLING

THE dribble can be both the most useful and the most harmful element in basketball. In 1928 the Rules Committee limited the dribble to one bounce. So loud and so widespread was the protest of coaches that the National Association of Basketball Coaches came into being as a result. A large representation of college and high school coaches from all over the United States met in Des Moines, organized, and unanimously protested the action of the Rules Committee. Their objection was sustained, and the dribble remained in the rules.[1]

EVILS OF THE DRIBBLE

Coaches recognize the evils of the dribble. They feel, however, that the dribble is so useful that the evils are to be controlled by coaching rather than by legislation. This seems to be a logical conclusion since the evils of dribbling operate more to the disadvantage of the team whose players are at fault than to the detriment of the game. Many of the bad dribble habits are enumerated here.

1. Probably the greatest evil of dribbling is the habit of dribbling too much. Some players will always dribble when they get the ball. These players, unconsciously of course, have the idea that they must retain possession of the ball just as long as possible. In other words, they will pass the ball as a last resort, but they will keep it if they can. It seems to be an inherent part of basketball for

[1] National Basketball Rules Committee of United States and Canada. *Minutes*. 1928.

players to desire the ball when they do not have it and to keep it when they get it. This habit is no doubt formed from playing by one's self too much. It is a fact that one can have much fun playing alone. A balance, however, is needed to develop a strong team.

Some teams have players who always dribble when they get the ball. It is good strategy to instruct a team to gamble on the possibility that such players will not pass and always to go for them when they dribble. Seldom have such tactics proved to be detrimental. So it is seen that such dribblers make the defensive work for their opponents a very simple matter.

2. There is always the problem of deciding how much a clever dribbler shall be permitted to dominate the play and to handle the ball. Certainly, the abilities of such a player should be utilized to the maximum. Clever dribbling makes for a spectacular game. However, individual play should not be emphasized to the neglect or breakdown of team play. After all, it is easier to concentrate on and defeat one good player than it is to win from a good team, even though that team is composed of one outstanding performer and four mediocre ones.

3. There is also the chronic dribbler. He is the player whose first move always, whenever he receives the ball, is to duck his head and bounce the ball. He never sees his teammates. It is he who never looks for a teammate after retrieving the ball from the backboard. He never makes an attempt to get the ball to the goal before his opponents get back on defense. He waits until everyone is back across the center line and then begins his pat-pat toward the goal. It was because of him that the Rules Committee originally passed the one bounce rule. It was because of him that the game was becoming a little drab and the action slow. It was because of him that many said the court should be cut in half— only half of it was being used anyway. His actions deprived his team of many opportunities to score. The chronic dribbler is a "blind" dribbler. Stop him at any time during his dribble and ask him if he has seen such and such a teammate. He is sure to answer that he has not. He needs practice in keeping his head

up and in consciously looking for possible passes to teammates. He must be reminded that a pass is always a faster method of advancing the ball than is dribbling.

4. Finally, there is the player with the one bounce habit. He is the player who does not look for teammates until after he gets the ball. While he is looking for a possible pass receiver, he bounces the ball once. He is usually one of the players who is handling the ball out in front of the defense. His one bounce habit deprives his teammates of the chance of carrying through any effective maneuvers that may have been started. An opening may have been made through the defense, but while one bounce is taken, the opening closes. A defensive player has been deployed out of position, but while time is consumed for the one bounce, the player recovers his position. A defensive player can take three steps during the time required for the one bounce.

Dribble Habits Coaching Problem, Not Rules Problem

It takes strong, sometimes even drastic coaching efforts to correct players who have formed these habits. But they are all coaching problems and should never call for changes in rules. One means of making players conscious of these faults during practice is to call violations when they occur and to award the ball to opponents out of bounds. A one bounce rule may even be invoked during practice to help cure dribbling evils.

Value of the Dribble

In spite of these bad features of the dribble, it is a necessary part of the game. The dribble is to basketball what the forward pass is to football. Whether it is used or not, it is an ever-present threat. Without the dribble, the game would be much rougher because the defense would have to be less cautious.

The dribble has at least five important uses:

1. It is needed to permit a player to break for the basket when he has the ball and there is a clear path before him to the goal

with no teammate ahead of him. A player would appear helpless if he had a clear path before him and yet could not advance the ball. He may not get to the goal for a shot, but at least he has had the opportunity to make the threat and he has caused other developments which may subsequently score a goal.

2. The dribble is needed as a threat to prevent the defense from becoming too aggressive. A player who has the ball and who has not dribbled it will be played rather cautiously by a wise guard. For the guard to become too aggressive and to play too close to the player with the ball is the same as inviting him to go around. Such over aggressive tactics by the guard often result in a foul by him.

3. The dribble is valuable in displacing a set defense. By means of the dribble a player may advance the ball up the court when he is the "front" man of his team on a fast break. Then as he approaches an opponent, if he is in the center of the court, he cuts sharply to one side. This draws the guard over to the side and permits a teammate to break clear toward the goal. At times when a pass is not possible out in front of a defense, the player with the ball may start quickly to dribble around an opponent. Then, when his progress is blocked, he quickly stops, pivots, and passes to a teammate. This teammate will take advantage of any displacement of the defense that may have occurred.

4. A player who is dribbling may often block out an opponent who is attempting to guard him. A player has gotten a break for the goal. He is dribbling toward it. An opponent comes up fast alongside. The dribbler sees or "feels" the approach of this opponent and steps over into his path. This maneuver by means of the dribble will cause the opponent to slow up, thus permitting the dribbler to continue to the basket for a score; or the opponent may be forced to foul the dribbler.

5. Finally, the dribble is most necessary to get the ball out of a crowded area when a pass is not possible. For example, a player retrieves the ball from the backboard. He is closely guarded by two opponents. A pass may be very dangerous under the circumstances. His best move, usually, is to force his way, by means of

the dribble, into an open unguarded spot on the court. On another occasion a player receives the ball. He may be anywhere on the court. He is closely guarded by one or more players. He does not have a teammate to whom he can pass the ball. His best move is to dribble into an opening. This situation occurs repeatedly after a player recovers a loose ball.

In all cases it should be clearly understood that the dribble is the last resort in any attack. Look for a pass first. Dribble if a pass is not possible.

Types of Dribbles

The dribble may be classified under two common heads: the low bounce dribble and the high bounce dribble. The high bounce is used only when a player is dribbling without any opposition whatever. It is good as a change of pace so that an opponent will be deceived as to the speed of approach of the dribbler. It is never used when opponents are near, when going around an opponent, when dribbling through or within a set defense, or when one is fighting his way out of a scramble of players. The low bounce dribble should always be used in these situations. One is touching the ball more often with the low bounce dribble. It is, therefore, possible to change direction, speed, or even to stop more quickly. The control of the ball is more constant, so that a change in the tactics of the opponents may be met with dispatch.

Dribble Technique

Because the low bounce is really the important dribble, the technique for only this type of dribble is considered here.

As a rule, the feet are spread as in the fundamental position. This gives excellent lateral balance and permits the dribbler to change direction most quickly.

1. Body Position.

A half knee bend is assumed. Since the trunk is bent forward at the waist in order to bounce the ball close to the floor, the deep

Fig. 30.   Luisetti dribbling. Notice in particular that the gaze is not focused on the ball.

knee bend prevents the dribbler from falling forward. The ball for the most part should be bounced well out in front of the feet to remove any possibility of kicking it or getting too far over it. The deep knee bend tends to make this maneuver possible.

2. Position of Eyes.

The eyes must be focussed on the players on the court ahead and to each side of the dribbler. He should always be ready to make a pass when a receiver is in position or to protect the ball against a surprise attack. He should see the ball out of the periphery of his vision. This makes it necessary for the chin to be well out from the chest. The head, in other words, is pulled back much in the fashion of that of a rabbit crouching in the grass, but ever alert to detect the approach of an enemy from any direction.

3. Handling the Ball.

The ball is bounced by a short, quick, light slapping motion of the wrist and fingers. The hand at all times is so close to the ball that this motion actually amounts to a quick push. It is similar to the movement used in shooting the one hand push shot, except that the position is inverted. Players should learn to dribble equally well with either hand. They are then effective in going around opponents on either side and in dribbling in any direction.

4. Free Hand as a Guard.

The hand which is not being used to dribble the ball acts as a guard or protection for it. This hand is held out in readiness to take the ball at any time. This tactic puts the forearm in a practically horizontal position. The elbow is to the front of the body and is pointed out to the side. The forearm and elbow thus give excellent protection against attack from a player who may come at the ball from the side of the free arm. Excellent dribble form is shown in Fig. 30.

5. Dribble Tactics.

The ball should not bounce higher than eighteen inches from the floor. For quick maneuvering, the bounces are much shorter than this. Many coaches teach that the ball should always be directly in front of the median line of the body.[2] The position of the ball, however, will depend entirely upon the play situation. For instance, if one is dribbling around an opponent, he will most certainly have the ball out to one side.

For speed dribbling, the ball is pushed away from the body at a very acute angle with the floor. To slow up and to change direction, the player bounces the ball more perpendicularly to the floor. Clever variations of these tactics tend to throw a guard off balance and to permit a dribbler to get around him and to out-maneuver him rather easily. Add to this a zig-zag movement made by alternating the dribble from one hand to the other and you have a dribbler who is a terror to any opponent. These tactics may be likened to the strategy of the movement of a broken field runner in a football game.

POINTS FOR COACHING EMPHASIS

The important coaching points to emphasize in first presenting the dribble to a squad are:

1. Maintain a low crouch, at least a half knee bend.

2. Keep the eyes on the players in front and to the side. See the ball out of the periphery of the vision.

If these two directions are followed, most of the other phases of the technique will be complied with automatically.

DRIBBLING AROUND AN OPPONENT

Because of its importance, the technique of dribbling around an opponent is treated as a special phase of dribbling. Many players are unsuccessful in their attempts to dribble around an opponent because they violate some of the simple but absolutely essential principles involved.

1. *The technique of going around an opponent when the player with the ball is dribbling toward the opponent.* The dribbler should

[2] Ruby, J. Craig. *How to Coach and Play Basketball.* Champaign, Illinois: Bailey and Hines Publishers. 1926.

use all the maneuvers of zig-zagging, change of pace, alternating hands, etc., as described on the opposite page. It is not necessary that he dribble fast until he starts around his guard; then he should use all the speed and quickness at his command.

The dribbler should not start around his guard until he is within three feet of him. It is not difficult for the guard to block the path of the dribbler if he starts around at a greater distance away. If the dribbler gets closer than three feet, the chances of interception of the ball are too great.

In the approach, the dribbler must be alert to a change of position of the guard. The guard may charge. This movement, however, is to his disadvantage. It is much easier to get around a charging guard. The guard may retreat. It is practically impossible to get around such a guard. The dribbler in this case should follow up this retreat until he is in a position to make an easy shot. More often the guard stands still with his feet even and spread laterally in a typical wrestler's stance. The job in this case is to go in one direction around the guard when he is caught leaning, or with his weight tending to move in the opposite direction. The zig-zag, alternating hands, the faking to go one way, and then actually moving in the opposite direction accomplish this feat. Some dribblers perform a veritable dance in front of the guard as they go through these tactics. The tendency, if the dribbler is effective in his movements, is for the guard to dance with him. The dribbler then should watch for a mis-move by the guard. The moment the guard is caught off balance, the dribbler must move like lightning to get around him. Here is where real quickness and keen judgment on the part of the dribbler are necessary for success.

Tactics as Dribbler Darts around Opponent.

As the dribbler makes his final dart to get around his guard, two very important moves are needed. If, for example, the dribbler is going around to his right, first he bounces the ball at the start with his left hand. He will have faked to the left, so that the ball will be over to his left in a position to be played with the left hand. The ball must be batted directly across in front of his body. Stating this another way, the ball is slapped across in front of the body and at right angles to a line connecting the guard with the dribbler. This is done in order to get the ball completely out of reach of the guard. It is necessary for the guard to make a complete recovery if he is to break up the dribble or even block the path of the dribbler. Too many dribblers make the mistake of bouncing the ball forward rather than across as they go around. This leaves the ball unprotected and does not take advantage of the overbalanced condition of the guard. It helps the guard to recover from his mistake and, many times, to intercept the ball.

The next move is for the dribbler to step forward to the right with his left foot. (Remember it is assumed that the dribbler is going to his right.) At the same time, the ball is bounced with the right hand. This places the body of the dribbler between the ball and the guard. Even though the dribbler is thwarted in his attempt to get around, the guard has no chance to get the ball.

As the dribbler steps with his left foot, he should dip his left shoulder and hold his left arm out in the protecting position described on page 159. This gives further protection to the ball and places the dribbler in such a position that he will go clear around the guard. He is thus complying with the rules concerning the dribble. He is not likely to commit a foul in this situation, but is more likely to be fouled.

If the dribbler can get completely around his opponent, he should immediately move to a position between his opponent and the goal. This maneuver blocks the guard entirely out of the play and assures the dribbler of an opportunity of going to the goal for a shot, so far as this one guard is concerned.

2. *The problem of going around a guard when the player with the ball is standing in front of the guard is solved in much the same way.* In this case the offensive player fakes by leaning as if to go in one direction and then, depending on the movements of his opponent, the player goes around either in that same direction or in the opposite. There may be considerable maneuvering before the dribbler can get a favorable opportunity to dribble around.

As the player starts to dribble around his guard, he carries the ball directly across in front of his body and.at right angles to a line connecting the defensive and the offensive player. He bounces the ball with the hand farthest away from the opponent. From this point the technique is the same as for the player who was approaching his opponent with a dribble.

DRIBBLE DRILLS

1. Two Drills for Beginners.

1. Dribbling is one of the best practice schemes to develop quickness and coördination. Players may work individually or in pairs with one ball. First one bounces the ball without much movement at the beginning. Then the ball is given to the other to do likewise. Gradually players may increase their activity until finally one of the pair acts as a guard and attempts to get the ball from the dribbler. During this type of drill short, quick bounces should be used.

2. A beginners' drill commences by forming the players into as many lines as there are balls. The front player in each line stands on one side line. The lines are equal distances apart. The coach stands on the opposite side of the floor. At a given signal the players in the front of each line begin dribbling across the floor. The players should dribble slowly as there is no desire for speed at the beginning. Also, they should not alternate hands at first. Three points should be emphasized: 1. a low crouch, 2. look at the coach throughout the dribble, 3. tap the ball lightly. As proficiency is gained, speed is attained, and the other versatile movements are introduced.

2. Dribble Race.

A dribble race is useful for dribble practice after some proficiency in dribbling is gained. The common straightaway dribble, however, is frowned upon. It is doubtful if any dribble value is gained from such practice.

Instead, the squad is divided into two equal groups. The groups

line up on either side of one of the baskets. The front player in
each line is just behind the end line and is given a ball. Four
obstacles (chairs make effective dribbling posts) are placed in
front of each line. They are located on either side of the center
line of the court and are staggered so that it is necessary for a
dribbler to zig-zag as he goes around each obstacle. The dribbler
is required to go around these obstacles as he dribbles the length
of the court.

At a given signal the players in the front line start to dribble
the length of the court. A goal is shot at the opposite basket.
The dribblers return, zig-zag around the obstacles, and finish by
shooting a goal. They must continue shooting at each end until
a goal is made. After shooting the last goal, the player passes the
ball to the next player in line, who goes through the same routine.
The group wins that finishes first.

3. Dribbling the Gauntlet.

When the players are able to dribble adeptly, a competitive
dribble through a squad of players may be used. Six players are
lined up one behind the other. They face toward one end of the
court and are spaced equally between the end lines. The first
player in the line is placed ten feet from the end line. The rest of
the squad lines up behind the end line. The front player is given
the ball and tries to dribble through the six players without
losing possession of the ball. The six guards who are attempting
to break up the dribble may not retreat. They may move forward
or laterally. When the dribbler gets by a guard, that guard has
finished his assignment.

As the dribbler approaches one guard, the next guard back may
not move forward until after the dribbler has successfully gotten
by the guard in front of him. The next guard who is waiting to
attack the dribbler may move laterally at any time.

When the dribbler finishes his attempt to dribble through the
six guards, the front guard in the line goes to the end of the line
of those waiting to dribble. The dribbler becomes the last guard
in the line. The others move up one position.

In addition to these drills, which are used only during preliminary practice, the All-purpose drill and the Individual Guarding drill, as described on pages 85 and 87 are used for dribble practice.

The drill for rolling the ball back and dribbling in for set-up, as described in Chapter XI, is also useful.

CHAPTER XIV

METHODS OF TIPPING THE BALL

WITH the elimination of the center jump, the art of tipping the ball may seem to be a superfluous accomplishment. However, there are at least two center jumps in every game. Jumps after held balls range from four or five to over forty per game. A matter of even more importance is the tipping of the ball on rebounds at the basket. The observation of short players who consistently out-maneuver their taller opponents on jumps, while at the same time the taller players reach a higher point, has made it quite evident that there is considerably more to jumping than merely reaching to a great height.

TIMING THE JUMP

The most important factor in tipping the ball is to time the start of the jump so that the ball may be tipped when the player is at the highest point of his jump. In tipping the ball after a held ball or after a toss-up at center, if the official tosses the ball in accordance with the requirement of the rules, the jumper should start his jump just as the ball reaches its highest point. The rules require that the ball shall be tossed higher than either player can jump. Officials, however, are prone to toss the ball too low. This destroys what would normally be good timing in jumping and causes jumpers to "steal" the ball by tipping it before it reaches its highest point. Players are inclined to jump too soon; therefore considerable practice time should be spent in tipping the ball, particularly at the basket.

Effort Directed Vertically

Next, all effort should be directed vertically. The ball should be watched at all times. The player should get as nearly under the ball as possible, so that he may take full advantage of his height, reach, and jump. As the arm is extended above the head, it should not be swung in an arc from its natural hanging position. This would dissipate in a horizontal direction a part of the effort, would cause loss of height in the jump, and would tend to swing the body sideways. As the arm is raised, the hand should be kept as close to the body as possible until it is extended above the head. Then it should be directly above the head if possible. By keeping the hand close to the body throughout this movement, not only is all effort directed in a vertical direction but it will be more difficult for opponents to interfere with the jump.

Art of Jumping

A good crouch will help the player to get a forceful spring from the floor. More particularly, when the player is waiting for a rebound from the basket, a crouch will prevent opponents from crowding too closely and from interfering with the jump. A quick forceful flexion of the ankle joint is necessary in effective jumping. Some players find a preliminary short hop gives them greater height. The weight should be carried on the balls of the feet for best results.

Rope skipping is a very effective exercise to develop foot work and ankle flexion.

Tipping Ball at Lowest Point

The ball should be tipped with a slight wrist movement only. It should not be batted by means of an arm swing as such a movement would cause a loss of height in jumping. If the fingers are held close together, greater extension can be obtained. The fingers should contact the ball at a point slightly above its lowest point.

It must be remembered that the ball is approximately ten inches in diameter. If the fingers are placed along the side of the ball, then almost five inches of height are lost. In jumping, a fraction of an inch is often the difference between controlling the ball and losing it on the jump.

DRILLS

Three drills are used for practice in jumping to control the ball:

1. First, the squad is divided into groups of three, so that three players of nearly equal height are together. One player acts as an official to toss the ball between the other two, who jump for it and play until one gains complete control in the fundamental position. This drill makes a good contest. The best jumpers in each group then compete against each other until the best jumper on the squad is found. The drill may be repeated to find the next best jumper, and so on.

2. Next, three players take positions about a goal. One tosses the ball so that it will not score a basket, and then the three jump to tip the ball into the basket. Each is expected to tip the ball when it comes down in his territory. The three do not compete against each other. The players may be moved away from the goal after a time so that they get practice in rebounding while in motion.

3. The third drill is the regular held ball formation. This is described in Chapter XXVI, together with explanations of game situations that arise at different positions on the court.

CHAPTER XV

METHODS OF INDIVIDUAL GUARDING

THE DUTIES OF THE GUARD

N O MATTER what type of team defense is taught, every player must be thoroughly drilled in the elements of individual guarding. The team's defense depends for its strength upon the defensive ability of each individual. It is important that the players get a clear grasp of what is expected of them when on defense. The job of the defensive player will vary according to whether the coach is conservative or aggressive. Aggressiveness, daring, initiative should be encouraged at all times, and so the duties of this type of a guard are set down here. These are listed in the order of their importance and sequence on the court when a team loses possession of the ball.

1. *It is the duty of the guard to get the ball.* If the opponent is successful in recovering the ball off the backboard, an aggressive attempt should be made to take it away from him. In other words, the players should not drop back immediately on defense without even a struggle. There really is no excuse for committing a foul in the back court, but it is still possible to tie up the player with the ball. With this idea foremost in mind, aggressive basketball, characterized by initiative and freedom all over the court instead of in only one half of it, will be encouraged and developed. It will be noted that this is not a conservative, cautious type of defense, but rather a daring, gambling type. Methods of carrying out this idea will be shown later in Chapter XXV.

2. *It is the duty of the defense to delay the opponent in the back court.* It may not be possible to obtain possession of the ball

from the opponent, but at least he can be delayed by the attempt until the whole of the defensive team has an opportunity to get into position. If the opponents are delayed in the back court, then the defense will be able to get between the opponents and their basket. One of the most effective ways to combat a fast breaking offense is to prevent it from getting out of the back court too quickly.

3. *It is the duty of the defense to prevent a close-up shot.* If a guard must make a choice between covering an opponent near the basket and one farther away, he should always cover the one nearer the basket. If the opponent is to get a shot, at least make him take the longer one. His percentage of hits will be lower from the greater distance away from the basket.

4. *Finally, it is the duty of the defense to prevent any shot at all.* If the situation happens to be such that two offensive players are pitted against one defensive player, the defensive player, while always first guarding the basket, should, if possible, "jockey" and feint to prevent any kind of a shot. Any time that an opponent has the ball in the front court he is a possible scorer. Therefore, the player guarding him should try to prevent him from taking a shot. There are some exceptions to this statement, as are pointed out in Chapter VI under strategical situations. Generally, however, this is the safest rule to follow.

The Facilities of the Guard

Many coaches think that the hands and the feet are the only tools of the guard.[1] Quite often, however, other factors prove much more effective. For purpose of emphasis, the four main facilities of the guard are listed here in the reverse of the order in which they are most used.

1. *The guard should use his voice.* Some coaches do not want talking players, but talking players are confident players. Talking helps to build team morale and team spirit. It gets players over

[1] Lindley, Frank. "Basketball Theory, System, and Style." *Athletic Journal,* Vol. XVII (January, 1937) p. 16.

their timidity. Where a team defense is used, instead of a man-to-man defense, talking is a means of keeping the defense functioning coöperatively. In addition to these points, talking to an opponent at the right moment tends to disconcert him, to cause him to change his mind, and even to make him miss a shot. A continuous din of chatter is not at all effective and is not even heard after a time. But a yell at the psychological moment is to be encouraged. I have seen players blush from the unexpectedness of a yell just as they were about to shoot or pass. Often they have thrown the ball away as a result.

2. *The guard should make use of the dramatic effect of his eyes and his expression.* The most effective feint can be carried out by the expression alone. It is possible to hypnotize your opponent by a strong, fixed, threatening gaze. He may even throw the ball to you. Often a player is able to dominate a situation entirely by means of good facial dramatics. Most players give away their intent with their eyes; so by watching carefully the eyes of the opponent with the ball, you can anticipate his movements; or by fixing your gaze upon him, you can confuse him in his movements.

3. *The guard should use his feet.* Many players, when they reach for the ball, are unable to move their feet at the same time. From the standpoint of avoiding fouls and keeping in a strong defensive position, it is more important to move the feet than the hands. The Technique of foot movement follows below.

In addition to the above, the feet can be made defensive weapons by slapping a foot to the floor to confuse an opponent who is on the point of shooting. The feet can be used to block the ball. Even though this is a violation, it is sometimes desirable to block a pass with the feet.

4. *The arms and hands are usually considered the main defensive weapons of the guard.* The technique of guarding follows below, where a full explanation of the use of the arms and hands in guarding will be given.

Individual Guarding Methods

It is assumed here, in describing individual guarding methods, that the guard is always guarding the player with the ball. Under all other situations a defensive player is waiting in position for an opportunity to guard.

1. Position of Feet.

The position of the feet for guarding is the same as in the fundamental position. This uniformity is maintained throughout all of the discussion of individual techniques. One foot is ahead of the other. If the nearer side line is to the guard's left, then his left foot is always forward. Conversely, if the nearer side line is to the guard's right, his right foot is always forward as he faces his opponent. This advanced foot should be pointed at the median line of his opponent. The rear foot will thus always be nearer to the long axis of the court. Such a position will place the guard so that he is always closer to the long axis of the court than is his opponent and between his opponent and the goal. If a line were drawn from the basket to the median line of the opponent with the ball (assuming the opponent is facing the basket), the guard would have his forward foot on this line and his rear foot on the side of the line toward the center of the court. This position makes it practically impossible for the opponent to get around the guard by going between him and the long axis of the court. It, therefore, forces the opponent toward the side line with both his passes and his movements. Since one of the threats of the opponent is removed by this position, the guard may play with less caution and still make his position impregnable. Defensive play is greatly weakened when the guard abandons this position. He becomes so engrossed in his attempts to get the ball that he forgets to maintain, or is maneuvered out of, a sound defensive position.

2. Low Crouch Desirable.

Next, a low crouch is desirable, using slightly more than a quarter knee bend. This permits the guard to maintain a more stable equilibrium (the center of gravity is closer to the floor and can be kept between the feet) and to shift and attack his opponent more quickly without losing his balance. One of the most common and most serious faults in guarding is to maintain an erect position.

3. Hand Position and Movements.

The hands are carried so that the hand nearer the side line is forward and in front of the guard. If the guard is blocking a shot or if the opponent is poised to shoot, the palm is facing the opponent. The hand is raised above the height of the shoulder. It should not be held stationary, but should be alternately drawn back and thrust out toward the opponent. This action is confusing and does not give the opponent a sight by which to gauge his shot. If the opponent is not poised to shoot, then the guard should attack the ball, attempt to get a held ball or to knock the ball out of the opponent's hands. In doing so, he should swing his arm under and up at the ball. The palm will be in a supine position or facing upward. Greater extension and better muscular coördination is possible when the palm of the hand is held up under these conditions.

The other hand is held out from the side of the body. The arm is slightly bent at the elbow and usually the arm makes an angle of about forty-five degrees with the vertical. This hand is used to block attempted passes toward the center of the court. Since the body of the guard is closer to the long axis of the court than is the body of the opponent, passes to this side are somewhat difficult.

4. Focus Attention on Eyes of Opponent.

The guard should look directly into the eyes of his opponent. He can, of course, take in the whole of the opponent, the ball, and other players on the court by utilizing his peripheral vision; but for purposes of intercepting or anticipating the movements of his opponent, more can be learned by focussing attention on his eyes. It is the unusual player who does not betray his intentions with his eyes. Then, too, sometimes an opponent will return an intense gaze of his guard to the extent that he is practically hypnotized by it. The eyes can be a powerful factor in guarding, if only they are used.

5. Method of Shifting.

Last, as the guard moves to meet changing situations, he should always remember to move with short, quick steps and never to cross one foot over the other, but always to skip. The long stride has no part in guarding technique. The long stride means that a guard has the whole of his weight on one leg for too long a period of time. This fault permits an opponent to change direction more quickly than his guard does and thus to maneuver the guard into a weak guarding position.

Figures 31 and 32 show players in correct guarding positions. In Fig. 31 the guard is blocking the ball when the opponent is poised for a shot. In Fig. 32 the guard is attempting to force his opponent and at the same time he is alert to block attempted passes. In each case the alertness of the guard and his fighting expression is noteworthy.

ADVANTAGES OF THE BOXER'S STANCE IN GUARDING

This, then, is the position of the guard with respect to his opponent. His stance is usually called the boxer's stance in contrast to the wrestler's stance, which is taught by many coaches.[2] There are so many advantages to the boxer's stance that it is important here to point them out for the sake of sound technique.

1. By use of the boxer's stance the guard can get closer and yet stay farther away from his opponent than by use of the wrestler's stance. This seems a paradox. However, his forward foot can safely be within a foot or two of the opponent when a thrust is

[2] Meanwell, W. E. *Basketball for Men.* Madison, Wisconsin: Democrat Printing Company. 1923. Pp. 96, 97.
Ruby, J. Craig. *How to Coach and Play Basketball.* Champaign, Illinois: Bailey and Hines Publishers. 1926.
Iones, Ralph. *Basketball for Coaches and Players.* (Out of print.)
Holman, Nathan. *Winning Basketball.* New York: Charles Scribners Sons. 1935.

FIG. 31. Correct guarding stance. Blocking a shot.

FIG. 32. Correct guarding stance. Forcing the play. Reaching for the ball.

made at the ball. The rear foot will be as much as four to six feet from the opponent. In the wrestler's stance, both feet are the same distance from the opponent, and it is not possible to get closer than within three or four feet of the opponent without giving him more than an equal opportunity to get around. Three feet is hardly close enough to force an opponent aggressively or to challenge his possession of the ball.

2. By use of the boxer's stance, then, the guard may aggres-

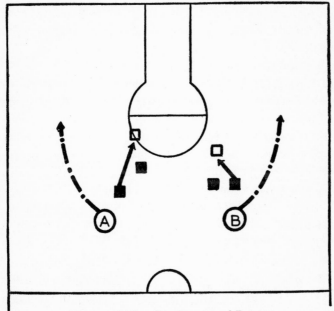

DIAGRAM 8. Guarding Stances and Retreat
A, Boxer's Stance; B, Wrestler's Stance

sively force his opponent to do something with the ball or to take a chance of having the ball knocked out of his hands or of permitting a held ball. If the opponent attempts to dribble around, the guard in his first step has retreated much farther to the rear than is possible by use of the wrestler's stance. Thus it is very difficult to dribble around the guard when he is using the boxer's stance properly. This situation is best shown in Diagram 8.

3. By use of the boxer's stance the guard allows the opponent

just one good passing lane, and that is to the outside, or toward the nearer side line. By the use of the wrestler's stance the guard is vulnerable to passing at six different points: a. between his legs, b. directly over his head, c. under the left arm, d. under the right arm, e. over the left arm, and f. over the right arm.

It will be remembered that the arms in the boxer's stance are carried so that the arm nearer the side line is held up to block shots and to prevent passing directly over the head. The other arm is out away from the body with the fingers pointed toward the floor. In the wrestler's stance the arms are held out away from the body and when in an "on guard" position, they are parallel to the floor.

4. It is much easier to shift forward and backward with the boxer's stance. A skip step is used so that perfect balance is maintained at all times. Using the wrestler's stance, one must run in short spraddled steps, which throw the balance first to one side and then to the other. By proper timing, the opponent can watch his opportunity to go around the guard to his right when, for instance, his weight is thrown entirely on his left foot.

5. The wrestler's stance has one advantage over the boxer's stance. It is somewhat easier to shift laterally by means of the wrestler's stance. But since it is much better technique always to shift back first and then to the right or left, this does not appear to be an important handicap to the use of the boxer's stance.

From the foregoing, it seems strange that any other than the boxer's stance in guarding should ever be taught and used.

Guarding Situations

Because of the fact that an opponent with the ball may be dribbling, may be shooting or passing, may be pivoting, may be feinting—any of these movements—may have his back to the guard, or may be some distance from his guard when he receives the ball, the guard must be able to meet many situations. He may even be required to guard two opponents for a time, or he and a teammate may have three opponents to guard.

Since these situations require special techniques, they will be discussed individually here. Each technique becomes a drill, which may be used in the practice of the fundamentals of guarding.

APPROACH AND ATTACK OF AN OPPONENT

The individual guarding drill, page 87, is the best drill for teaching the approach to an opponent who has received the ball and is some distance (six to ten feet) away from the guard. The practice here is first the approach. Next to playing too high, over-rushing an opponent so that he may dribble around is the most common fault of a guard. As the guard approaches his opponent, two paces away, he should not fail to use the skip step movement and maintain his crouch.

If the nearer side line is to his left, then his left foot is forward. If the opponent is exactly midway between the side lines, the guard may advance with either foot. Right handed players will usually advance with the left foot.

If the approach has been successful, the opponent has not been able to dribble around the guard and so is held in position. The guard may now aggressively force his opponent into action. Any advance that is made for the ball (unless the ball is knocked out of the opponent's hands or a held ball results) should be followed by a retreat in order to regain the proper guarding position, to be ready for another thrust for the ball or to offset a counter attack by the opponent. That is, if an attempted shot is blocked, the guard has thrust his hand out at the ball and into the face of his opponent. In doing so, he must rise up and usually step forward. He will, in recovering, step back and resume his crouch to prevent the opponent from dribbling around. Likewise, if the guard takes an underhanded cut at the ball, he steps toward his opponent and crouches much lower than usual in order to get his full reach and at the same time maintain a good balance. After the thrust he should retreat to his original position and be ready for the next move. His voice and feinting movements will prove very effective here.

Preventing an Opponent from Dribbling Around

Now, if the opponent attempts to dribble around the guard, the first move of the guard should be to retreat *directly* toward the goal until he is in a strong guarding position between the opponent and the goal. Then—and not before—he may attack the ball. The guard should always turn as he retreats, so that he faces the opponent. This prevents the opponent from reversing the direction of his dribble and, by so doing, causing the guard to spin helplessly in a circle.

The common fault in this guarding situation is for the guard to shift laterally as his opponent starts around. Such a movement either draws a foul or permits the opponent to get to the goal for a score.

Any position on the court may be taken for practice in this situation.

Breaking up the Dribble

For stealing the ball from a player who is dribbling, two movements are most common. The guard thrusts at the ball from the side or sneaks up on the dribbler from behind. In either case the technique is the same. First, the guard should not attempt to get at the ball until he is at least one-half a step ahead of the dribbler. Second, he should be moving with the dribbler. Third, he must move with short, quick, choppy steps. Long strides will permit the dribbler to evade the guard too easily and are the cause of most of the fouls that are committed on the dribbler. Fourth, the guard must run crouched over so that his head is at a lower level than the shoulder of the dribbler. Fifth, there are two methods of striking at the ball. If the guard is not quick enough or fast enough to intercept the ball, he should swing from under at it with the hand that is farther away from the dribbler. If the guard is quick, he may have a chance to steal the ball from the dribbler. He should get in as close to the dribbler as possible. The hand nearer the dribbler should come up under the arms of the dribbler.

In this way the dribbler's arm may be blocked from bouncing the ball and the guard can continue the dribble with this nearer hand. This is one of the prettiest plays in basketball, but it requires a quick player to steal the ball from an opponent without fouling or causing contact.

Always the guard should plan to get into a position between the dribbler and the goal in order to prevent a setup shot if he finds that he is not fast enough to intercept or bat the ball. A player without the ball is nearly always able to move faster than a player with the ball.

This maneuver may be practiced by dividing the squad into couples, one a dribbler, the other a guard. The drill is started at the center of the court. The dribbler is given a full stride start ahead of his guard, and then the guard attempts to catch him and to steal the ball.

BLOCKING A ONE HAND SHOT AT THE END OF A DRIBBLE

If a guard finds that he cannot quite catch the dribbler or assume a position between him and the goal, he should do his best to block the shot without committing a foul. If the guard attempts to block the shot from behind, it is very difficult to avoid a foul. He may hit the ball, but in so doing he is almost sure to charge or to hit his opponent's shoulder or arm and spoil his shot. The one exception to this is probably the case where the guard is an exceptionally tall player and the dribbler is short or of only medium height. In order to block the shot, the guard should get between the dribbler and the long center axis of the court.

As the dribbler starts his shot, the guard should attempt to block the ball by using the hand farther away from his opponent. This technique will cause him to turn facing his opponent. It will prevent guarding over the opponent's shoulder and will thus obviate the possibility of a foul. As the one hand goes up to block the ball, the other hand should be carried at about the height of the diaphragm. If contact should result, the guard may use this hand as a buffer to break the force of the contact and ease both players to the floor without any chance of a bad spill for either.

By using this technique, the guard is in a position to meet any clever tactics on the part of his opponent. Should the opponent fake his shot at the goal and not jump into the air but stop instead, in order to displace the guard, the guard is in a position to meet the situation. He must, of course, first guard against a possible shot. He has therefore—if the opponent was at all clever in his fake—jumped into the air to do this. But his movements caused him to rotate so that he faces his opponent. This prevents him from over-running his opponent and going on out of bounds. He is in a position to cover any subsequent move of his opponent. Figures 33 and 34 show this situation. In Fig. 33 the guard has jumped into the air to block a possible shot. In Fig. 34 the guard has recovered and is facing his opponent who faked the shot in Fig. 33.

GUARDING OR ATTACKING FROM THE REAR

If at the end of a dribble a player is rushed by a guard, such a player will often pivot so that the guard is behind the player with the ball. After recovering a rebound from the opponent's basket, a player will attempt to dribble toward the side line and may be stopped in a corner of the court with his back to the guard. These are guarding situations that occur many times during the game. It is next to impossible to guard directly from the rear without committing a foul. Consequently, if the guard plans to attack the ball aggressively, he should do so by approaching his opponent from one side or the other. At the same time he should take a position which will prevent the opponent from pivoting away from him. If it so happens that the player with the ball has not dribbled, then the guard must also take a position that will prevent the opponent from displacing him and dribbling in toward the basket.

The technique for this is as follows:

1. If the opponent has stopped with one foot ahead of the

Fig. 33. Guarding maneuvers, first step. Blocking a shot at end of a dribble. Guard has had to run to get into position.

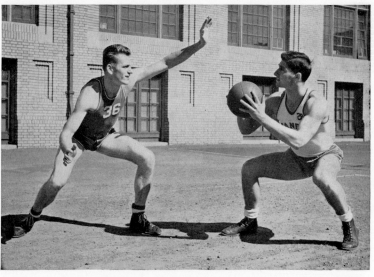

Fig. 34. Guarding maneuvers, second step. Guard recovered and in guarding position after jumping to block shot.

FIG. 35. Guarding from the rear.

other—that is, in a two count stop—the guard should straddle the rear foot. If the opponent has stopped with neither foot in advance of the other—that is, in a one count stop—then the guard may straddle either foot. It is better for him to straddle the foot nearer to the center of the court.

2. He should place his hand on the knee of the leg which is between his opponent's feet. The arm should be held stiff and unflexed. No contact should be made with the opponent, but the knee should be below the rump of the opponent. This position is full protection against a retreat or pivot of the opponent away from the guard. It will not be possible to assume the position against players who crouch low, but erect players may be easily blocked from progress toward the goal.

If the opponent attempts to pivot away from the guard, he will swing into the arm between his legs and will be thrown off balance, provided the guard holds a firm position.

3. The guard must crouch low. His head and body must be to the side of the opponent. His head should be under his opponent's arm. He may step as far forward as possible with his other foot.

4. In reaching for the ball he should swing under at it. If he can knock it out of his opponent's hands, he has an equal chance to recover it. If he can trap it with his hand, a held ball is the result.

This whole maneuver may be executed without contact on the part of the guard. The player with the ball may cause contact and a foul by butting into the guard in his attempt to pivot. Figure 35 shows a player guarding from the rear.

In the case of a player's being trapped in a corner in the back court at the end of a dribble, the guard may choose to try for an interception. In this case he should not rush the opponent at all. Rather he should stand about six to eight feet away from him and directly behind him. From this distance he is better able to see where the pass is going and he has more time to spring for it. If the guard is too close to the opponent, a pass can be faked to draw the guard out of position. Such a fake will not be successful if the guard stays away.

Two on One—One Guard on Two Opponents

Many times during a ball game a guard finds that he is forced to guard two opponents. Four rules should guide him in his movements.

First, if a line is drawn connecting the two opponents, the guard should always stay on the side of this line which is nearer to the goal.

Second, as the ball is passed from one opponent to the other, the guard should always turn through the lesser arc in guarding the ball. He should always stand and move so that he can see both of his opponents at all times.

Third, he should always keep his back toward the goal. If he does not adhere strictly to the second and third of these rules, his opponents may have him spinning in a circle until he is dizzy.

Fourth, if both opponents are outside a fifteen foot square in front of the basket, the guard should usually play mid-way between the two opponents. If one opponent is in the square and one not, the guard must play closer to the one in the square. If both are in the square, then he must favor the one closer to the basket, even though that player does not have the ball.

The guard can never afford to rush one of the players unless he has more than an equal chance to get the ball. He must use all his ingenuity to force his opponents to make a mistake if possible. If the opponents are outside of the fifteen foot square in front of the basket and one is dribbling, the guard should stop the dribbler far out in the court if possible and then drop back to prevent the other player from receiving a pass under the goal. If the guard is successful in this move, help from his teammates can reach him sooner than if he permitted both players to advance unmolested to the goal. It is, of course, the best practice for the two offensive players to advance to the goal as quickly as possible and with little or no hesitation.

Practice for this type of guarding may be set up by dividing the squad into groups of three. One player is assigned to guard. The other two are offensive players. The offensive players should both start from at least thirty feet from the goal. The game of "two on one," as described on page 92, may also be used to stimulate interest in this practice.

This drill may be made identical with game situations by using a second guard. This guard will delay in the back court until the offensive players are ten feet ahead of him. Then he will go to the rescue of his teammate. This will put pressure on the offensive players to act without delay. The guards will get excellent practice in teaming together in a situation of this kind. The guard who is defending the goal should be the leader. Whether he covers the player with or the player without the ball will depend entirely on the position of the players at the time his aid gets to him.

If both offensive men are outside the fifteen foot square in front of the goal, the guard will be approximately mid-way between them. In this case the teammate will first get between the goal and the ball before directions are given. Then he will guard the nearer opponent. It usually works out, however, that the guard who has been fighting the two opponents will cover the player with the ball.

In any case this guard should call out his directions just before his teammate gets into guarding position. It is an excellent plan to give directions with respect to the man with the ball. "I get 'im," means "I'll take the man with the ball." "You take 'im," means for the teammate to cover the player with the ball. An understanding of this kind prevents confusion and misplays.

THREE ON TWO—THREE OFFENSIVE PLAYERS AGAINST TWO DEFENSIVE PLAYERS

The movement of the defensive players in this defensive drill forms the basis for the movements of the team defense which is described in Chapter XXIV. It is a simple beginning of the team defense.

Here the first move is to form the defense at the goal, then to

work out from that point. For purposes of description of the movement of the guards, Diagrams 9 and 10 may be used. The three
offensive players are shown in their most widely scattered positions
in a triangle about the goal. One guard should always be "in the
hole." The other will be guarding the player with the ball.

In order that one guard may always be near the basket and between the ball and the goal, these two rules should govern the
movements of the guards:

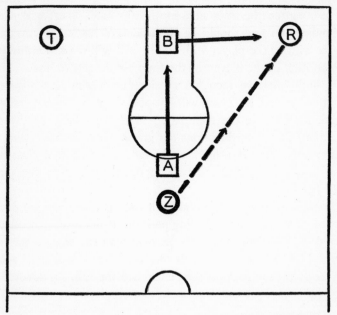

DIAGRAM 9. Three-on-Two Guarding Movements. First Situation

1. Whenever the ball is passed behind a guard, *i.e.*, from **Z** to **R**
in Diagram 9, that guard shall move directly to the basket. The
other guard shall cover the player who has received the ball. It is
possible for a player of only average quickness to move from as far
as the outer edge of the free throw circle back to the goal before
the ball can travel from **Z** to **R** to **T**. He must, however, move directly, not first start toward **R**. The guard in moving back to the
basket should face the ball as he moves.

2. As long as the ball is passed out in front of the guard, he shall cover the ball; i.e., if Z passes to R, Diagram 9, A moves back to the goal and B covers R. If now R passes back to Z, Diagram 10, then B will continue to cover the ball because the pass is all in front of him. A will remain in his new position under the goal, so that he is between the ball and the goal. If A were to go back out to cover Z, a pass could be made to T, and T could get

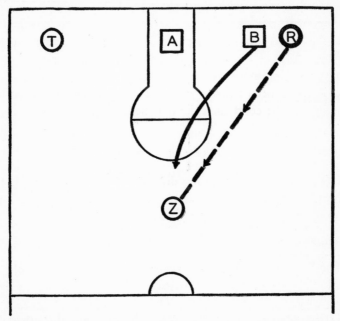

DIAGRAM 10. Three-on-Two Guarding Movements. Second Situation

a shot for goal before B could move to a position between him and the goal.

These two rules provide for the greatest economy of movement of the two guards and at the same time the greatest protection against a score. The logic of these movements may be demonstrated to the satisfaction of the most skeptical by using three of the best offensive players available against two of the slowest and weakest guards.

SUMMARY OF TECHNIQUES

In summary and for purposes of emphasis in introducing the techniques of individual guarding, these few basic points should be stressed first. All the other phases of guarding will follow without difficulty or confusion if these four points are stressed exclusively at first.

1. Always assume a boxer's stance. When on the right side of the court, advance with the right foot. When on the left side, advance with the left foot.

2. Assume at least a quarter knee bend and bend forward at the waist.

3. Always move with short, quick steps.

4. Keep between the opponent and the goal and nearer to the long axis of the court than the opponent.

GUARDING DRILLS

In addition to the guarding drills listed in Chapter VIII, the following are used for introducing guarding technique and for emphasizing certain features of the techniques.

1. Shadow Boxing.

The foot and hand work in guarding is similar to the foot and hand work in boxing. For this reason the squad is divided into pairs, and shadow boxing is indulged in. It is good practice to have one player represent the offensive man and the other the defensive player. Two tactics may be used: the guard will try first to touch his opponent's chin with his open hand; then he will try to touch the knee of his opponent. This attempt will encourage a good crouch.

A little of this practice will cause the players to have a great deal of respect for boxers because this drill is very strenuous.

2. Mass Drill in Foot Work.

Line the squad up along the side line. Players should be spaced so that their outstretched fingers do not touch. Now, according to the proper command, they will advance in skip steps with the right or left forward as directed; move to the right or left; throw the hand high in the air to block a shot, and then retreat; thrust under to bat the ball out of an opponent's hand; or turn to the right or left and rush back to the goal to prevent a dribbler from getting around them. This is a good scheme for teaching defensive foot work simultaneously to a large group.

PART III

TEAM PLAY

CHAPTER XVI

GENERAL PRINCIPLES OF TEAM OFFENSE

THERE are probably as many theories of offensive play as there are basketball coaches. At least, each coach has his own peculiar scheme by which he hopes to have his players work the ball into a position for an easy unguarded shot at the basket. Regardless of whether his system resembles one of the many accepted schemes of offense, he will have his own unique variations, which either represent the fruition of some of his early basketball dreams or are an attempt to utilize to best advantage the abilities of players who report to him.

Regardless of whether the coach is an advocate of a ball control game, a double pivot post offense, a fast break offense, a three-out and two-in pattern, a figure-of-eight movement, percentage basketball, or of no set pattern of offense at all, he must adhere to certain general principles if he is to develop a well balanced offense.

The principles presented here are, first, those which every coach must include in his offensive set-up and, second, those which should be included if a team is to be adequately prepared to meet any kind of opposition, if the players are to derive the greatest educational value from the game, and if an interesting spectacle is to be presented. These principles will be enumerated and described, then applied to a system of offense. The first three of them are always present in the play of every team. The others may or may not be present. In order that the team shall be equipped for any emergency and equally strong against any type of defense or team personnel, all of the principles should be provided for in the organization of team play.

1. Protection.

Every offense must provide for protection against mistakes or unexpected breaks in the game. In essence this means that the player with the ball should always have someone between him and the opponent's goal. It means that someone must always be in a position, or responsible for getting into a position, to guard the goal against a normal or unexpected attack by the opponents.

There are many schemes of providing for this protection. No one can be considered best. The one to be used will depend upon the philosophy of the coach, the pattern of offense adopted, and the ability and general characteristics of the players available. If the coach is very conservative in his thinking, he will always have two players back for protection. Other coaches have one player as a safety and a second player who should be ready to drop back in case of need. These players may or may not be the same players all the time. This choice again will depend on the philosophy of the coach, the pattern of offense, and the ability and general characteristics of the players available.

Some coaches choose a player for the job of safety man. He is the watch dog of the basket. Such a player is usually tall, heavy, and strong. He is primarily a defensive man. He seldom shoots, is not recognized as a scoring threat. His main job on offense is to stand outside the defense and handle the ball when necessity requires it.

2. Agreement with Fundamentals.

It is, of course, recognized that it is useless to practice painstakingly on fundamental drills and then never apply those fundamentals during a game. Nevertheless, this mistake is often made. For example, coaches may spend hours drilling on the technique of the hook pass and then never use the hook pass in any part of their offense. Again, intricate passing drills are devised, the movements of which have no relation whatever to the movement of the offense that is used in a game. Such practice not only wastes time but develops playing habits which are often contrary to those desired for game use.

3. Timing.

The sequence in the movement of players is without doubt the most difficult part of offensive basketball. It is difficult for two reasons: first, because each player has an individual battle on his hands with the opponent that is guarding him; second, he must not only maneuver so that he can get into an unguarded spot to receive the ball, but he must also time his maneuver so that he gets to the proper unguarded spot at the proper time. In other words, his individual movements must be synchronized with those of his teammates.

There is not in basketball the rhythm and instantaneous movement of all players that is so necessary in football. In football, as a rule, every player gets going at the snap of the ball. The ball is not in play for a scrimmage until it is passed back by the center. The team in possession of the ball is king.

In basketball the picture is different. The ball is continuously in play, and possession of it is being contested at all times. The players may be anywhere on the court. As a consequence, their movement is never in unison. Rather a jerky, stopping, darting, direction-changing type of movement is the more effective. In order that this may be synchronized, it is necessary, first, to have some rules for governing the movement of the players and, second, for the players to see the ball and to know the position of all the other players on the court at all times. (See Diagram 11.)

4. Flexibility.

The offense with which a team is equipped should be adaptable to any kind of defense. Coaches have been heard to remark, "I'll play your team if you won't use a zone defense. We don't meet that kind of a defense in our conference. I don't know how to penetrate it, and I don't have time to find out." Such a coach would have a "pleasant" time in a conference where he would meet almost every conceivable kind of defense. The best plan is to design an offense that can be readily and effectively adapted to any kind of a defense.

Many coaches spend the week before meeting a certain team devising a particular play to use against that team. They assume that their opponents will defend in a certain way. If their opponents happen to surprise them with a change in their defensive tactics, then their attack flounders helplessly. The situation is just as bad as with the football team that is prepared to meet only a six man line defense and is surprised by finding that the opponents have switched to a seven man line.

The team that is flexible enough to meet a rushing defense, a man-to-man, or any variation of a team defense is the team that is always the greatest threat at all times.

5. Action.

By action, as used here, is meant movement of both the ball and the players. Many teams depend too much upon the quick passing of the ball to displace defenses. This is particularly true when a team meets a zone or team defense. As a matter of fact, one of the most effective methods of penetrating a team defense is to have the players mill about the court, while at the same time the ball is being passed rapidly in and out of the defense.

This double feature of the offense not only is one of the most effective ways to get players into the open but is also very pleasing and exciting to watch. Nothing is more monotonous than to sit and watch the passing of the ball without any apparent movement of players and with little or nothing accomplished.

Action connotes aggressive play, taking chances, fast breaks, attempts to score, not playing keep-away or teasing. One should not erroneously assume that only when a zone defense is employed is there lack of action. It happens just as often when a man-to-man defense is employed. The point is that an offense is really weak and vulnerable to the extent that it lacks this quality of action. An opponent that does not take advantage of such an apparent weakness is merely playing into the hands of the offense and helping with his own defeat. This point is discussed at length under *Strategical Situations* on page 54.

6. Coördination.

A team's play will be most effective and efficient if all phases of play are well coördinated.

For example, if a fast break is used, it should be possible to fall smoothly right into the play of penetrating the defense in case the fast break is stopped. On an out-of-bounds play that does not produce a shot, it should be possible to continue the regular offense without delay or any change of positions of players. One should fit into the other. The same should be true after recovering a held ball. The organization of the movements of players should be such that they can swing from one phase of the game to the other without any hesitation or waiting for players to get into their proper places.

This suggests continuity, which was first introduced by Carlson.[1] This addition to basketball offense is one of the most valuable contributions that has been made to the game. The possibilities of development of continuity of play have hardly been touched. A method of coördinating all the phases of the game will be shown in the pattern of offensive play which is discussed on the following pages.

7. Non-Mechanical.

To treat a player as if he were a pawn or an automaton is to thwart the development of personal initiative, of freedom, of the exercise of judgment. It is not to be inferred that a mechanical offense is not effective—it is, and it wins games. But it is also dictatorial in nature and contrary to the democratic features of a non-mechanical offense. The mechanical offense does not utilize the educational opportunities that are present in the sport.

For these reasons the game is more fun for the players, and more valuable to them if their offense is not composed of set, unvarying, stereotype plays. Hager's percentage basketball is an ex-

[1] Carlson, H. C. *You and Basketball*. Braddock, Pennsylvania: Brown Publishing Company. 1929.

ample of a strictly mechanical game.[2] His players could play only one position. Each was drilled in separate and distinct habits. If a play was tried and the movement blocked, the ball was thrown back to the key man; each player went back to his particular position and then, when all was ready, that play was repeated or another was tried.

This method of organization, even though it is successful, must be recognized as highly a-social and certainly not much fun for a player who has any independence and initiative. It is also true that this type of play is more easily defended against than any other.

Players with less ability, when given freedom in their play, are better able to cope on even terms with a team trained in such a style of play. The success of a mechanical offense depends on the ability of the team using such an offense to force its opponents to play its style of game. If this is not permitted (even by a much weaker team), then the mechanical team is usually disorganized and demoralized.

It is much better practice to first give a team a general, continuous movement for the ball and the players. Then the team should be taught play situations. These involve certain movements designed to meet the various possible defensive positions that may be encountered. If these are mastered, players will learn to recognize opportunities for the offense to take advantage of defensive weaknesses that become apparent during the progress of a game. This method certainly is not mechanical, but highly educational in every respect.

These are the seven principles upon which the following offensive system is built. This offense is given as a suggestion of what can be done. It has been used for years in actual coaching and has proved to be highly successful in every way. There is no limit to the possibilities of offense that can be built on these principles. Several others have been developed and have been used successfully in conference play. The author's methods classes each year have developed a system that was entirely original.

---

[2] Hager, Bob. *Percentage Basketball.* Corvallis, Oregon: Oregon State Agricultural College. 1926.

CHAPTER XVII

THE STANFORD FREEDOM OFFENSE

THE system of freedom offense will be described in the order in which it is presented to a squad and developed in actual practices. The general pattern of movement, without reference to or practice of scoring opportunities, is first presented. The "guard-through" offense which has been so successfully used at Stanford is shown in Diagram 11. This is used early as a passing drill. While the players are learning passing techniques, foot work, and so on, they are at the same time learning the general offensive movements. The drill, as shown in Diagram 11, presupposes that each player will learn to play from all of the five positions on the court. It will be shown later how to adjust the system to fit the specific material when there is a wide difference in the ability and characteristics of the players. It should be emphasized, however, that it is surprising how easily the players adjust themselves to all five positions on the court. For this reason one should not decide too hastily to have players specialize on one position.

Positions of Players

From the diagram it is seen that the players are distributed equally over the playing area on the front court. They are scattered as widely apart as possible in order to deploy the defense. Some player should occupy one of these positions at all times when starting the offense in the front court. In this way it is easy for any player to know where to expect his teammates to be. If the players become bunched, the chances are that when they scatter all five places will be occupied.

197

The players at **X** and **Z** should as a rule occupy the inner third of the court. They will, of course, work toward the side as well as toward the center. Occasions will also arise when they will cross, exchanging sides. One will at times stand behind the other for protection. In any case, for safety in passing the ball, the players should never be farther than fifteen feet apart.

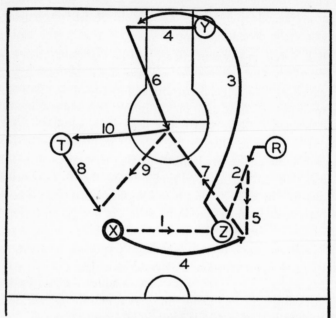

DIAGRAM 11. Stanford Freedom Offense—Guard-Through
Continuous Passing Movement

As they stand in front of the defense, they should not get closer than six feet to the center line. This will permit one player to go behind the other to receive the ball in case this maneuver becomes necessary for purposes of protection. These players may, if the defense has retreated, be as far as fifteen to twenty feet away from the center line.

The players at **T** and **R** should as a rule play just back of the free throw line so that they have plenty of room to dart out to meet the ball. At the same time they will have enough distance between them and the end line so that, if their opponents play too close to them, they can cut behind and toward the basket to receive a high pass for a shot at the goal. They should also play at least six feet from the side line. This distance will give them sufficient space to pivot toward the side with an opportunity to get around their opponents by going to the outside. They should not crowd toward the free throw circle as is the usual habit. The center of the offensive front court should be left unoccupied so that it may be used for cutting across for breaks to the basket.

The player at **Y** may play on either side of the free throw lane and anywhere along the free throw lines. He should move from one spot to the other in order to keep his opponent busy locating and covering him. He should do this also with the hope that he may be able to get his guard screened off in such a position that he can receive a pass from a teammate with a subsequent opportunity for a shot. This player may, if he chooses, move into either corner. He may be used, depending upon his ability, as a free lance player with permission to move anywhere that he chooses without regard to the other four players. This particular feature of this offensive movement will be gone into in detail a little later.

Continuous Passing Movement

The sequence of movement of the players and ball in the offensive play of Diagram 11 is as follows:

X and **Z** may maneuver out in front of the defense, passing the ball back and forth and criss-crossing from one side to the other until they can get a pass to **T** or **R**, who likewise have been working to get into a position to receive the ball. **Z** then finally passes to **R** who comes to meet the ball and, if his opponent is guarding him closely, steps over in front of his opponent just before darting out for the ball. **Z**, after passing, fakes to the inside by stepping with his left foot and then darts for the basket between **R** and the free throw circle. As he passes **R**, **Z** should slow up and look back over his right shoulder. He should then proceed slowly to a position on either side of the free throw lane.

As Z passes R, X should come over toward R. He is the safety man and protector for R. His exact position will depend on the activity of the opponents. He must in any event get to a position from which he may receive the ball from R. As X moves over behind R, Y moves out of the path of Z on the opposite side of the free throw lane.

During this movement R has held the ball and has been looking for an opportunity to make a play. He now passes to X.

As the ball is passed to X, Y darts out toward the ball. His movement should be timed so that he receives the ball while he is moving and just as he reaches the free throw line.

During the whole of these movements T has made no definite moves. He now starts out to the position occupied by X. T, who is on the opposite side of the court from where the ball penetrated the defense, is the secondary safety man. He is responsible for going to the rescue of X should X need help. Otherwise T is the fourth man in the offensive threat.

Y has three seconds to look for a possible play from his new position. He passes to T and moves out of the circle with his pass and over to the position originally occupied by T.

The ball is now out in front of the defense whence it started. The sequence of movements of both the ball and the players in Diagram 11 is numbered for clearness. The five positions are occupied. R is the only player who has not changed his position. After passing the ball back out to X he moved back to his position behind the free throw line and continued to maneuver for an opening so that he would be in readiness to receive the ball again. Z has replaced Y, X has replaced Z, T has moved to position X, and Y to position T.

METHOD OF PRACTICE

The ball moved from X to Z to R to X to Y to T. It is now in a position for the whole process to begin again. It is best to continue the movements in one direction until the interchange of positions and the passing sequences are learned.

After the movement is learned in one direction, it is a very simple matter to reverse the situation and then for the players to move in either direction according to whether the first pass is made to **R** or to **T**.

The next procedure is to practice this passing sequence and player movement against opposition. The defense may be either a man-to-man or a team defense. It is best not to permit the defense to be too aggressive at first. The purpose is to develop the offense; therefore smoothness of and confidence in the offense is the first thing that is desired. As this is gained, then the opposition may be made stronger.

TYPES OF PASSES TO USE

When opposition is used against the movement, the problem of the kinds of passes to use and the proper time to make a pass must be met. Guidance and early insight in this respect will hasten the effective development of the offense. These suggestions may be helpful:

Passes between **X** and **Z** can be either two hand underhand, one hand underhand, two hand push passes, or bounce passes. The pass from **Z** to **R** is usually a bounce pass. This is particularly true if **R** is closely guarded. The pass from **X** to **Y** can be a hook pass or a high floating pass or a bounce pass. **Y**'s pass to **T** can usually be a straight two hand push pass.

This passing movement is an effective means of playing keep-away in the last few minutes of a ball game. There is always the threat of a score. The players are breaking toward the basket so that the defense is being constantly moved and thus an unguarded spot is being created at all times in order that a safe pass can be made.

In this sequence of passes the most difficult one to make is the one to **Y**. It may not always be possible to execute this pass, and therefore the ball may travel directly from **X** to **T**. **Y** in this case will move to his new position at **T** just the same.

CHAPTER XVIII

SCORING SITUATIONS

FOUR scoring situations are presented next in the sequence of the development of the offense. These four situations give the basis for a well balanced attack against either a man-to-man or team defense. A movement is shown around either side of the defense, through the center, and diagonally from one corner to the other.

At first only one movement from each situation is given. As this is mastered and as opposition is used against the offense, many possible variations creep into the play incidentally and of necessity. When the set play as outlined will not work, then the possible variations or counter movements are best presented. A few of these will be suggested as each situation is discussed. As the teammates get accustomed to the movement of the offense and to the habits and characteristics of each other, they will take advantage of all the opportunities that the mistakes of their opponents offer. When this condition develops, the greatest freedom of play has been reached, and the players are able to exercise their own initiative in offensive play. This is the end that is desired for a most effective offense against any kind of a defense.

SITUATION No. 1. THE GUARD-THROUGH PLAY

In Diagram 12, Z has passed to R and followed up his pass in typical "guard-through" fashion. The sequence of movements is as described in the explanation of the continuous passing movement. R fakes to Z as Z passes him and then raises up and tosses him a high pass over the head of R's guard. Z should slow up after breaking by R and look back over his right shoulder. This pass can be made to Z only if Z is able to get away from his guard or if the guard is in the position as shown by the square at C or if the guard becomes careless in his vigilance over Z. This last usually happens when Z passes R and then slows his pace.

As Z receives the ball, he should, if he can, go right to the goal to score. Usually this is not possible; so the movement as shown is the one that will work most often. Y retreats to the opposite side from R and then cuts out toward the free throw line as Z

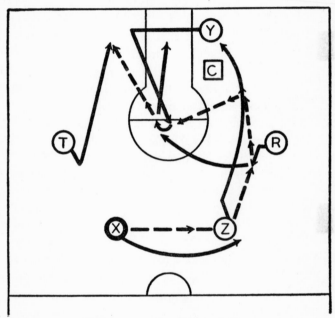

DIAGRAM 12. Guard-Through Play

attempts to go in to the goal. Z passes to Y. This is either an underhand pass, a hook pass, or a floor bounce. Z, if he has gone in to the goal too far before stopping, may even pivot and then pass to Y. Y will of course shoot if he is open and no pass, to a player closer to the goal, is possible.

When T sees that the ball has been passed to Z and that Y has darted to the free throw lane, he does not continue out as a safety man, but cuts back to the goal as shown. He is in a position to receive a pass from **Y** if he can evade his guard. It will be noticed that the passing moves in a triangle about the goal. This scheme will usually be found to be the most effective means of handling the ball to get an unguarded shot and to prevent interceptions.

As the ball is passed to **T**, **R** moves over into the free throw area. He is in a good position to get any wild rebounds of the ball and to receive tip-outs from his teammates when the opponents crowd too closely under the goal. **X** remains back as a safety.

If from this final set-up of the players the ball is passed out to **X**, then **R** would come out as a guard, **Z** would move over to **R**'s position, **Y** would remain in the center area, and **T** would return to his original position. These players are all nearest to these spots so it is logical that they should occupy them. The regular movement of the offense is then ready to start over without any delay and thus can quickly take advantage of any favorable breaks.

It should be remembered that, if at any time during the progress of the play the threat to the goal is blocked, the ball may be thrown out to the safety man either directly or by first passing to some other player, and then the same movement or some other more advantageous one may be started.

SITUATION NO. 2. THE CENTER PIVOT PLAY

In Diagram 13, **R**, after receiving the ball, has not been able to pass to **Z** under any circumstances. Nor has it seemed expedient for him to attempt any other scoring maneuvers; so he passes the ball out to **X**, who has moved over in anticipation of just this emergency.

X then passes the ball in to **Y**. This pass must as a rule be a high pass or a bounce pass. It should be a high pass if **X** must get the ball over an opponent's head. A low pass is used if **Y** is closely guarded. No pass at all can be made if the defense has massed in the free throw area.

When **Y** receives the ball, there are many variations of play for him. He can pass to either side, turn and shoot with either hand, pivot and dribble in for a set-up pass to **Z** along the lane line, or, as a last resort, **Y** can pass out to **X**. The play that makes scoring the easiest is a bounce pass behind the back to **Z**. It will be found that this may be done successfully many times during a game. It is even possible (when **Y** knows that **Z** is getting into an unguarded position) for **Y** merely to tip the ball blindly back over his head to **Z** when he receives a high pass from **X**.

Y of course follows up his pass, and **R**, when he sees the ball go to **Z**, breaks for the goal from his side of the court. **T** who has

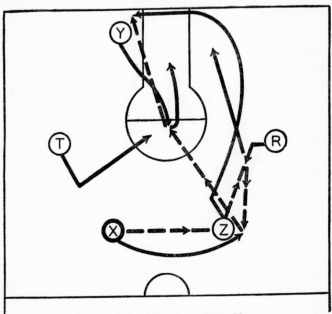

DIAGRAM 13. The Center Pivot Play

gone out as a second safety man when the ball was passed out to **X** now goes to the free throw line to receive a possible tip-out. The set-up at this point, so far as the distribution of players is concerned is the same as in situation No. 1. The basket is surrounded by three players, a tip-out man is in position and a safety man is back. Whereas the pass to the guard going through was the key to the situation in the first play, the pass to the free throw line is the key to this second play.

SITUATION No. 3. THE DIAGONAL PASS PLAY

In the third situation it has not been possible to pass to the guard going through, nor for the center to make a scoring move from the free throw line. The ball therefore is thrown out to **T** (Diagram 14). As **Y** passes to **T**, **Y** moves over toward that side of the court.

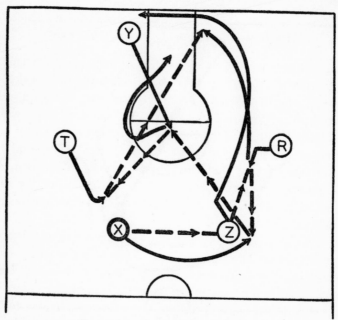

DIAGRAM 14. The Diagonal Pass Play

The fact that the ball has moved from one side of the court to the other and that **Y** moves over toward the ball tends to cause the defense to favor that side of the court. This gives **R** an opportunity to get into a scoring position. As **T** receives the ball, **R** who is out beyond the free throw line turns quickly and breaks for the basket. **T** presumably shoots for the basket. In reality he makes a high pass, which is timed so that **R** may receive the ball while high in the air. **R** shoots while in the air and in a favorable position for an easy set-up shot. The follow-up and tip-out positions of the players after the pass to R are shown as before.

T may of course shoot from his position. If his guard has played him very loosely, Y may even be able to screen for him. T may also find that a quick pass to Z in his new position under the goal is possible. If no play at all is possible, then the players are all in position to proceed with the continuous passing and scoring threats.

SITUATION No. 4. THE GUARD-AROUND PLAY

This last situation is a slight variation of the original movement, but it works in very well with it and prevents the defensive team from opposing the offense in a mechanical way. It also provides a scoring threat from the opposite side of the court from which the ball starts in toward the basket. The purpose of this play is to take advantage of a defense that tends to over-shift toward the ball to the extent that the guard through and the center pivot play are impossible of execution. It also takes advantage of the carelessness of defensive players who focus their attention on the ball and neglect their opponents.

On this play Z passes to R and starts as if he were going through as before. Instead he stops and drops back to act as safety man. Diagram 15 shows the movement. Y, since Z does not come through, does not retreat to the opposite side of the court. Instead, when he sees that Z has not come through, Y goes to the corner behind R. R fakes to the inside and then pivots and passes or makes a backward bounce pass to Y.

When T sees that Z has not gone through, he fakes to go out and then darts across the free throw circle to receive a pass from Y. X during this whole procedure has delayed movement in order that all attention may be turned from him. As Y passes the ball to T, X sneaks around under the basket to receive a pass from T. The tendency is for X to be too hasty in his movement; so he must be retarded at the start of practice of this play in order to make it successful.

Of course it is often possible for **Y** to shoot from the corner or for **T**, if he gets an advantageous position in relation to his guard, to dribble to the basket for a set-up.

Y, after passing to **T**, cuts for the basket for a return pass or to rebound. **T** follows down the center after passing to **X**. **R**, who has remained in a position to receive a pass from either **Y** or **T**, now goes to the free throw line for a tip-out. **Z** remains back as the safety man.

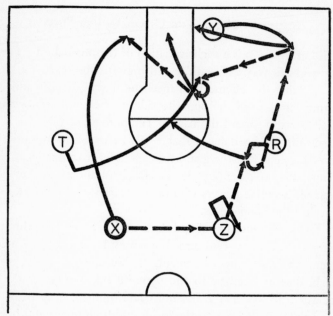

DIAGRAM 15. The Guard-Around Play

These situations are given as examples of the basis for a balanced offense. They represent a method that has been used successfully. It should be emphasized that there is nothing mechanical about this pattern of play. No signals of any kind are necessary. One situation with all the possible variations merges smoothly into another and without any delay whatever.

As a rule, a defense will be able to stop the first thrust that is made through it, but if the offense continues the movement, the

defensive players in following their men or in shifting will sometimes get into a weak position for effective guarding. When the
offense becomes skilled in handling these movements, they will be
able to take advantage quickly of any miscues that are made by
the defense and turn them into scoring opportunities.

Methods of Practice

In practicing this series of plays against opposition, it is wise to
begin with less than five defensive players. When practicing the
guard-through plays, two guards (for R and T) are all that should
be used. The players in these positions will then gain proficiency
in making under pressure this pass to the guard going through.

When the center pivot play is used, a single guard against Y is
all that is necessary. Y will then learn to take advantage of the
opportunities presented by his guard. Next the opposition may be
increased to three. These three should play against the positions
at R, Y, and T. Of course, it is not possible to play a man-to-man
game under any of the above circumstances, but this is not desired
at this point. Finally, five defensive players can be thrown against
the offense, and the offense then begins to work the play that seems
best fitted to the defensive situations. This practice is called "offense
through defense." Best results are obtained when one team is not
kept on defense too long. The defense tends to lose interest and
get careless. At first the defensive team should not be too strong
because it is desirable to make the offense work successfully and to
build up confidence in the players. Later two of the strongest
teams should be pitted against each other. Then a contest may be
made of the practice. Each team may be on offense for five or ten
minutes. The number of goals made in this time is recorded. This
scheme tends to arouse greater interest in the practice.

Adjusting the System to the Material

In many schools it is not always possible to find five players who
can successfully interchange positions as indicated by the above
offense. It is often the case that one player works well as a center,

so that it is desirable to make a specialist of such a player. Differences in the height of players often necessitate such an adjustment. Again, some coaches desire to charge one player with the task of being the safety man.

Adjusting the movements of the players to fit this idea or condition is shown in Diagram 16. In this set-up X is always the safety man. X and Z may, of course, change positions so that the attack may go in on either side. X shuttles back and forth in front of the

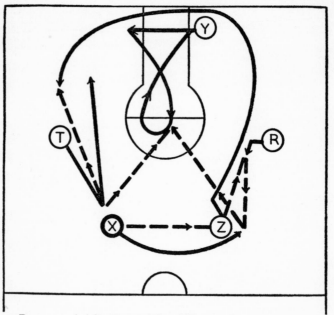

Diagram 16. Adjustment of Guard-Through Movement to Fit
Special Player Situations

defense, but never goes to the basket. Y plays the center position exclusively and never interchanges with any of the other players. Z, R, and T are the versatile players who interchange places in this altered movement.

As Z passes to R, it will be noted that his movement is the same as in Diagram 11 up to the time that Y receives the ball. As Y passes to T, Z must move out to the position originally occupied by **T**. **Y** moves out of the free throw circle and then, if he is not able to continue in the play, moves back to a position along the free throw lane. He is ready to enter into any subsequent attack.

Y, on the guard-around play as shown in Diagram 15, will go to the corner as before, but **Z** will be the player that always cuts to the basket if **X** is to continue as the safety man.

These changes in the movement of the players in no way alters the general scheme or philosophy of the offense. The same general plays are just as effective, and the movement of the ball is the same. However, there is not the same versatility or complexity of offense. It is therefore easier to defend against such an altered offense, since only three of the offensive players are real, aggressive, scoring threats.

CHAPTER XIX

VARIATIONS OF STANFORD FREEDOM OFFENSE

IN EVERY league or conference where competition is very keen and where teams are scouted closely, it is desirable to have variations of offense. These variations can be used for surprise attacks, or even as the main basis of offense at times. They not only prove effective but they also help to strengthen the regular offense. The introduction of slight changes may so confuse the opponents that, when a team returns to its old offense, this offense seems to work just as well as if it were something new.

Variations have proved to be most successful when they are designed to coördinate with the speed of movement, general timing, and fundamental theory of the original offense. This is undoubtedly due to the fact that a team becomes conditioned to a certain tempo. When this tempo is altered to any great extent, it seems quite difficult for all five players to synchronize their movements. As a result a team usually loses its scoring power immediately.

In the original system of offense as presented here, two fundamental factors characterize the movements. First, all movement is continuous; and second, the attack is emphasized by a quick dart toward the ball by one of the players in front of the defense. All variations that are presented here have these characteristics. This second feature seems to be the one that sets the cadence of the movement. Repeated efforts have been made to devise movements and variations which would alter this second point; it was felt that such a change would be devastating to the defense. However, when such variations were tried, the results were always more disastrous to the offense than to the defense. It has been noticed that

other teams have had this same experience when they have de-
parted from the original fundamental characteristics of their offense.

Teams should not attempt variations until they have mastered
the details of their basic offensive movements. If the movements
are sound, the opponents will not as a rule be able to stop them
before the team itself has perfected all the details. If a team is
loaded with too much offense, it will be delayed too long in
effecting smoothness of play. One movement, well executed, will
produce far more scores than many movements which are so
poorly timed that by inefficient execution they defeat their own
purpose.

It has been found also that the players return to their original
offense in a pinch. The additional offense becomes in fact a variation which is resorted to only occasionally.

During a period of three years the following variations were developed and used. The third year, with a veteran and well-trained
team, all the variations were in use throughout the season. This
will give some idea of the time and conditions under which new
material may be given to a team. In each case the name of the variation describes its movement. It will also be observed that no signal is necessary to determine which variation or movement will
be used. The variations are so coördinated that, when a player
starts a movement, there is no confusion or doubt as to what move
is under way. It may seem that such simplicity would be too easy
for the defense, but this has not proved to be the case.

The Diagonal Offense

Diagram 17 will indicate the continuous movement of the
diagonal offense. X passes to Z and immediately cuts diagonally
toward R. The fact that X cuts is a cue to Z that he must be the
safety man and cannot cut after his pass to R, as in the case of the
guard-through movement. X sets a screen for R. Z passes to R and
fakes to go to the goal in order to cause his guard to retreat. Z
moves over to receive a return pass from R. Y moves to the corner

behind **R**. **R** passes to **Z**. **R** fakes to his right in order to set up his guard for the screen and then cuts around **X**. **T** replaces **X** at the guard spot. **Z** passes quickly to **T**. **T** in the regular scoring situation feeds **R** if possible. **X** holds until **R** breaks to the free throw line and then is ready to cut to the goal in case of a defensive shift. **Y** holds in the corner ready to rebound in case the pass to **R** from **T** is successful. **Y** then replaces **R**. **X** replaces **Y**, and **R** re-

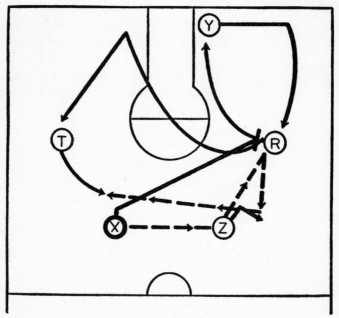

DIAGRAM 17. The Diagonal Offense

places **T**. Thus all five offensive spots are covered and the continuous passing is not interrupted.

A variation of passing in this movement is shown in Diagram 18. Here the only difference in the movement of the ball is that **R** passes to **Y** in the corner instead of to **Z**. **Y** then passes to either **Z** or **T**. **R** cuts immediately after passing to **Y**. Again the players interchange positions as before. **R** replaces **T**. **T** replaces **X**. **Y** replaces **R**. **X** replaces **Y**. It is evident that the play may move to either side. **Y** may take a position on either side of the free throw lane at the start. While no scoring plays are shown here for either of these passing movements, several possibilities should be obvious. For example:

When **X** cuts diagonally, he should look for a pass from **Z** or even from **R** because **R** will have the ball before **X** arrives for his screen. **R** may dribble around **X**. **Y** may pass to either **X** or **R**. **T**

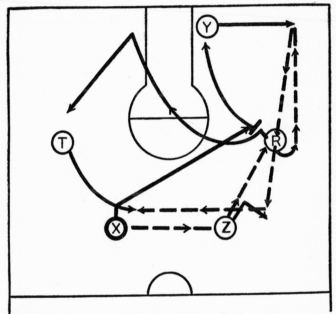

DIAGRAM 18. Variation of Diagonal Movement

may see an opportunity to break to the free throw line after **R** has moved out of this area. These are just a few of the many possibilities for scoring moves.

THREE-OUT OFFENSE

Diagram 19 shows the continuous movement for the three-out offense. The three-out offense is built up from the regular guard-through movement. The center **Y** is the one who determines whether the set-up shall be three-out or not. If **Y** chooses to move as shown, instead of replacing T as in the regular guard-through (see Diagram 11), then the three-out situation is formed without any other signal. Y may come out between X and T, or he may go to either side. Z, when he sees Y out in front, moves over to replace T.

An offensive thrust should start without delay; otherwise any advantage by this change in the offensive formation will be lost.

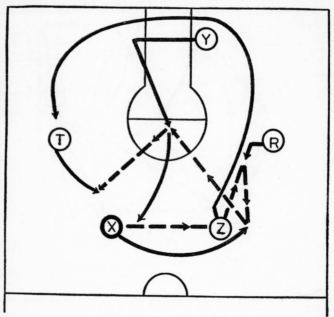

DIAGRAM 19. Three-Out Offense from the Guard-Through Movement

The movement from the three-out set-up may have many variations. Diagram 20 shows the new arrangement of the players after the movement in Diagram 19 and a typical play that has been used from this formation. It will be noted that the same idea as in the original guard-through is used. T passes to Z and breaks toward the ball. Z may pass back to T if he is unguarded. Z passes to Y. R breaks across the free throw lane to receive a pass from Y. X holds until R receives the ball and then darts as shown. R has the option of passing to T or X or shooting.

If he can do none of these things, he will pivot and pass back to Y or dribble out to replace **X**. **X** would then turn back and replace **R**. **T** would remain at the center spot and the passing could continue from the regular guard-through set-up.

In this play **R** may cut early or late. He may move in time to receive a pass directly from **Z** or he may hold as originally indicated. **T**, as he cuts in, may also move around between **Z** and the

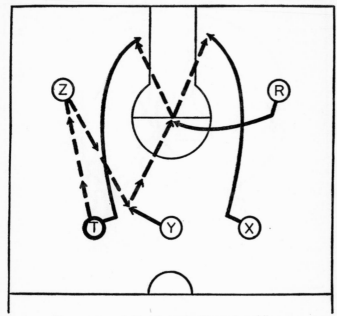

DIAGRAM 20. A Play from the Three-Out Offense

side line if he chooses. This is an effective move against a man-to-man defense.

THE NEW GUARD-THROUGH

The new guard-through was devised for two reasons. The defense on the regular guard-through had a tendency to play the guard very loosely as he broke through. The new guard-through movement took advantage of this situation for a scoring play. When used against a man-to-man defense, it forced a shift of men or else gave an opportunity for an excellent set shot over a screen.

Diagram 21 shows the new guard-through movement. The fact that the guard ran between the ball and the side line gave the opposite forward, **T**, his cue for his movement. This variation in movement strengthens the center movement of the regular guard-through. The opponents after a time began to look for **Y** to break to the free throw line. This change gave a little uncertainty to the movement of **Y**.

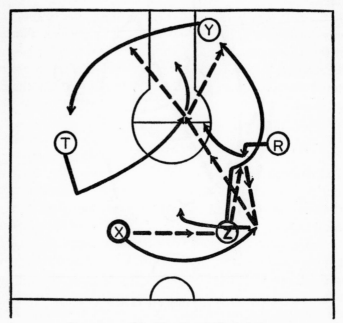

DIAGRAM 21. The New Guard-Through Play

X passes to **Z**. **Z** passes to **R**. **Z** fakes to go inside of **R** but circles around him. **Z** may receive the ball from **R** and get a set shot over **R** as a screen. If, after hesitating, **Z** does not get the ball, he continues as shown. **T** starts out to replace **X**, as shown. **R** passes to **X**, and **T** cuts to the free throw line to receive a pass from **X**. **T** should continue across the circle if necessary in order to get into an advantageous position to receive the ball. He may also break earlier and receive a pass from **R**. As **Z** approaches the goal, **Y** moves over as shown, unless he is already on the side of the free throw lane away from the ball, and looks for an opportunity to receive a pass. If the scoring play does not go through, that is, if **T** must turn and pass back to **X** or if he does not get the ball at all, then **Y** replaces **T**, **Z** replaces **Y**, **R** replaces **Z**, and **T** replaces **R**. **X** will move over to his original position, or if the ball is passed to him, he may find it necessary to dribble back across the court.

If the play does go through after **T** receives the ball, then **T** may shoot or pass to either **Z** or **Y**. It will be noted in this case that there are three offensive players around the goal for rebound work and that **R** moves over on the free throw line to receive tip-outs, or even a pass from **T** who may pivot and feed him the ball and act as a screen for him.

THE CUT-BACK PLAY

The cut-back was designed to draw attention away from the center **Y**. In most of the offensive movements, **Y** had been breaking out to the free throw line. The defense was conditioned to look for such a move each time. By means of the cut-back, a change in defensive tactics was made. While from Diagram 22 it will be noted that the cut-back involves the movements of only two players, **X** and **T**, it has nevertheless proved quite effective as a check on stereotyped defensive movements. The movement, of course, may be used on either side of the court. **X** passes to **Z** and then breaks for the goal. **X** looks for the ball all the time. **Z** passes to **R**. **R** looks for an opportunity to feed the ball to **Y**. **Z** fakes to go in, but drops back to receive the ball from **R**. **X** stops abruptly as shown and cuts back to meet the pass from **Z**. **T** has started out to replace **X**. As **X** receives the ball **T** reverses and cuts for the goal to receive a pass from **X**. Of course, **X** has several alternatives as may be seen. If no pass to **X** is possible, then he replaces **T**, and **T** in turn replaces **X**.

It must be evident that all the variations of movement shown here are used as check plays on the original guard-through offense. The guard-through was so firmly established after three years of use with little or no variation that the defense against it was stereotyped. Naturally as opponents grew accustomed to this type of offense, their defense became more effective against it. These variations tended to confuse and disorganize the routine which opponents had fallen into. Thus not only did the variations score

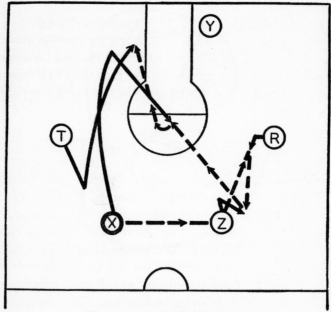

DIAGRAM 22. The Cut-Back Play

many goals, but the old offense became more effective by the introduction of this element of uncertainty.

THE DOUBLE REVERSE PLAY

The double reverse (name influenced by association with Pop Warner's system of football) is really a play from the regular guard-through; it can be used most effectively against a man-to-man defense. The timing and sequence of moves up to the point where **Y** receives the ball are the same as in the regular guard-through (Diagram 11). In Diagram 23, **X** passes to **Z**. **Z** passes to **R** and then cuts for the basket. **Y** moves across the free throw lane unless he is already there. **X** moves over to receive a pass from **R**. **Y** breaks to the free throw line. **X** passes to **Y**. **T** has started to replace **X**. **T** may at his option cut toward **Y** and then quickly swing around him to lose his opponent. **Y** fakes to **T**, who stops

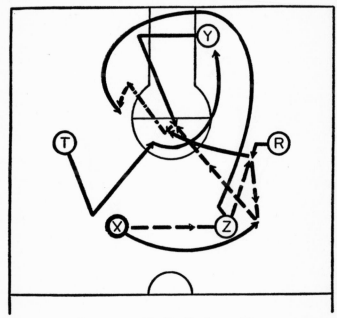

DIAGRAM 23. The Double Reverse Play

and screens for **R**, and passes to **R**, who moves as shown. **R** dribbles out of the circle. **Z** has retreated across the free throw lane as **T** made his dash. **Z** now circles around **R** in order to lose his guard. **Z** uses **R** as a screen and shoots for the basket or passes to **T** under the basket.

Y may shoot or he may give the ball to **T**. If no play is possible and **Y** must get out of the circle with the ball, he will dribble out or pass back to **X** and then go out to replace **Z**. **T** replaces **R**.

R replaces **T**. **Z** replaces **Y**, and play may continue without delay.

This play must move with precision in order not to violate the three-second rule. A stop watch has been used to check the legality of the play, and it has been found that there is plenty of time to execute the play if **T** cuts back as the pass is made to **Y**.

CHAPTER XX

SCREEN PLAYS

THE freedom offense, which has been presented here as a sample of offensive play, is designed primarily to combat a team defense. This type of defense is the most difficult to penetrate; hence it was used as a basis from which to build an offense. All of the features necessary for scoring against a normal man-to-man defense are present. Therefore, for playing against such a defense, it is necessary to stress only the particular points which are most effective against a man-to-man defense.

It often happens in the case of either the man-to-man or the team defense that the defensive play is so perfect that it is not possible for a player, through his own efforts, to get into an unguarded scoring position. When this situation prevails, then it becomes necessary for one player to come to the assistance of another. This is done by means of screen plays. Their sole use is to help a player get into an unguarded scoring position. Screen plays are most effective against a man-to-man defense. However, they may be used against a team defense.

A screen play is nothing more than the coöperation between two or more offensive players in such a way that the freedom of movement of a defensive player is legally interrupted. The common execution of a screen consists in an offensive player legally placing himself in the path of a defensive player so that the defensive player runs into the offensive player. This interference permits the player who is being guarded by the defensive player to become unguarded and free to receive the ball for a subsequent shot at the goal unless another defensive player quickly carries on for his teammate.

Rules for Screen Plays

There are many types of screen plays. The most successful and most difficult to defend against adhere to the following five rules:

1. *The player who is to do the screening should approach the defensive player from behind.* He should thus move away from the basket to his position behind an opponent. Under this circumstance the defensive player who is to be cut off from the opponent that he is guarding is unaware of the approach of the player from behind. This movement from behind requires quick coöperation and team play on the part of the defense if the advantage of the screen is to be offset. It is very difficult for the defense to shift players in a situation of this kind. At least one of the two offensive players involved in the maneuver is sure to be left unguarded.

Diagram 24 will best illustrate the effectiveness of this principle of the screen. In this diagram, player **Y** comes up behind guard **E** to screen for **T**. **Y** may take any position he desires so long as he does not make contact with **E**. **T** cuts for the basket and **E** runs into **Y**. Unless **D** shifts to cover **T**, **T** will be free to receive a pass near the goal for a shot. If **D** shifts to cover **T**, then **Y** cuts to the center as shown and is in a position to receive a pass. It will be difficult for **E** to shift to cover **Y** because **E** is out of position. He is not between **Y** and the goal.

2. *The player for whom the screen is set must not move until the player setting the screen is stationary.* In Diagram 24, **T** must not cut for the basket until **Y** has taken his position behind **E** and is stationary. This timing is absolutely necessary; otherwise a foul for blocking by **Y** is unavoidable.

3. *The player setting the screen (**Y** in Diagram 24) must not move until after the player for whom the screen is set (**T** in Diagram 24) has passed behind him.* If **Y** should move too soon, he would either commit a blocking foul or he would destroy the effectiveness of the screen by permitting the player guarding **T** to escape the trap set for him.

4. *The first move of the player for whom the screen is set (**T** in*

Diagram 24) should be directly at his guard (**E**). This move gives the guard no alternative but to move directly backward and directly into the trap set for him. In the diagram, **E** would move back into **Y**. **T** would then cut around **Y** and toward the goal. This maneuver is absolutely necessary if the guard is playing farther than three feet away from his man.

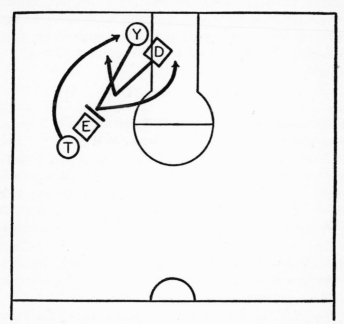

DIAGRAM 24. Illustrating the Rear Approach for a Screen

5. *While it is not absolutely necessary, screen plays are nevertheless most effective if they are set for the player who has the ball.* When a player has possession of the ball and is within twenty-five feet of the goal, his guard is more likely to play rather close to him. This fact, as stated in rule 4 above, reduces the possibilities of the guard's escaping the screen that is set for him. The player with the ball may then pass to a teammate and cut around his screen, or he may even dribble around his screen.

All other types of screens are so much easier to combat that they will not be discussed here. Several will be shown that are a natural part and variation of the four scoring situations described in Chapter XVIII. Sometimes they work well, but they do so only because the defense is not alert, for there is little if any deception or surprise about them.

A system of screen play movements which fits into the Stanford freedom offense and which conforms to the rules just stated is shown in Diagrams 25, 26, 27, and 28. These are called longitudinal, diagonal, guard-through, and lateral screens. The names describe the movement of the player who sets up the screen.

THE LONGITUDINAL SCREEN (DIAGRAM 25)

When he receives the ball from **X**, **Z** does not pass to **R**; instead **R** comes up behind **B** who is guarding **Z**. As **R** gets set, **Z** passes back to **X** and then starts toward **B** and cuts around. **Y** in the meantime has gone to the opposite side of the court in order to draw his opponent away from the basket. After **Z** goes behind **R**, **R** cuts to the free throw line as shown.

If **X** can not pass to either **Z** or **R**, he passes to **T** who attempts to get the ball to either **Z** or **R**. If **B** and **C** shift men, then **R** will be the unguarded player. As a matter of fact, it is hoped that the defense will shift men, for the pass to **R** and the subsequent possibilities are much more favorable for the offense.

If neither **T** nor **X** can complete a pass to one of the players going in to the goal, **T** passes out to **X**. **X** moves over to **Z**'s position. **T** takes **X**'s position, **Y** moves out to **T**, **R** replaces **Y**, **Z** replaces **R**, and play can be resumed without delay.

THE DIAGONAL SCREEN (DIAGRAM 26)

In this play, **Y** furnishes the screen for **R**. The movements and sequences of passes can be readily followed in Diagram 26. This play starts like the guard-around play, but **Y** instead of going to the corner comes up behind **R**'s guard. If a scoring play is not successful from this set-up, **R** and **Y** merely change places, and the

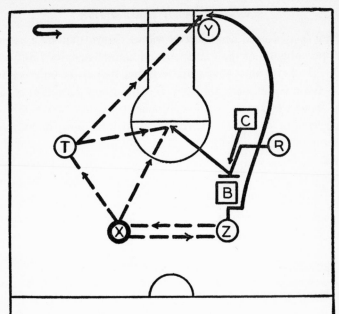

DIAGRAM 25. The Longitudinal Screen

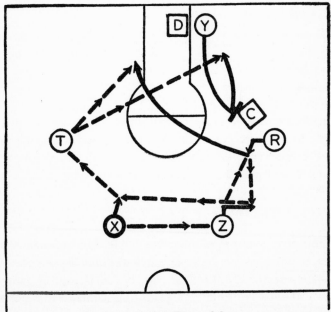

DIAGRAM 26. The Diagonal Screen

offense continues without interruption. The timing of these plays will be much smoother if the player who sets the screen will call out when he is in position and is stationary.

The Guard-Through Screen (Diagram 27)

This screen play is more or less of a supplement to the diagonal screen. It has two players, Z and Y, screening for R. It starts in the same way as the guard-through play, but instead, Z and Y screen for R. Using two players for a screen makes it practically impossible for the guard C to extricate himself in order to follow R. This makes a shift absolutely necessary if R is not to be given an open shot for the basket.

T comes out to replace X in the regular guard-through movement. After R cuts across the free throw lane, Y follows around and across as shown. Z remains in position all the while and, if no other pass is possible, Z is usually open to receive the ball. The sequence of passes and movements may be seen in Diagram 27.

If no scoring movement develops at all, R replaces T, Y returns to his position, Z replaces R, X replaces Z, and T replaces X. All positions are occupied, and play continues.

The Lateral Screen (Diagram 28)

The lateral screen is really a continuation of the diagonal screen, but on the opposite side of the court. R, when he sees that he is not open to receive the ball, comes over to screen for T and the play revolves about T as it did about R when the movement originated.

Key to Movement

In order to avoid confusion in these plays and to insure coördination of movements of all players, the player at position Y is usually designated to initiate the movements. When it is decided that screen plays are to be used during the progress of the game, the other players look for the key movement of the center, Y.

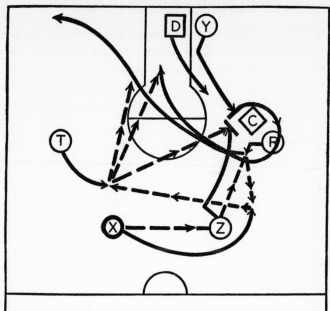

DIAGRAM 27. The Guard-Through Screen

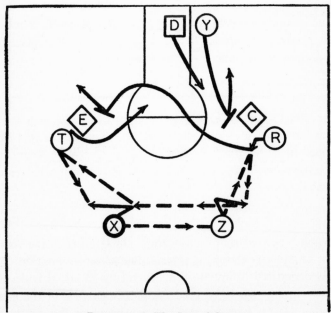

DIAGRAM 28. The Lateral Screen

It is not at all difficult for the other players to keep an eye on the center. He is behind the rest of the defense so that the defense is not so likely to anticipate what is to be thrown at it next. If **Y** moves to a corner, then a longitudinal screen is the logical order. If **Y** comes up behind **R** or **T**, then a diagonal or a guard-through or lateral screen is in order. It really makes no difference which one

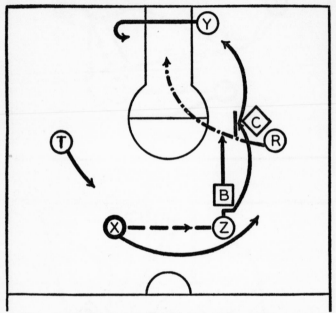

DIAGRAM 29. Screen from Regular Guard-Through Movement

of these screens develops, for each fits in with this movement of player **Y**.

OTHER SCREENS

In addition to the above types of screens which, as already stated, are the soundest types, a number of others, less effective, develop out of the natural variations from the Stanford freedom offense. These are shown without explanation in Diagrams 29, 30, 31, 32, and 33.

It will be noted that the screen in Diagram 29 follows naturally as a variation of the guard-through movement and that when the

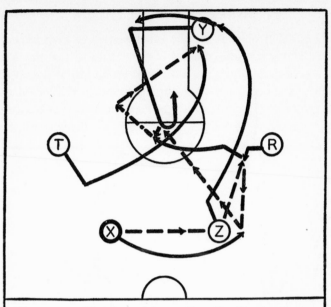

DIAGRAM 30. Variations of Center Pivot Play Showing Screen
Possibilities

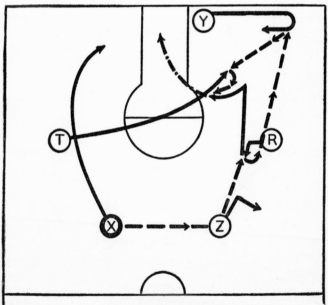

DIAGRAM 31. Forward Using Man with Ball as a Screen in the
Guard-Around Situation

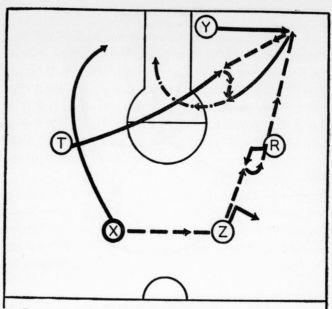

DIAGRAM 32. Center Using Man with Ball as a Screen in the
Guard-Around Situation

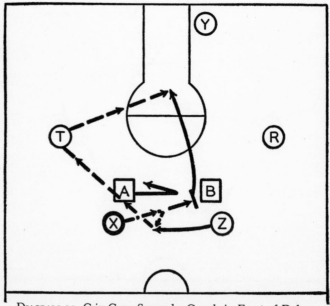

DIAGRAM 33. Criss-Cross Screen by Guards in Front of Defense

defense gets careless in covering men it works effectively. Player **R**, of course, knows that if **Z** stops just back of him it is his cue to use **Z** as a screen and that he should dribble into the goal.

Diagram 30 is a variation of the center pivot play. There are of course many varied screens that may be developed from this set-up. In this particular scissors play, **T** cuts by **Y** first and is quickly followed by **R** if the ball is not passed to **T**. This play has been carefully timed so that it is possible to execute all the maneuvers within the limits of the three-second rule.

Diagrams 31 and 32 show possible screen plays from the guard-around situation.

Diagram 33 is a possible screen movement which involves no help from a teammate. The criss-crossing of **X** and **Z** out in front of the defense has merely maneuvered an opponent into a weak position, and a score may result.

CHAPTER XXI

FAST BREAK

MANY coaches do not believe in fast break offense at all. They feel that it breeds careless and wild handling of the ball and that it makes sound fundamental play impossible. Other coaches use the fast break whenever the opportunity presents itself. In other words, they use it only as a threat. These are not the theories presented here.

It has been found from actual tabulation of scoring during games that scoring by means of the fast break has added more to the scoring threat of a team than any other factor. It is the easiest way to score points because by means of the fast break the ball is gotten down to the basket from the opponent's end of the court before all of the defense has had an opportunity to organize and mass itself about the goal. A team, therefore, is not required to work the ball through the whole defense in order to score.

It has been found through observation of games and the testimony of other coaches that it is more difficult for a slow-playing team to play fast than it is for a fast team to play slow. Therefore a fast-playing team, if it can set the tempo of play, will easily demoralize and make erratic the slow, deliberate team.

The constant threat of a fast break tends to weaken and make conservative the offensive play of the opponents. If they are afraid of the fast team, they will be more cautious about sending players in to rebound. They will leave more players back for protection against the fast break.

For these reasons the fast break should be made the primary weapon of a team. When a player gains possession of the ball, he should look first for a possible fast break. The slow break should be used only as a last resort.

Basic Principles of the Fast Break

Certain characteristics are necessary in the personnel of the team if it is to use the fast break successfully. The tendency is to give up the idea of a fast break too soon, before it has been thoroughly tried and before the players have had an opportunity to adjust themselves to this style of play. The best advice is, don't give up too soon. Even the players who have grown up playing the ball control, conservative, cautious type of game eventually swing into the rhythm of the fast break, and they always like this style much better. It is more fun to play. It gives them greater freedom. It encourages them to be daring. It invites them to use their own initiative. They score more.

In order for a team to use the fast break successfully the following rules are essential:

1. *The team must have defensive rebound strength.* The defense must develop the knack of blocking their opponents away from the goal. The use of the team defense has been found to be the most effective means of concentrating strength about the basket. Three players about the basket, one on either side and one in front, can completely encircle the basket. These three players are sufficient to set up about the basket a wall which will be difficult for the opponents to penetrate. It is thus seen that the defense and the offense, where the fast break is used, are very closely tied together.

It is, of course, essential that at least two of these three defensive players be tall and if possible rugged. The third, if he is small, must be a good jumper, very quick, and adept at blocking opponents away from the goal. One good small player in this trio is not a bad asset. He is able to pick up many loose balls and to snatch stray bounding balls before the opponents can get them.

2. *After rebounding the ball from the backboard, the ball must be passed away from the goal without delay.* The fast break will

be successful in proportion to the speed with which the rebound men get the ball away from the backboard and out to a teammate.

3. *It is absolutely necessary that the other two defensive players start on the fast break before their teammates get the ball and before their opponents start on defense.* In other words, these two players, usually the forwards, must anticipate possession of the ball by their teammates and accordingly must get started toward their goal in advance.

It will now be seen why it is so necessary for a team to have dependable rebound strength. If the two men who form the front line of defense cannot depend on their teammates to secure possession of the ball, they will not dare to break prematurely for their own goal. They will be needed to help rebound. Consequently the threat of a fast break is lost.

4. *The two players of the defense at the goal who do not get possession of the ball must dart on offense as soon as possession of the ball is a certainty.* These two players are no longer needed for defense. They must have confidence in their teammate's ability to handle the ball safely. The player who secures the ball from the basket will be the last one down the court. He is the safety man.

5. *Finally, the secret of the success of any fast break is to run like lightning to the other end of the court.* The tendency is for the players to wait for the ball. They should have faith that the ball will come to them. It is their job to get going.

Primary Fast Break Movements

The movements of the Stanford fast break are shown in the following diagrams. Speed and directness of the run to the basket are emphasized here. These fast break movements are begun as passing drills after the first week of practice and are practiced daily until the players become fast-break minded. The play will be erratic at first, but soon the timing will become more precise and the movements and passes perfectly coördinated. Errors are to be expected at first and should not be criticized so severely that initiative and daring are destroyed.

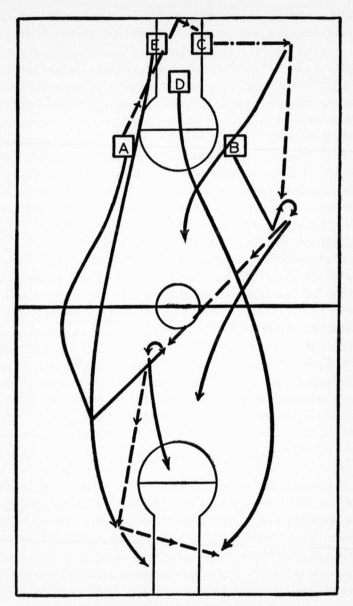

DIAGRAM 34. Basic Fast Break Movement

Diagram 34 shows the first movement that is taught. It is the one that must usually be employed against a team well coached against the fast break. It also gives the best coördination of the movements of the players in the fast break. It is not the fastest method of fast break. It is, however, the one used when the opponents are between the goal and the forward who is farthest down the court.

The players take the positions as shown for rebounding. To start the play one of the forwards shoots the ball against the backboard. As the shot is made, both forwards start for the center of the court and toward the side lines. As C recovers the ball, B, who is on the same side of the court as C, turns back to receive a pass from C. A continues down the court until B receives the ball, then cuts back toward it and receives a pass from B. Cutting back to meet the ball leaves little danger of an interception.

After C recovers the ball, D starts down the center. He gradually moves toward the side line to which the ball has been passed. If B is not open for a pass, then D is a possible pass receiver. If D does not receive the ball, he hurries toward his own basket.

At the same time that C started on offense, E broke for the basket along the opposite side line. He is the logical player to receive the ball from A. The fact that A cuts back toward the center of the court to meet the ball tends to draw attention away from E. Many times during a game he will get an unguarded shot from under the goal. But he must not forget to do one thing, and that is *run, run, run.*

A, after receiving the ball from B, should pivot in making his pass to E. This will insure against molestation from an opponent. E may shoot or pass to the center D. This movement will synchronize perfectly if every player will RUN.

Each player follows the pass that he makes. C is the safety man. B goes to the free throw line for a tip-out. A follows in at the center, while E and D are on the sides. If for any reason the fast break does not go through to a score, the players are all in perfect position to continue their freedom offense. E will be on one side,

A at center, **D** on the other side, while **C** and **B** will be in the guard positions.

Method of Practice

The fast break may be practiced by several teams, one following the other in drill fashion. After all teams have dashed in turn from one end of the court to the other, they may reverse the process by starting at the opposite end. It is a good plan after the end of a fast break to have the team continue playing by moving immediately into the regular continuous passing movement. In this way the fast break movement and the offense-through-defense movement will become associated so that there is no delay in changing from one to the other.

The fast break drill is an effective method of finishing a practice period.

Diagrams 35, 36, 37, and 38 show variations of the fast break movement. These diagrams can be readily interpreted by using the explanation and sequence of movements described for Diagram 34 as a model.

Diagram 37 shows what is probably the fastest method of getting the ball to the basket. Only two long passes are involved. It is even possible sometimes for the guard, **E**, to pass the length of the court to **B**. This is the type of movement that should be used when the forwards get ahead of their opponents in their break for the basket. It will be used most often after interceptions or recoveries. The ball in this case should be thrown fairly high and ahead of the forward rather than directly to him. If it is thrown high, there is no danger of interception, and the forward will have time to run to get the ball. These long passes should all be one hand passes.

Diagram 38 shows **C** batting the ball back over his head to **B**. This can be tried only when **C** and **B** learn to coöperate well. It is, of course, a very quick way to get the ball away from the back-

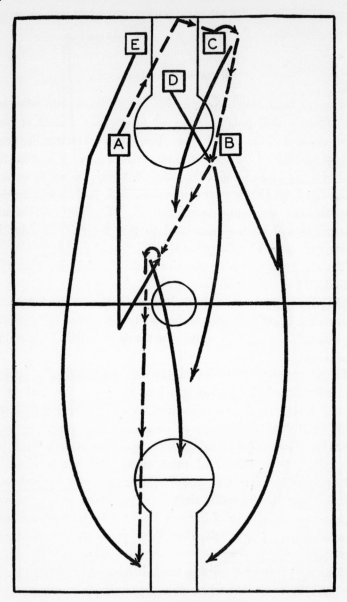

DIAGRAM 35. Variation from Basic Fast Break Movement. First Pass to Center

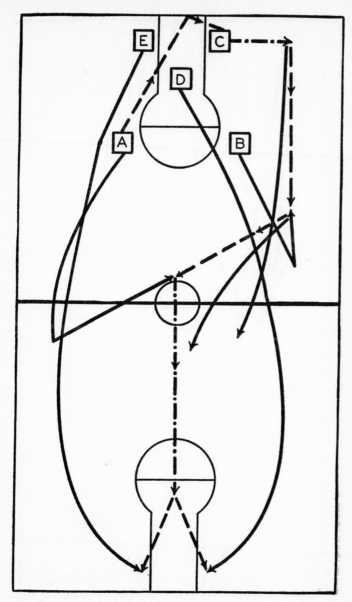

DIAGRAM 36. Variation from Basic Fast Break Movement. Forward
A Dribbles Down Center of Court

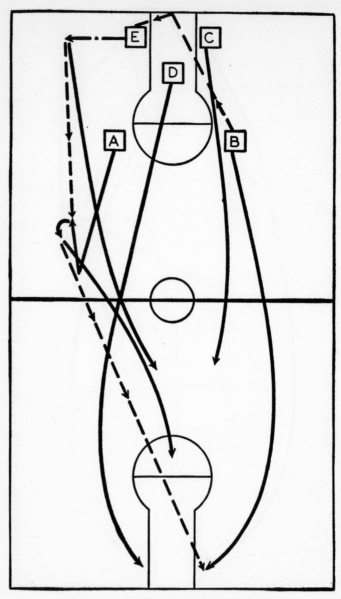

DIAGRAM 37. Direct Method of Fast Break

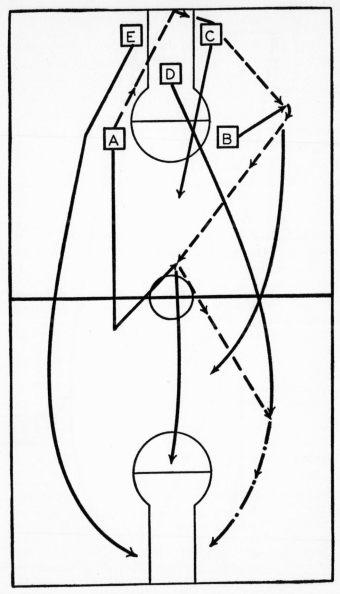

DIAGRAM 38. Fast Break Movement. Guard C Starts Play by
Batting Ball to Forward B

board. It deprives opponents of an opportunity of slowing up the quick break at its start.

The type of a fast break described above is very daring. It leaves no player back to protect the one who recovers the ball from the backboard. The diagram also shows the players breaking straight down the court, a practice which is contrary to most methods of fast break.[1] It is, however, an extremely fast fast break and it has not been found necessary to use protection for the player who recovers the ball from the backboard if he is taught proper methods of protecting the ball. In practically every game, our fast break scores as many goals for us as does our offense-through-defense movements.

The moves of the opponents on offense will not always leave the defensive players as ideally located as they are shown to be in the diagrams for the fast break. At times, too, the forwards may be around the goal while the guards or the center may be in the forward position. The center will often be in a guard position. This should in no way affect the fast break. The players should practice breaking from all positions so that they are prepared for any game situation.

Fast Break Offense after Recovering a Missed Free Throw by Opponents

There should be just as much effort used to fast break after recovering a missed free throw by the opponents as when recovering a missed shot for a field goal. As a matter of fact, the methods are the same except that in the case of the free throw the players always start from the same definite positions.

For clarity in explaining the offense after a free throw, it is necessary also to describe the defense. In Chapter XXVI (page 317) reference is made to the explanation given here.

The rules provide for an equal distribution of players along the free throw lines. Teams as a rule will place their four tallest men

[1] Browne, W. H. "The Fast Break Offense in Basketball." *Athletic Journal*, November, 1936.

Lambert, Ward. *Practical Basketball*. Chicago: Athletic Journal Publishing Company. 1932. Pp. 130-44.

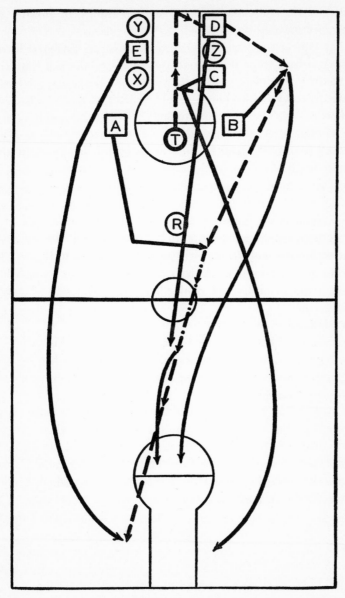

DIAGRAM 39. Fast Break after a Missed Free Throw

in the positions nearest the goal. Thus tall men of one team offset the height advantage of the tall men of the other team. The location and movement of the defensive and offensive players are shown in Diagram 39. The players indicated by circles are members of the team shooting the free throw. No attempt has been made to distinguish them. E and D should be tall men good at jumping and rebounds. They must prevent their opponents from tipping in baskets. In case they have difficulty in this respect, A or B or both may have to come to their assistance by booming for the ball from behind or down through the free throw lane.

C need not be a big player. It is his job to step across into the free throw lane and back toward the free throw line. In this way he prevents the free thrower from getting tip-outs or following up his shot. He also is in a position to recover any wild rebounds.

If the ball bounds to the right as shown, B goes to the side to receive a tip-out from D. A darts down the court as soon as the direction of the ball is determined. He cuts across to receive a pass from B.

C and E will be somewhat delayed in getting a start down the court because they have jobs to perform first. For this reason A will as a rule have to dribble once or twice to give them a start and then float a long pass to one of them. The follow-up moves of each player are shown.

One variation of this movement may be used as shown in Diagram 40. In this diagram, one forward stays at about the center of the court. This should be a tall and clever forward. The ball is tipped to A as shown. He turns and attempts a long high floating pass to B who takes the ball on the run to score a goal. The other players follow up the play as before.

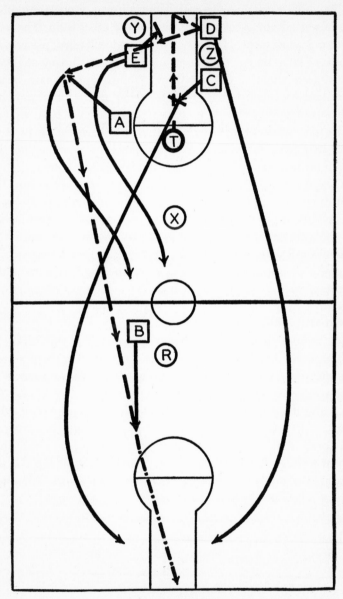

DIAGRAM 40. Fast Break after Missed Free Throw, Showing
"Sleeper" B in Back Court

CHAPTER XXII

OTHER OFFENSIVE SITUATIONS

OUT-OF-BOUNDS PLAYS

A S A result of the elimination of the center jump, there are now three out-of-bounds situations. When the opponents force the play in the back court, it is now necessary to have some understanding among the players concerning out-of-bounds movements after the opponents score a goal. Out-of-bounds situations that occur at the end line in the front court, along the side line in the front court, and at the end line in the back court will therefore be considered. Since out-of-bounds problems occur as often as any other play in a game, it will pay dividends to prepare for them. For example:

1. It has been found valuable to practice with organized plays in order to get scoring opportunities when the ball is thrown into the court. However, it should be emphasized that quickness in taking advantage of any momentary let-down on the part of the opponents is the best out-of-bounds offensive thrust.

2. If a team has been going through a set formation from out-of-bounds time after time, the opponents shortly begin to wait until the formation is set for action. An alert team will take advantage of this delay. While its opponents stand waiting, it will score without setting up its formation.

3. It should also be stressed that the player who throws the ball into the court from out-of-bounds should immediately get into the court. He is usually the unguarded player. This is particularly true when the ball is out of bounds at the end line in the front court. When the ball is passed into the court in this situation,

248

the opponents usually turn toward the ball and have their backs to the player who threw the ball into the court. He is thus the logical one to receive a return pass. Many goals have been scored by this kind of alertness and quick thinking.

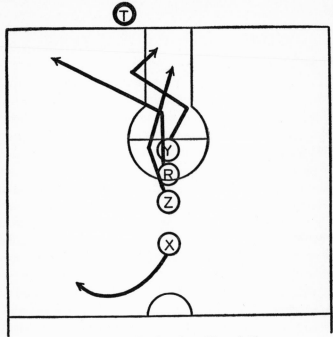

DIAGRAM 41. Tandem Out-of-Bounds Play

THE TANDEM PLAY

Diagram 41 shows a very effective movement when a team is awarded the ball out of bounds at the end near the goal in its own front court. The player who takes the ball out of bounds should be one of the coolest and most experienced players on the team. The same player should always take the ball out of bounds in this situation. The other players form a line behind the free throw line. This may be called a tandem formation. The center is usually placed at **Y** because of his tipping ability. The next player, **R**, is

a forward. Z is the taller guard and the better scorer. X is the
safety man and is usually the smaller, quicker guard. T, who is out
of bounds, is an excellent passer and a very cool and steady player.
When play is called, all players start to move slowly forward. Y,
after taking a step forward, first moves to the right and then to the
left and finally quickly cuts back to the right and jumps for the
ball. If Y is open, T will lay the ball at about the height of his
jump for a tip shot. In this case R will follow the shot, and T will
get in bounds as quickly as possible to follow up the play.

If the ball is not passed to Y, then R darts quickly to the left
to receive a pass from T. T immediately jumps in bounds to receive
a return pass. Y who jumps for the ball continues to a position on
the side of the basket opposite the ball. R of course has the option
of shooting or passing to some other teammate who may be
unguarded.

If a pass to R is not possible, then Z will be found at a position
just in front of the free throw line. After the maneuvers of Y and
R, Z is usually in a position to receive a pass from T.

As a last resort, the ball may be passed to X. He should always
get into an unguarded position to receive the ball. This may be
far in the back court, or he may see an opportunity to break in for
a shot. In any case, it is absolutely necessary for him to be on the
same side of the court as the ball. A cross court pass is likely to hit
the backboard, bound back out of bounds, and thus be awarded
to the opponents.

This play should not be hurried. Five seconds affords plenty
of time for all of its phases and variations. To hurry the play is
likely to prevent it from unfolding properly and from timing
smoothly.

Diagram 42 gives a variation of this type of out-of-bounds play.
In this play Y remains stationary. He acts as a screen for R and Z.
They both start directly forward. R darts to the side of the court
toward the ball. As Z approaches directly behind Y, he cuts to the
opposite side. If neither R nor Z succeeds in breaking into the
open, Y is almost sure to be unguarded. The fact that R and Z

are on the move around **Y** usually draws attention away from him. If **Y** receives the ball, he may shoot or pass to **R**, **Z**, or **T**. **T** of course has stepped onto the court immediately after putting the ball into play.

These two types of plays are usually most effective against a

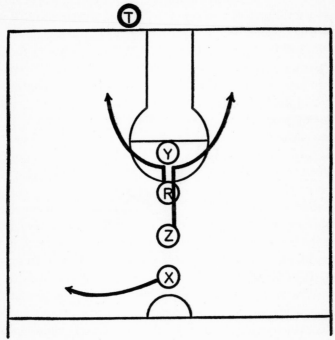

DIAGRAM 42. Variation of Tandem Play

zone defense and may sometimes be useful against man-to-man play. It will be noticed that, if no score or shot results from either of these plays, the players are in position to swing immediately into their regular offense. In Diagram 41, for instance, **T** and **Y** will be in the forward position, **Z** at center, and **R** comes out with **X** at guard.

Box Play

As a variation, two types of screen plays which can be used against a man-to-man defense, or when the ball is along the outer third of the end line, are shown here.

Diagram 43 shows a double screen on **X**. It is essential that the

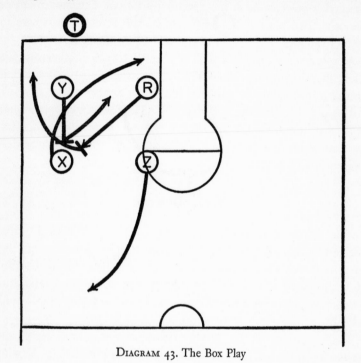

DIAGRAM 43. The Box Play

players quickly take the positions shown. **Y** is the center, **R** the forward. **X** is the faster guard, while **Z**, the big guard, plays safety this time. **T** is the experienced ball handler, as before. When "Play" is called, **Y** and **R** move up behind the player who is guarding **X**. When they become stationary in these positions they call, "Cut!" to **X**. **X** starts straight toward his guard and darts around as shown. In a close man-to-man guarding game he will usually get clear to receive the ball for a shot.

After **X** has cut toward the basket, **Y** darts toward the free throw circle. If the defense shifts men, **Y** is almost sure to be unguarded. As a matter of fact the play is more effective when the defense does shift.

R either remains stationary throughout or else moves over toward the side line as shown. Usually, however, **R** will be unguarded if he remains in his screening position. The movement of the other two players, **X** and **Y**, causes the defense in its care to protect the goal to forget momentarily about player **R**.

As a last resort, the ball may be thrown to player **Z** who is the safety man and who is directed to go anywhere on the court that assures him freedom in receiving the ball.

The play is called the box play. The player who takes possession of the ball out-of-bounds should yell, "Box!" in plenty of time for his teammates to assume their positions before the ball is awarded to him out of bounds.

Screen Plays

The screen play is shown in Diagram 44. When **T** calls, "Screen!" the players should take the relative positions on the court as shown. Here a good side shot player is placed at **X**. Usually he is the guard who is the best shot. **Y** and **R** are the center and forward respectively. They should stand close together and should take up as much floor space as possible. **Z** is the safety man.

Two variations of this play are used. In one **Y** and **R** remain stationary. The ball is thrown high over their heads to **X** who shoots from his protected position. If the guard of **X** moves behind **Y** and **R** to cover **X**, then **X** cuts around by the side line, as shown, to receive the ball. This play has proved to be very effective and assures a team of a shot practically every time it is used.

In the other variation player **T** calls, "Cut!" This is a signal for **Y** and **R** to criss-cross as indicated in Diagram 45. **R** moves first and takes a position to screen for **Y**. When **R** becomes stationary, **Y** fakes to his left and then darts for the basket to receive a pass from **T**. If the defense shifts men, **R** will usually be open for a pass. The player who was originally guarding **Y** will be out of position to guard **R** successfully. In this maneuver **X** remains stationary and is quite often left unguarded.

This play can be used when the ball is out of bounds anywhere along the end line in a team's front court. The lineup is always directly in front of the player who has the ball out of bounds.

DIAGRAM 44. Screen Play for Out-of-Bounds in Front Court

SIDE LINE PLAYS

When the ball is out of bounds along the side line and in the front court, the players take their usual offensive positions (see Diagram 46). The center **Y** is under the basket and is on the side of the free throw lane nearer to the ball. The forwards are on either side. One takes the ball out of bounds, the other moves over to the edge of the free throw circle. The guards take positions near the center line of the court and slightly toward the ball.

When the ball is declared in play, **Y** moves up behind the opponent who is guarding **T**. **T** may pass the ball to **Y**. The best move, however, is to pass the ball to **R** who has run toward it. **T** then forces his guard to run into **Y**. **Y** must remain stationary

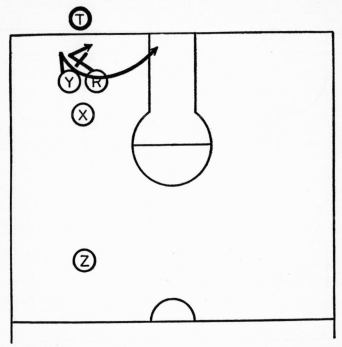

DIAGRAM 45. Criss-Cross from Screen Play When Ball Is Out of Bounds at End of Court

during this maneuver to make this play legal. **R** attempts a return pass to **T**. At this point **X** swings around to the goal as shown. He must not start until after **R** has received the ball. It is better for **X** to be late than early. By delaying, the tendency, even in a man-to-man defense, is to forget about the player who is farthest away from the ball. He can thus, sometimes, sneak in to the goal unnoticed by the opponents.

Z of course is back as a safety man, as in all the other out-of-bounds situations.

It will be noted here that, if the out-of-bounds play is not successful, the players are in a position to resume their regular offense without delay. R and Z would be the guards, Y and X the forwards, while T would be at center. A good rule to follow in assum-

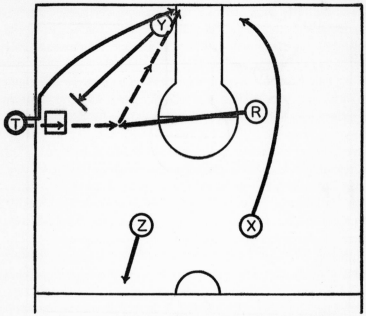

DIAGRAM 46. Side Line Play from Out-of-Bounds on Side

ing offensive positions is that the player nearest to an offensive position should take that position.

HELD BALL PLAYS

A careful study of held ball situations during games and of held ball practices advocated by different coaches has led the author to some rather interesting observations. This study was inspired by the fact that the results from gaining possession of the ball on the jump after a held ball had been unsatisfactory. Here are some of the facts:

1. *Possession is divided 50-50 between opponents.* It was found that, regardless of the size of teams, possession of the ball after a held ball had been declared was divided about 50-50 between teams.

2. *There are few organized plays.* Most of the coaches interviewed did little planning for held ball plays. Their main concern was to be sure that they had plenty of protection. At least two players assumed defensive positions. The other two fought as they saw fit for possession of the ball. For the most part these two players either tried to get a favored position so that the ball could be tipped to them or they dashed by toward defensive territory on either side of the players who were jumping for the ball. Their teammates would try to tip the ball to one side or the other. The player gaining possession of the ball would toss it back to one of his teammates who was in a defensive position.

3. *Held balls per game varied from 5 to 45.* Data were available from the Illinois State High School Tournament, the Big Six Conference, and the Pacific Coast Conference. Three factors seemed to determine the number of held balls per game: (a) The number of held balls varied indirectly with the ability of the two teams playing. As a rule more held balls occurred during a high school game than during a college game in spite of the difference in playing time. (b) The number of held balls varied indirectly with the aggressiveness of the defensive game played by the teams. If the teams were playing a conservative type of defense, taking no chances, not rushing their opponent, then few held balls occurred. If, however, a team on defense was "two-timing" an opponent at every opportunity and was cornering the player with the ball whenever possible, then the number of held balls increased. (c) The number of held balls varied with the type of officiating. If the officiating was hyper-technical, if the officials called held balls to prevent rough play, and if the officials were inexperienced and inefficient, then the number of held balls was high; but if the officials called held balls only when rule conditions for held balls

existed, if they gave a player an opportunity cleverly to extricate himself from a tight spot, and if they were seasoned officials who thoroughly understood play situations, then the held balls were few and far between.

For example, by attention to the points involved in 3(c), the Southern Division of the Pacific Coast Conference reduced the number of held balls per game from 30 to less than 10. This was accomplished over a period of three years.

Since there are almost as many held balls during a game as there are out-of-bounds balls (excluding out-of-bounds situations after a goal has been scored), and in view of 3(a) and 3(b) above, it would seem to profit a team to practice on organized plays in order to score and to gain possession of the ball a larger share of the time following a held ball. With this in mind, a definite effort was made to organize held ball plays. Many experiments were tried, and the results were highly successful. With the same team and against similar opponents, possession of the ball after held balls was increased from less than 50% to better than 80%. An average of two baskets per game, as against none before (this does not count balls batted into the goal on jump balls) was scored. These results obviously justify the provision of time for held ball practice.

Principles of Held Ball Play

Set plays after a held ball are somewhat more difficult than plays from a center jump. This is true because (a) there is usually not sufficient time to get organized, (b) one never knows in advance which two players will be jumping, and (c) the ball may be at any position on the floor. However, in planning held ball plays, these principles should be followed:

1. The jumper must be able to account for the position of all the players on the court. A simple set formation which will enable him to do this is much better than a hit or miss set-up for an advantageous position.

2. The jumper should delay as much as is legally possible in

order to permit his teammates to get into position. The other players must get to their places quickly on a held ball, else it will not be possible to use any kind of play effectively.

3. A formation which requires little or no movement is better than one which involves movements similar to center jump plays.

4. At least one player must be back for protection. If the ball is in defensive territory, then two players should be between the ball and the goal, unless it is quite evident that the ball will be controlled.

5. The ball should always be tipped high into the air so that the receiver must jump for it.

6. The jumper must choose instantly the player who will be the most likely receiver.

7. The opponents should capitalize on the fact that the twelve foot circles are a disadvantage to the team in defensive territory.

8. Whatever formations are used, if scoring is blocked by the opponents, it should be possible to go without hesitation or shifting of positions into the regular offensive movement.

HELD BALL FORMATIONS

The two following diagrams of plays will demonstrate how these principles were put into practice with the successful results above noted.

Diagram 47 shows the formation that is used anywhere in the front court. It may in fact be used anywhere on the court when it is evident that the tip will be controlled by Z or whoever may be jumping. The play is shown at the free throw circle to indicate the disadvantage of the defense in controlling this play.

Players Y, T, and R should rush for the spots indicated so that they may be side by side. This will force the opponents behind or to the side. The present rule does not permit them to enter the area of the circle until after the ball has been tipped. It can be readily seen that, if the two outside defensive men get to the side of Y and R and along the circle, then, if the ball is tipped to T, Y and R have position on their opponents. They can break for the basket after the tip and will be in a position to receive a pass from **T**.

The center player, **T**, in this formation should be the most experienced one on the team. Normally, most tips will go to him since he is in the protected position in the center. It will be his job to decide what move to make after he receives the ball. If **T** is to jump, then the next best player should take this center posi-

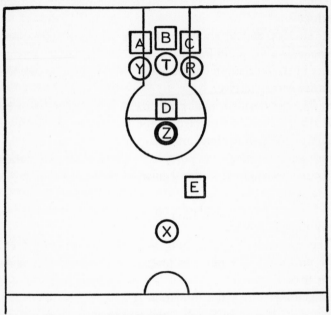

DIAGRAM 47. Held Ball Formation for Front Court

tion. These players should be designated so that there is no delay in getting into position. The center man should, if possible, be a tall player. Height will be of considerable advantage in controlling the ball. It is the job of the two players, **Y** and **R**, who flank **T**, to protect him against opponents. They should step into the circle with their outside feet as the ball is tipped and at the same time keep close to **T**. After he gets the ball they may break to the side or to the basket. In any case, they attempt to get to an open spot.

T has many alternatives, depending upon the defensive movements of his opponents. He may be able to shoot or even turn and dribble in to the basket. He may pass to either Y or R. He may tip the ball back to Z, who steps back after the tip. Z is often the unguarded player who may shoot, because when the ball is first tipped to T, D, the player guarding Z, will turn toward the ball. As a last resort, T may pass the ball back to X. It is the job of X to keep in an unguarded spot, even though it is necessary for him to retreat beyond the center line.

A back tip by Z to X should not be attempted unless Z knows positively that X is unguarded. For instance, by this formation Z is absolutely sure of the whereabouts of eight players. He cannot be sure of the location of E and X. If it should happen (as is often the case, particularly when the jump is not at the circle) that E will take a position somewhere in front of Z, then Z will know that X is directly behind him, far back and unguarded. It will thus be safe to tip back to him.

This same setup may be used even though the held ball does not occur in one of the three circles. The circle, however, strengthens this type of play a great deal because it prevents an opponent from taking a position between the jumpers and the three players in front of the jumper.

The opponents A and C may take positions between Y and T and between T and R. This will, of course, prevent a tip to T but either Y or R may receive the ball if it is tipped high and toward the side line.

OFFENSIVE MOVES AFTER HELD BALL

Should the ball be tipped or thrown back to X, the other players would break to position immediately so that the regular offensive movement might start. X should of course be alert for any opportunity to pass the ball to a teammate who may have maneuvered into a scoring position. Diagram 48 shows how the other players move into offensive positions when the ball is given to X and how the passing may start. Z may hesitate in the circle before moving out as the second guard.

When the ball is over to one side of the court, it should be remembered that a tip to the nearer side line is practically always possible. The opponents will, of course, first take position between the ball and the goal. This will place most of their players toward the inside of the court and of necessity will leave the space toward the nearer side line unprotected.

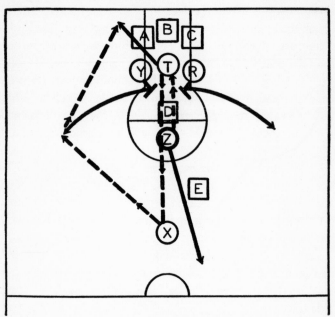

DIAGRAM 48. Movement of Players to Offensive Positions after a
Held Ball Tip

This formation and the various moves from it have been by far the most successful of any that we have ever used or seen. The fact that many scores were made directly from it and that, when-ever the tip was controlled, possession of the ball was secured in over eighty per cent of the cases is evidence enough of the use-fulness of the formation. Also, the fact that the opponents were continually attempting new ways to stop the formation was proof that they were puzzled to find an effective defense for it.

SCREEN PLAYS FROM HELD BALL

Diagram 49 shows another formation which was used on occasion, but with much less effectiveness. It is a more conservative formation in that two players are back at the beginning as safety men. It is slightly weak in that one player, **Z**, moves as the ball is

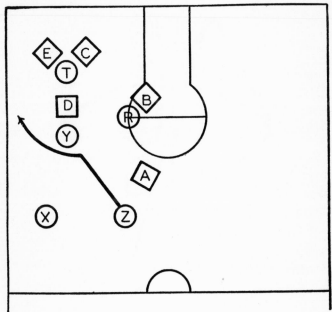

DIAGRAM 49. Screen Play on a Held Ball

tossed up for the jump. The jumper cannot be quite sure where as many players are located in this formation as he can in the other formation. As a result the percentage of recoveries was not as great from this formation. Few scores were made directly from it. The advantage of this formation is that it may be used anywhere on the court, regardless of whether the tip will be controlled or not.

If possible, a tall player should be used to receive the tip, and the tip should be made to **T**, who is the player with excellent judgment. **T** is always directly in front of **Y** and in a position to see all his teammates, so that he can choose the best move to make after he receives the ball. **Y** should tip the ball to the most protected side of **T**. **T** takes a position toward the inside of the court. He usually stands with his back to the goal and attempts to stand in such a position that, if the ball is tipped to him, his body will screen it from his opponent.

Just as the ball is tossed up, **Z** starts toward **Y** to displace his guard and then cuts toward the side line. If **Y** is to tip to him, **Y** need know only that the area just in front and to the side line is unguarded. He knows that **Z** is breaking to this spot every time.

It so happens in this formation that **Z** is the player who is most often open to receive the ball and to shoot. Even when it is tipped to **T**, he is usually double guarded so that he must bat or pass the ball immediately upon receiving it.

X remains back as a safety man. If it is obvious that the ball will not be controlled on the jump, then **Z** will remain back with **X** for protection, while **T** and **R** may do their utmost to gain possession of the ball.

In this formation, as in the other, the players are in a position to continue their offense without delay if a shot for basket is not possible at the tip. In this event, **Z** and **R** will be on the sides, **T** in the center, while **X** and **Y** will be back.

CENTER JUMP PLAYS

With the elimination of the center jump, center jump plays, except in a few instances, have lost their significance. It does not pay to take time to practice them, neither is there need for a variety of them. This was practically true for several years before the elimination of the center jump. So intense had the play about the center become that teams did not attempt to score from the tip; they merely fought for possession of the ball. For these reasons, only three tip-off plays will be shown here. They have been chosen out of the usual repertoire of twelve because it is felt that they offer a sufficient variety for most situations.

Principles of the Center Jump

In all tip-off plays certain general principles apply:

1. All players must do a good job of acting, so that the movement or intent of no player is indicated in advance of the tip-off.

2. The ball should be tipped up and not batted down at a player. This permits a player to time his movements and to adjust for any slight errors in them while the ball is in the air. A high tip will necessitate jumping for the ball, a fact which gives the team controlling the tip an advantage in getting the ball.

3. One player must always drop back toward the center of the court to act as a safety man in case something goes wrong with the tip. Usually this is the guard on the side of the court away from the ball.

4. The center practically always sneaks in to the goal on the opposite side of the court from which he tipped the ball.

5. The player receiving the tip should always be moving toward the ball.

Three Tip-Off Plays

Play No. 1, Diagram 50, is called the "front tip." Many variations of it have been used, but this one has proved to be the best adapted to most situations. In this play, and in all others, T and R take places about ten feet in front of the circle and ten feet to the side. The tendency of the guards to get too far away from the center must be watched. Fifteen feet is usually far enough.

In Play No. 1 the ball is tipped forward and to the side. The ball should be tipped far enough to fall outside of the twelve foot circle. T can displace his guard by faking to go to the side and then cutting across for the ball. R fakes to go toward the center, then quickly pivots and darts for the basket. Y sneaks to the basket along the opposite side. He is the player who is most often open to receive a pass from T. T has the option of dribbling down the center or of shooting or passing to Y or to R. As a last resort he may pivot and pass to Z, who comes up behind him as a trailer.

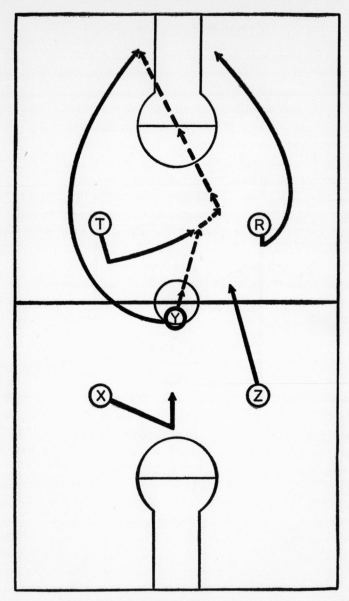

DIAGRAM 50. Center Jump Plays. The Front Tip

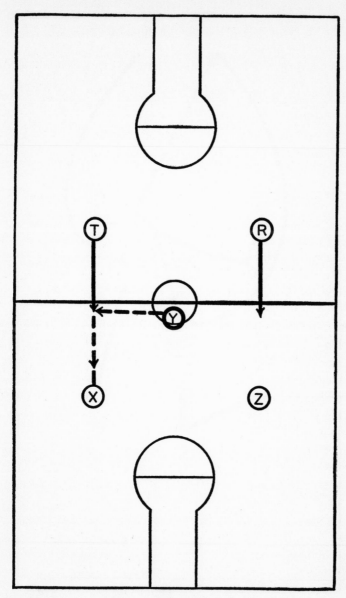

DIAGRAM 51. Center Jump Plays. The Safety Tip

X drops back and cuts across to the center. When he sees that the tip has been successful, he comes up across the center line for any subsequent play.

This is an excellent play when the tip is easily controlled. If opponents should place their guards in a tandem directly between the center circle and the goal, it may not be possible for **T** to cross over as shown. In this case the tip would be made directly to him, or another play would be used. The play, of course, may be reversed to the other side, in which case **R** would receive the tip.

Play No. 2, as shown in Diagram 51, is called the "safety tip." It is used when a team is not sure that it will control the tip. It is used merely to gain possession of the ball without any thought of a scoring play ensuing therefrom. **T** and **R** break along the side, about ten feet out from the center of the circle. Either one may receive the ball. If one of them gets it, he will bat it back to **X** or **Z**. If the team should not gain possession of the ball, there are four players back in defensive position.

Play No. 3, Diagram 52, is called the "double tip." It is designed to take care of the situation when the opponents are all crowding so closely about the center circle that no play is possible. In this case the ball is tipped high and far out along the side line to **X**. **X** should be about six feet from the side line. The ball must be tipped high so that **X** catches it above his head. This method will get the ball over the heads of the opponents and prevent interception.

T has a very important task to perform. He moves as though he intends to get the ball as in Play No. 1. Instead he stops behind the opposing center. When the center drops back, he will charge into **T**. At this instant **Y** breaks for the goal as shown. The success of the play depends upon the ability of **Y**, with the help of **T**, to get to the goal unguarded. **T** after performing his task moves toward the free throw circle.

R starts his movement the same as in the front tip play, but, as **X** receives the ball, he cuts back to a point in front of the free throw circle to receive the ball from **X**. It is important for **R** to be outside the circle so that there is no opportunity for his guard to

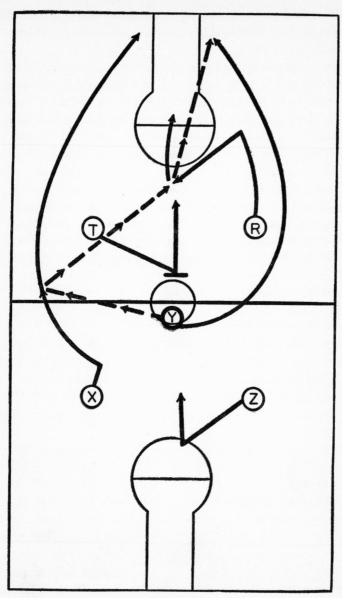

DIAGRAM 52. Center Jump Plays. The Double Tip

cover both him and the center, **Y**. **R** should pass to **Y** if at all possible. A hook pass, backhand bounce pass, or a pivot and underhand pass may be used.

After he has passed the ball to **R**, **X** continues to the goal as shown. In case **Y** is not unguarded, **R** may make a return pass to **X**. **R** may also pivot and then dribble to the goal himself. In case all forward movement is stopped, he may pass back to **T** from where regular offense-through-defense play may start. **Z** has played the role of the safety man. This play may, of course, be executed on the opposite side of the court.

These methods of getting possession of the ball after the center jump provide enough effective variation with the limited number of center jumps that are made under the present rules.

CHAPTER XXIII

GENERAL PRINCIPLES OF TEAM DEFENSE

THE DEVELOPMENT OF THE DEFENSE

IN THE early stages of the game of basketball, there was no such thing as a team defense of any kind. The game was built up entirely with specialists. Guards were players who could not score. They were the watch dogs of the opponents' basket. And woe betide any opponent who dared to break in toward his basket for a shot. It was the job of these guards to prevent scores. They performed this job in a vigorous and effective fashion.

Very little time was devoted to the teaching of guarding. As a matter of fact, not until the last year of my own college playing days did I receive any instruction in defensive play. Until 1910, defensive instruction was limited to the individual technique of guarding. All defensive play was some kind of man-to-man play.

Sometime after 1910, there crept into the game the idea of team defense in the form of a zone defense. With the advent of the zone defense, a new philosophy of defensive play evolved. Just as the idea of continuity in offense has made the greatest contribution to offensive play, so this new philosophy of defense has made the greatest contribution to defensive play. It has given rise to greater variety in defensive play and has brought about the development of defensive play to a point at which it is on a par with the offense. As a matter of fact the changes in defense have forced innovations in the offense. Along with this new idea, there have arisen two antagonistic groups among the coaches of the country: (1) those who advocate the use of the man-to-man defense and who think any other kind of defense ruins the game, and (2) those who are disciples of a zone or team principle of defense and who think that the development of types of this defense has been one of the greatest possible boons to the game.

The advocates of a man-to-man defense object to the zone defense on the ground that it masses its forces in a stationary fashion around the free throw area and thus allows no opportunity for the execution of cleverly designed plays. However, this objection is invalidated when one realizes that this very massing may be done (and is done) in a man-to-man as well as in a zone defense. It follows, then, that it is not the type of defense employed, but rather the aggressiveness and daring of the team that determines the nature of its defensive play. If a team is taught to play conservatively, it will tend to mass its defense about the free throw area, regardless of whether man-to-man or zone defense is used. As a matter of fact, the chances are that a team will play more aggressively and take more chances when playing a zone defense than when playing a man-to-man defense. Here is where the difference in philosophy regarding the two types of defense comes into the picture.

Two Defensive Philosophies

1. *In a man-to-man defense the primary responsibility of the guard is to watch the man (an opponent).* The ball is of secondary importance. Usually, the player to be guarded is assigned before the game begins. Therefore the guard, when his team loses the ball, hunts out this player to whom he has been assigned and stays with him until his team recovers the ball. He faces this player under all circumstances, except when rebounding. He has no concern for the ball unless it is in the possession of his particular opponent. The ball may hit him in the back or roll between his legs, but he does not for a minute relax his vigilance on his opponent. He realizes that one of the cardinal sins of defensive play is to lose his opponent or to turn his back on his opponent for one moment. His responsibility is a singular one. If his man gets away from him, there is likely to be a score. He cannot look to his teammates for

much help because each of them has a similar obligation. Therefore the element of team work, which is one of the fine social standards that ought to be developed through sport, does not enter into defense of this type.

2. *In the zone or team principle of defense, the primary responsibility of the defensive players is to watch the ball.* Every effort is bent toward getting the ball whenever possible. The opponent is of secondary consideration. No player is assigned to any particular opponent, but rather each player moves and plays according to the whereabouts of the ball. In his effort to get the ball, he will take chances and will do what many would consider to be unorthodox. A defensive player may take these chances because he knows that he has the support of his teammates to protect for him in case he fails in his attempt to get the ball. A team may mass its defense about the goal under certain circumstances, but it can just as effectively spread its defense all over the court— and does so more often than the man-to-man team. It has been my observation that the team employing the team defense is usually the aggressive team, even when ahead in the score.

One might criticize this type of play by saying that it is not sound fundamental defense. The answer is three-fold: (1) The same technique and fundamentals of guarding are taught as in man-to-man defense with the added direction to take chances and use freedom and personal initiative to get the ball whenever possible. (2) The dividends paid by this type of play in gaining possession of the ball and harassing opponents justify the procedure. (3) The fun that players get out of catching their opponents unawares and the appreciation of the coöperative effort of teammates make this one of the best socializing and educational elements in the game.

A Testimonial to the Team Defense

A typical reaction from a player who was playing against this type of defense one evening will best illustrate the above points. Bill Kinner, a member of the University of Utah team, was one of the outstanding players of the country several years ago. He was too good for any one player on our team, but by team play methods we were able to concentrate on him. Since he was the main strength of his team, we felt that, if we stopped him, we could win the game. We forced him at all times in the front court. He was clever enough often to out-maneuver one player, but there was always another to cover him and prevent him from dribbling in to the basket for a shot. On one occasion he had seemed to evade several of our players and yet, when he poised to shoot, his shot was blocked. In desperation he groaned, "How many players are on your team anyway?" This is often the reaction of players who come up against a team defense.

The principles of man-to-man defense are largely the principles of individual technique in guarding. These principles have been covered under *Methods of Guarding*, Chapter XV. Therefore the principles of team defense alone are here presented. The reader might conclude that an attempt has been made to build up a case for the team defense and that therefore only one side of a controversy has been given. Frankly, the writer, from long study, from years of observation of defensive play, and from playing both types of defense while in high school and college has reached the conclusions which have just been stated. The position with respect to the team defense has been stated dogmatically, deliberately so. Students of basketball have said, after watching my teams play, that part of the time they play man-to-man and part of the time they play zone, or team, the preferred term for the defense. My answer is that my teams never play man-to-man defense for the reason that they are always playing for the ball and not for the man. This may seem to some to be begging the question, but the real student of basketball must recognize that there is a fundamental difference in this point of view. It is a state of mind created within the player which certainly has a very decided effect upon his play and upon his reaction to play situations.

The Principles of Team Defense

There are six general principles of team defense:

1. *The focus of attention of the players is primarily upon the ball.* This is the fundamental difference between the man-to-man and the zone defense which has just been discussed. To illustrate this principle, a picture of the position of the players in a general

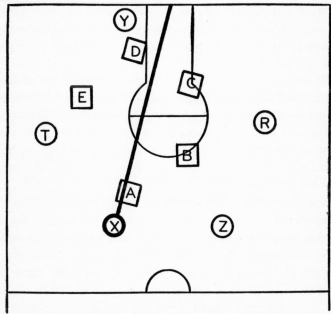

DIAGRAM 53. Showing Defense Concentrating on the Ball and about a Line Connecting Ball and Basket

situation is given in Diagram 53. The ball is indicated at **X**. A line is drawn connecting the ball with the basket. This, of course, is an imaginary line to the players under actual playing conditions. The players in general will tend to arrange themselves about this line, mainly between the ball and the basket. All are concentrating primarily upon the player with the ball. They attempt to detect from his actions and expression what he will do with the ball. If he becomes careless or gets into an indefensible position, the players near him will attempt to steal the ball or force a held ball. The purpose in grouping about the line drawn between the ball and the goal is to force all passing and movement toward the side line and out around the defense. In any defense, if it is possible to spread the players so that the attack can go between them rather than around them, the defense has been weakened, the possibilities of team coöperation have been lessened, and the chances for fouling have been increased. Even in the case of one player guarding another, if the offensive player with the ball can maneuver into a position between the guard and the goal, the guard is decidedly at a disadvantage. He will find difficulty in guarding without committing a foul.

2. *The players will adjust their positions (but not the focus of their attention) according to the positions and movements of their opponents.* It is a fundamental of basketball that all players should at all times know the location of all other players on the court. Players should therefore develop a wide peripheral vision. A defensive player should always play back of and well in toward the center of the court from the particular man that he is guarding.

The positions of the defensive players in Diagram 53 were set according to both the position of the ball and that of the offensive players as shown. To illustrate a change in position necessitated by a change in position of the defense, Y is placed in the corner as in Diagram 54. The positions of all defensive players are the same, except that of D. He has moved back toward the end line slightly and over very slightly toward the corner occupied by Y. It will be noticed that the concentration of players is still between the ball and the basket. As a general rule, it may be said that the nearer an opponent is to the ball or to the line connecting the ball with the basket, the closer the guard must play to him. D, in Diagram 53, is covering Y very closely. Y is not close to the ball, but is very close to the line connecting the ball with the basket. In Diagram 54, Y is in the corner and is far removed from both the ball and the basket. Consequently, in this situation, D is not so close to Y. Likewise E is covering T much closer than C is covering R. T is closer to both the line and the ball and is in a good position to re-

ceive the ball, whereas **R** is far away (comparatively speaking) from
both the line and the ball. A pass from **X** to **R** must risk interception by **B** and thus must be lobbed over his head. This pass would
give **C** plenty of time, not only to get into a position to guard **R**,
but would even give him an opportunity to intercept the ball.

In the next chapter the positions and movements of the defense

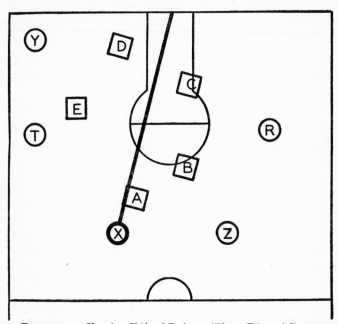

DIAGRAM 54. Showing Shift of Defense (Player D) to Adjust to
Position of Offense (Player Y). Refer to Diagram 53

will be shown for typical offensive situations. Here, suffice it to say
that defensive players should not be confused or drawn unduly
out of position by the position or movement of their opponents.
The defensive positions and movements should be governed, so
far as adjusting to the position of the opponents is concerned, by
the answer to this question, "Is the offensive player in a strong
offensive position where he can receive the ball with an opportunity to score?" If the answer to this question is "Yes," then the
defensive player must move close enough to the opponent to be

able either to prevent him from shooting if he should get the ball or to chance an interception. If, on the other hand, the answer is "No," then the defensive player need not be concerned about his position or his movements, but should hover about the line connecting the ball and the basket.

3. *Players should shift opponents whenever possible.* In general the players should keep the same relative positions with respect to each other. The players are usually placed in their defensive positions with the idea that they will be most effective in doing the tasks peculiar to these positions. The offensive play of most teams is so stereotyped and the movement of the offensive players is so limited in comparison with the movement of the ball that it is possible, for the most part, for the players to maintain their positions. (This type of defense has been one of the motivating factors for more complicated, varied, and flexible offenses.)

However, it is not always possible for a player to maintain his same general position on the court. In such cases he should not hesitate to move as the situation demands. As a consequence, a player who normally is on the right side of the court may be playing on the extreme left side of the court. A player out in front of the free throw circle may on occasion find himself back under the goal. Under these circumstances the players should shift back to their original positions as soon as it is convenient and safe to do so. Opportunity to shift back to original positions will usually present itself when the ball is away from the basket and on the opposite side of the court from the players who desire to change their positions. Of the two players changing positions, that player who is farthest from the basket should change first. This will always leave the defensive strength concentrated near the basket. If a shot is permitted as a result of the change, it will of necessity be a long shot.

Four movements will be shown here to illustrate the possibilities of shifting. In general, players may shift whenever the players they are guarding cross in front of and close to them. This closeness is a judgment factor, but usually if the players cross and are more than six feet apart, shifting may be difficult and even dangerous.

In other words, the opponents are not close enough to permit a shift in this case.

A simple shift, of course, is that of the players out in front of the defense who criss-cross or move in a figure eight pattern. Diagram 55 shows this situation. X passes the ball to Z and then cuts around behind him. A would follow X across. When A bumped into B, B would shift to cover X, and A would guard Z. B should

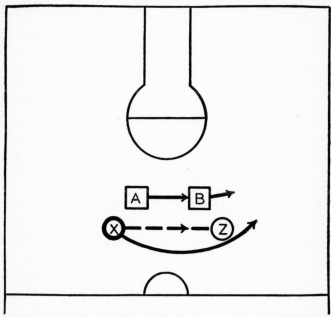

DIAGRAM 55. Showing How Defensive Forwards (A and B) Shift
When Guards (X and Z) Cross

not move until X has passed beyond Z and is outside of B. This same type of shift would occur along the side line as shown in Diagram 56.

If, however, as in Diagram 57, X, after passing the ball to Z should take a diagonal route behind B, then A must drop back with X. If, as X approached R, R should cut to the center as shown, then A and C would shift men. A would cover R while C would fight hard toward the center and back toward the goal to

get between **X** and the goal. This is a partial screen situation, and
for the moment **C** is not in a good guarding position.

If **X** in Diagram 57 had gone behind **C** and into the corner so
that no shift was possible anywhere, then **A** would have dropped
back with him and for a time would be in the back line of defense
rather than out in front in his original position. As long as the
ball remained at **Z**, he probably could not shift back, but when

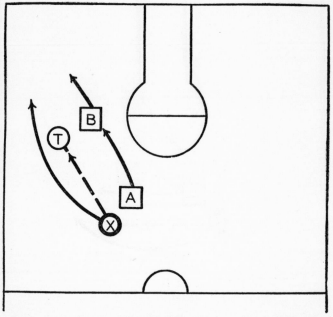

DIAGRAM 56. Showing How Defensive Forward (A) Shifts with
Guard (B) When Offensive Guard (X) and Forward (T) Cross in
Front of Them

the ball moved to the other side of the court, he could watch his
chance to get back into position. These are all comparatively simple
shifting situations.

Diagram 58 shows the most complicated type of shift that may
occur. The shift is complicated because it involves four players
rather than two as is usually the case. In this situation **Z** passes to
R and moves in a line between **R** and the center of the court. **B**

and C cannot shift because Z and R do not cross as the players in
Diagram 56. (Had Z gone around R, then B and C would have
shifted, and this would have been the only shift necessary to cover
the situation.) B must drop back. Here two moves may be made:
either B may stay with Z as would be the case under the general
statement concerning shifting, or a bold maneuver may be at-

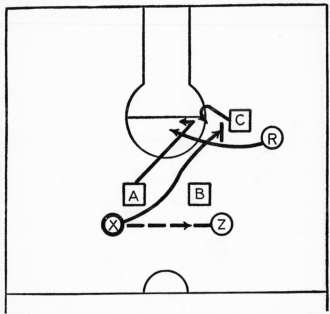

DIAGRAM 57. Showing Situation in Which Defensive Forwards (A
and B) May Not Shift. X and Z Did Not Cross in Front of Them.
Instead A and C Shift Players

tempted as is indicated. This, you will see, results in every player's
maintaining his same relative position.

B moves back until he gets behind the ball. (This assumes, of
course, that R retains possession of the ball. If he were to pass it
back to X then B would not continue back but would immediately
come out toward the ball.) At this point D calls, "Shift." B stops
and moves toward the ball, attempting to help C get a held ball
from R. D shifts to cover Z; as a matter of fact, he need move

very little unless **Z** should go to the corner. **E**, who has moved over into the lane a little as **R** received the ball, now shifts to cover **Y**. **A**, who has dropped back as **R** received the ball, moves back until **T** shows up in front of him. **B**, as stated before, is ready to cover **X**.

This maneuver involves a four-way shift which is quite complicated. Shifts of this kind require practice in team defense as well

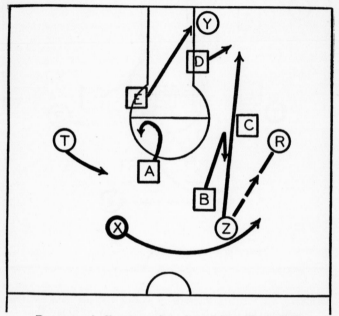

DIAGRAM 58. Showing a Complicated Four-Player Shift

as careful analysis of offensive team movements. Difficult as this may seem, our teams, after a little practice, make the shifts deftly and without a hitch. It will be seen from the foregoing that individual responsibility can always be assigned for all situations. However, in the case of a team defense, it is always a team responsibility, which is of course of much greater educational value to the players than is a rote man-to-man assignment.

In all cases of shifting there must be smooth team play, and the defensive players must be talkative. The shifts should always be called (otherwise no shift should be made) and in every case should be called by the player who is behind. He is in position to see all the moves and to size up the situation best. If at any time during play there is confusion concerning shifts, no shifts need be made until there is opportunity to talk over the situation.

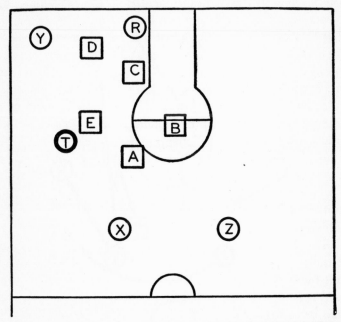

DIAGRAM 59. Showing Principle of Guard Keeping Between Opponent and Goal and Not Worrying about Man Behind Him

4. *Always guard the opponent who is in front of you.* Players have a tendency to worry about the opponents behind them. For example the center often is confronted with the problem of seeing a player in the corner and one under the goal. Diagram 59 will illustrate this situation. T has the ball. D has moved over to guard Y, but he senses player R behind him. In this case and in all other situations of this kind where all five men are in position on defense, D should not hesitate to go after Y. Likewise he should not worry about R who is behind him.

One exception may be stated to the rule of always guarding the player in front. Diagram 53, on page 275, will illustrate this exception. Whenever **Y** plays along either free throw lane line and does not go beyond the intersection of this line with the free throw circle, **D** should play in front of him. Most coaches, even in this instance, have the guard play behind his opponent. However, it has been found by repeated experimentation and observation, both in practice and in games, that, when the two players are of approximately the same height, the guard will be more effective if he plays in front. There is absolutely no danger of passing over the guard's head for a score. The distance back to the basket is too short. If the offensive player waits until the ball has passed the guard, he cannot recover it before it goes out of bounds. In all other cases the guard can move to intercept passes. Practice in such guarding strategy renders the offensive player useless.

The guard should take a position facing slightly toward the side line and practically on a line connecting his offensive player and the ball. This position keeps his opponent in his visual field and permits ready shifting. If the opponent goes out into the circle or toward either side line, then the guard must play behind.

This is the only exception. In all other cases it will be noticed that the guard is between the opponent and the goal and always guards the player in front of him.

5. *Whenever the ball is passed behind a defensive player he should move toward the goal.* Such a move always places the defensive player or players in a position to defend the goal. They are in position to do rebound work if necessary or to guard opponents near the goal in case they have been left unguarded as the result of a necessary shift due to the movement of the ball or the players. Diagram 58 is an illustration of the converging of the defense toward the goal under the above conditions.

It is sound defensive technique for a player who is guarding the ball to drop back when the ball is passed to an offensive player behind him. Dropping back prevents the offensive player who made the pass from breaking by the defensive player to receive a return pass. This would be the situation in Diagram 58 with respect to the offensive player Z and defensive player B. The moment Z passes the ball to R, B should drop back and should keep between Z and the goal until Z moves past R, who has possession of the ball.

The distance that a player must move back depends entirely upon the offensive situation. Every offensive player must be accounted for. There should never arise (under normal conditions when all five defensive players are in their organized guarding positions), a situation in which one defensive player is required to guard more than one offensive player. This would mean (again referring to Diagram 58), that, if Z stayed out in front of the defense instead of running in as indicated, neither A nor B would drop back farther than the initial safety move of one step. They would know that every opponent behind them was accounted for because there would be at least two players out in front of them. Just as soon as there were not two players out in front, then A and B would know that their three teammates behind them had four opponents to guard. It is therefore necessary to converge toward the goal until each opponent is personally accounted for.

6. *The defense should always be formed from the goal first.* This is tantamount to saying that, if under any circumstances an opponent must be left unguarded, it should be the one who is farthest from the goal. There will be many occasions during the progress of a game when all of the defense is unable to get into position before the opponents bring the ball to the front court and in scoring position. This is particularly true when teams are using a fast break offense. The center, who is usually assigned the duty of playing under both baskets, is often the player who is last to get back into a defensive position.

When it happens that only four or even three players are in defensive position as the opponents attack, these players, regardless of where they normally play, should see that the defense around the goal is intact. The players who are last to return to defense in these cases will fill in the places that are thus left vacant. They will then shift into their regular defensive positions at the first safe opportunity.

CHAPTER XXIV

STANFORD TEAM DEFENSE; SET-PLAY SITUATIONS

THE Stanford team defense is built upon the six general principles of team defense as discussed in Chapter XXIII and so may be taken as an example of the application of these principles. The defense is designed with three objectives in mind. First, it is intended to develop to the fullest extent the educational values of coöperative group effort. Second, by virtue of coordinating and supporting the movements of the players in an attempt to gain possession of the ball at all costs, it encourages the greatest possible daring. Third, it is organized to permit its offensive movement to begin, without delay or lost motion, the instant the team has gained possession of the ball. The defense may thus play with the same principles of movement whether it is massed about the goal or whether it is deployed the full length of the court.

As a starting point for elementary teaching and demonstration of the defense, the setup shown in Diagram 60 is used. Game situations will materially alter positions, and these changes will be discussed in turn. However, most of the present-day offensive patterns place three offensive players inside the defense and two, usually the guards, outside the defense. Since this is true, the initial positions of the defensive players are considered with three defensive players forming a triangle of primary defense about the goal and two defenders, the attacking element of the defense, constituting the secondary line of defense, stationed out in front of the free throw circle. The defense will be developed and explained from these stationary positions.

SELECTION OF PLAYERS FOR EACH POSITION

Not only the positions of the players on the court but also the placement of the players in the five defensive positions are of tremendous importance. The position that an individual plays on offense need have no bearing whatever upon what or where he plays on defense. The players should be placed entirely on the basis of their ability to do a particular job well.

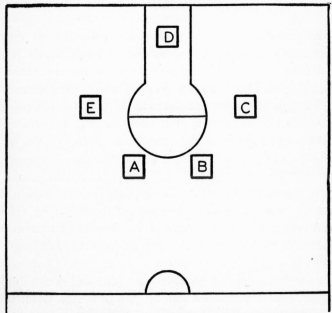

DIAGRAM 60. Initial Positions of Players for Stanford Team Defense

The players in positions **A** and **B**, Diagram 60, should be very quick and aggressive. They are the ball hawks and should be urged to take chances under most circumstances. If they are tall and rangy, they are the more valuable, because opponents will have greater difficulty in passing around and over them. They will make unexpected interceptions. However, height around the goal should not be sacrificed for the sake of having height in this front line or secondary defense.

The player at **D** should be the quarterback on defense. He should be thoroughly trained in all the vagaries of the defense. He is back of practically all the play and is in a position to see all the play situations as they develop. Therefore it is logical that he should be an efficient floor general on defense. He must have confidence in his knowledge of defensive situations and he must be able to convince his teammates of his ability so that they will have confidence in his judgment and his directions. He must talk; he must have pride in a shot-proof defense; he must demand hard, relentless defensive play from his teammates. And finally, he must be tall. If he is also big, he is an even greater asset, but he must be tall because the bulk of the rebound work will fall on his shoulders.

Of the other two defensive men, **C** and **E**, at least one of them should be tall and rugged. If a team has only two tall players, they should both be in the defense line around the basket. One will be at **D** and the other usually at **E** because most teams seem to concentrate their attack on the right side of the court. This will place the player at **E** under the basket for rebound work more often than the player at **C**. There are times, however, when certain idiosyncrasies may make it desirable to place this second big man at **C**. Lefthandedness, for example, would be a desirable asset to the player at **C**. Such a player would have a distinct advantage in passing the ball out from the goal to start a fast break after rebounding.

If a team has three tall players, it is desirable to use one of these at **A** or **B**, provided he is quick, instead of placing all three in the back line of defense. The tall man in front is very useful in receiving long high passes on a fast break. A small man is very unsatisfactory when long high passes over the head of an opponent are desired. However, a small man in the back line of defense adds spice to the big men. While he cannot do a great deal of rebound work against taller players, nevertheless he can do a very effective job of screening players away from the goal so that the taller men can rebound.

If perchance a coach is fortunate enough to have five tall players, no one of whom is under six feet three, then of course he has no height problems to worry about.

Positions of Players after Shots

It is the job of the three players around the goal to form a barricade so that opponents may not be able to make rebound shots. After opponents shoot, one player should be in front of the goal and one on either side. The particular offensive situation before the shot may not make it possible for **D** always to be in the center, but the triangle about the goal should always be maintained. A more effective job of guarding the goal can be done if these three players will not crowd closer to the goal than six feet. They should spread themselves as much as the rules will permit and they should assume a low, crouched position.

Players **A** and **B** should retreat to the free throw line. They will usually be at either end of the free throw line. Their duty will be to recover balls that come back over the heads of their three teammates. They will also be ready to rush to the goal to assist their teammates on rebounds in cases where opponents seem to have an advantage and where their teammates are crowded too far under the goal or even out of bounds.

The extent to which **A** and **B** must come back to help rebound will depend entirely upon the effectiveness of the three-man barricade about the goal. If **C**, **D**, and **E** are able to handle rebounds successfully, then **A** and **B** need not retreat to the goal at all after shots. On the contrary, the moment a shot is made they should start on offense.

When playing conservatively and in the early stages of learning the defense, **A** and **B** should always drop back to aid **C**, **D**, and **E** on rebounds, and they should not advance farther than ten feet from the edge of the free throw circle.

Preliminary Defense Practice

When the defense is taught to a group for the first time, practice should begin with simple situations. The players should mass conservatively about the free throw area. An offensive team should be placed on the floor around the defense with the forwards along the side line, the guards out in front, and the center near the end line and along the free throw lane line. The offense should not be permitted to move at first. The ball may be passed from one player to another. After each pass is made, the ball should be held momentarily so that the defense may move and have an opportunity to check its position before the next pass is made.

With the defense massed and the offense stationary in the fashion described, it will be much easier to learn the methods of moving so as to focus attention on the ball. The players will gain confidence in this type of defense more quickly than if they were thrown against a live offense with the inevitable opportunities for confusion.

Next, let one offensive player, the center, move at will from the basket to either corner or to the free throw line. This will give the player in the center of the back line of defense an opportunity to adjust his position according to the position of the offense.

Next, permit the three players, forwards and center, within the defense to move at will. This will allow the three back defensive players to adjust positions for movements of the opponents and also give them practice in shifting men whenever the opportunity presents itself.

Finally, a regular offense-through-defense scrimmage is in order with all five offensive players permitted to move and play in any way that will earn a shot and a score. The defense should still mass about the free throw area in order to reduce the effective offensive area. The defense will thus be able to cover more effectively the area which it encompasses and its shifts will be much easier to see and to make. It will not be necessary under these circumstances for the defensive players to change their relative positions. In directing the defensive practice, it is well to sit above the floor if possible. A much better view of movements as a whole can be secured from a balcony, for example, than from the level of the floor.

As the defense gains confidence and proficiency, the players should spread more, should become more aggressive and daring, and more complicated offensive situations should be introduced.

The players should be ready for any emergency whether it be forcing a team in the back court, out at the center line, or adjusting to some offensive trick; whether it be out-of-bounds plays, held ball maneuvers, screening plays, or stalling for time. Nothing will surprise a team that is thoroughly grounded in the general principles of defense and in general situations that may arise. However, it is one thing to talk about these points, and another to practice them.

The practice of team defense is usually taken up after the drills in offense have started, but once the defense is presented, it will require as much time for practice as the offense. Of course, the two may go hand in hand so that double time is not necessary.

CHAPTER XXV

APPLICATIONS OF THE TEAM DEFENSE

THE defense has been shown for the type of offensive formation that is most commonly used, i.e., two guards out, the forwards along the side line, and the center along the free throw lane. The defense for this setup is used as the foundation upon which and from which all other movements evolve. Only static situations can be shown in the following diagrams. Situations involving movement need present no difficulties, however, if the six general principles are thoroughly mastered.

THE CENTER PIVOT PLAY

Before the advent of the three-second rule, the center pivot play was one of the most popular types of offensive movements. Now with that half of the free throw circle from the free throw line toward the center circle no longer restricted by the three-second rule, except when the player in this area has the ball, undoubtedly this play will again become very popular. The defense for this type of offense is shown in Diagram 61.

With player **Y** stationed at the free throw line, **D** must play behind him and slightly toward the same side of the court as the ball. **D** may, however, play any weakness that he finds in **Y**. For example, most players—because coaches do not teach ambidexterity—can pivot and dribble in only one direction and shoot with only one hand. When this weakness is evident, then **D** may overshift to the player's strong side and thus absolutely stop his movement in that direction. This was a weakness of Guttero, the great center from University of Southern California. He could pivot and dribble to the basket in one direction only, and he never became adept at shooting with his left hand. If a team has a weak player at either forward spot, R or T, then the guard of either of these players can help to concentrate on Y, who is nearly always the key player.

In this play it is practically impossible, with the defense set as shown, for X or Z to pass to Y, so that the pass must be made to T

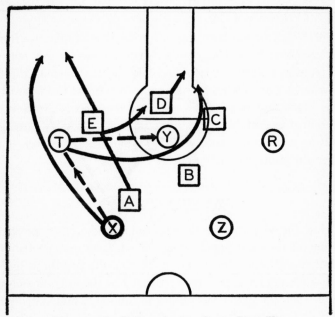

DIAGRAM 61. Defense Against Center Pivot Play

(or R), who in turn passes to Y. Even this pass is made difficult because B drops back, as the ball goes to T, and can often help to cover Y so as to prevent a pass to him.

X, after passing to T, usually cuts around him. The shift between A and E is evident here. If T passes to Y, he may cut around him as shown. The shift here is between A and D.

There are, of course, opportunities at all these points for forcing a held ball by disregarding the offensive players without the ball and two-timing the player with the ball. This move should be encouraged whenever possible. Play from this formation tends to make the game somewhat congested and therefore lends itself admirably to "tying up" the player with the ball.

There are many other variations of this formation, but this explanation should give the reader the general scheme of meeting it.

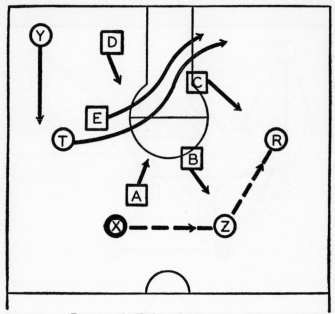

DIAGRAM 62. Defense for Two on a Side

TWO ON A SIDE

Diagram 62 shows a formation from which two types of movement are used rather generally. One is a figure eight made by R, Y, and T, and the other is a figure eight made by all five players. This movement has been made famous by Dr. Carlson [1] of Pittsburgh.

The defense is shown as it should be used for the static position of the players with the ball at X. When the ball is passed to Z, T

[1] Carlson, H. C. You and Basketball. Braddock, Pennsylvania: Brown Publishing Company. 1929. Ch. 5, pp. 75-121.

cuts as shown and **Y** usually moves out to replace **T**. **R** will move out a step or two and may receive a pass from **Z**. If **T** receives the ball, **Y** may cut for the goal.

If the movement of the offense is timed correctly, **C**, **D**, and **E** will not be able to shift men, and their consequent movements are indicated in the diagram. If, however, the movements of **Y** and **T** are not properly synchronized, then **D** and **E** may shift men,

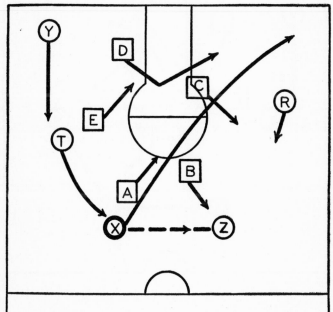

DIAGRAM 63. Defense Against Five-Man Figure-of-Eight

for neither would move very much. **D** would move from one side of the free throw lane to the other, while **E** would drop back a couple of steps to make sure that **Y** did not break for the goal and would then come out to cover him when **Y** replaces **T**.

These movements would now be repeated from the other side with **R** cutting across the free throw line. The defensive movements would be similar, but from the other side of the court.

Diagram 63 shows the same formation, but with a figure eight movement by all five offensive players. Even though there is more offensive movement in this formation, there is actually less defensive movement. One reason for the limited defensive movement may be the stereotyped movement of the offense. The defense does little more than make a catch step in one direction for safety purposes, and then hops back to its original position as the offense reverses itself and finally becomes exhausted, discouraged, and takes a long shot.

The ball starts at X. It is passed to Z. X cuts diagonally as shown. T replaces X. Y replaces T. R moves out a couple of steps, and X replaces Y, but on the opposite side of the court. The formation is now ready to reverse itself by having Z pass to T and then move on a diagonal to the spot originally occupied by Y.

The defensive moves are shown in the diagram. A need move back only far enough to prevent a pass from Z to X and until D can pick up X. A can, after this movement has continued for some time, fail to drop back at all and take a chance on intercepting the pass from Z to T as the movement is reversed. D moves forward and then back on the opposite side of the free throw lane. E moves back to the spot occupied by C, but on the opposite side of the lane, and C moves out to cover R. B covered Z as A dropped back.

When one analyzes these moves in terms of the position of the ball, he will see that the defense is quite sound. Even if Y cut for the basket instead of moving out, the play would be well covered. As a matter of fact, both C and E should be alert to just such a variation. If Z passed to R and R to X, the defense would still be sound. Therefore, what might appear to be risky shifting proves to be sound defense and a tremendous energy saver. It so happens that the movement and timing of this formation is not effective against this team defense. It was primarily designed for a man-to-man defense.

THREE-OUT, OR DOUBLE PIVOT OFFENSE

A three-out offense creates the most radical change in the fundamental setup of the team defense of any offense that is met. The three man triangle about the basket must be broken up. With three offensive players out toward the center line in front of the defense, it becomes necessary to match them with three defensive men and thus weaken the defense about the basket. However, if the three players out in front were not covered, one would always be open for a shot.

The exact method of matching an offensive formation of this kind with the proper defense depends entirely upon how the three-out offense is formed. If it is a set formation into which the opponents arrange themselves before they attempt to penetrate the defense, a very definite defensive organization may be planned in advance. If, however, the three-out offense comes about as an incidental part of the offensive movement, so that any players may make up the three who are out in front and so that they may come from any position on the court, then the defensive maneuvers to meet this offense can be set up in a general way only. Both methods of forming a defense for three-out offense will be discussed.

1. Mechanized Three-Out.

Most three-out offenses are more or less stereotyped; so the defense for this type will be discussed first. A typical formation for a three-out offense is shown in Diagram 64. Y and R may range anywhere from the corners of the court to positions along either side of the free throw lanes. The center man of the three players in front is usually a key man, although there may be many variations of the organization of these three.

There are two points in the defense against this type of offense that have not been previously covered. The first concerns the organization of the three defensive players out in front. If the offense is a mechanically organized one, the defense is planned so that the two big defensive men are still left in the back line around the goal. The player who is assigned to be the third player out in front is the small guard. If all men in the back line of defense are large, then the quickest guard should be assigned to the front line duty. The center man of the back line should never be used in the front line since he is the quarterback on defense. He must stay in the back in order to direct maneuvers.

The guard **E**, who is the third defensive man out, should move directly out from his side of the court. This arrangement will always keep side by side the two original front men, **A** and **B**, who are

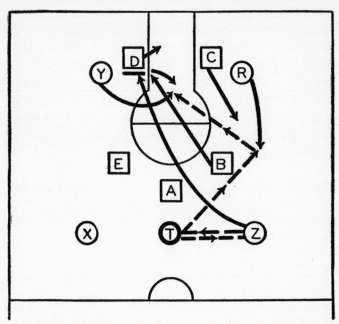

DIAGRAM 64. Defense Against Three-Out Offensive Formation.
Diagonal Movement with Screen

accustomed to teaming together. **E** is also ready to drop back into his regular spot when the occasion demands. What has actually happened then is that our original defensive setup has merely rotated a short distance in order to cover each offensive player.

The second point has to do with covering and following the three offensive players out in front. Since there are now only two defensive men around the basket, opportunities for complicated shifts are not present, and such shifts must not be attempted. Only simple shifts are reasonable and possible. This means that any time that one of the three front offensive men breaks toward the goal, a defensive man must follow him. This rule holds true whether the offensive man cuts diagonally, as Z in Diagram 64, or whether he goes straight toward the end line from his position. The importance of calling "Three out" in this connection will, of course, be obvious, so that the players all may know that a different setup now exists.

If screens or criss-cross movements are attempted, as shown in Diagram 64, then the obvious shifts, as shown and as previously described, must be made. Likewise, if the three men in front use a figure eight movement, A, B, and E should always shift. Further, they should crowd close together in order to force any offensive thrust to the side line and around to their outside rather than permit any opportunity for the opponents to split their ranks and make an offensive attack down the center.

It will be noted that against this type of offensive formation, with the ball in possession of the center man, the defense behind the ball forms a box. The idea here carries out the principles of grouping about a line connecting the ball with the basket while at the same time covering the opponents. Even if Y and R were to move to the corner, C and D would still tend to hover toward the center.

If the man on one side holds the ball, then the three front players are staggered as shown in Diagram 65. D must move over to cover Y a little more closely, while C can move farther away from his man since the ball is on the opposite side of the court.

A common movement is shown with the accompanying defensive checks. Here T and Z cross so that A and B shift. B must drop back with T. A natural shift occurs next for B and C. C must follow R until T comes around him. B will then be between R and the goal so that C should call, "Shift." X moves along the side line and must be followed by E. There is no opportunity for a shift. D of course guards Y.

2. Incidental Three-Out.

When the offensive movement of a team changes from two-out to three-out and back as an incidental part of the team play, so that the change may occur under varying circumstances, then the defense must be ready to change with it and without confusion. In this case, no one particular player may be assigned to the duty of being the third man out.

The only safe rule to follow under these circumstances is to assign to third-man-out duty that defensive player whose opponent

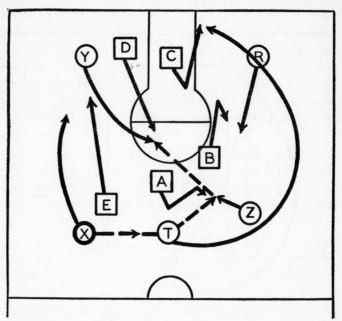

DIAGRAM 65. Defense Against Three-Out Offensive Formation.
Figure-of-Eight Movement

moves out to become the third-man-out in the three-out offensive situation. For example, if an offensive player on the side of the court moves out in front of the defense, then the man who is in the position to guard that player would move out with him. If the center should move from near the basket to a position out in front of the defense, then the player guarding would move out with him unless a natural shift occurred on the way. In this case an attempt is made whenever possible to shift so that the center man of the defense, who is the defensive quarterback, may be left back under the goal.

Some teams may analyze the defensive organization and attempt to pull the key men out of position. Where this is done as a deliberate move, after which the offense begins its attack, it is nearly always possible to arrange for shifts, even though they appear to be unorthodox, in order to keep the defensive men in their original positions.

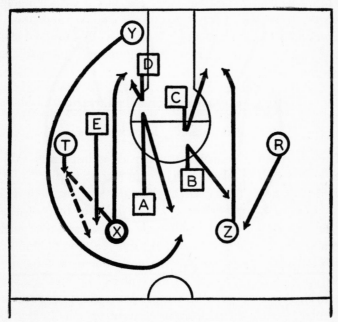

DIAGRAM 66. Defensive Maneuver to Keep Player D in Position Under Goal

One example of how such a maneuver was tried and how it was successfully met is shown in Diagram 66. The ball was passed from X to T. Then X and Z moved toward the goal to take up pivot post positions on either side of the free throw lane. T dribbled out in front of the defense. R and Y moved out as shown. B and C have obvious shifts. A and D shift, although Y is left unguarded momentarily and near the ball. E moves out with the man, **T**, who has the ball, and becomes the third man out with **A** and **B**. Since no scoring effort was made until the new setup was arranged, there was no hesitancy in making these shifts. It will be appreciated here, of course, that this is not an incidental move but rather a deliberate attempt to displace key defensive men. Since there was no scoring threat from the move, its value and effectiveness was lost. In this instance of the double pivot post the defense is playing directly in front of the post men and between them and the ball. The effectiveness of double post play is entirely nullified when the defense plays in front. In spite of the contention by many coaches that such tactics will not work and are not sound, several years of experience in successfully using these tactics have proved their value.

SPECIAL DEFENSIVE TACTICS

DEFENSE AGAINST SCREEN PLAYS

There are just two maneuvers to be made against screens. When one offensive player places a screen for his teammate and this teammate then cuts for the basket, there are two things to be done. First, the defensive players must shift men. When they shift men, the defensive player whose progress was impeded as a result of the screen is not in a sound guarding position. In other words, he is not between his opponent and the goal. Consequently his first effort should be to move toward the center of the court and back toward the basket, so that he can get between his opponent and the basket. The farther the players are away from the basket when the screen is formed the more difficult is the defensive job of the player who is screened. If the screen is close to the basket, then the movement is limited, and this one player can get into a guarding position.

This situation is shown clearly in Diagram 67. **R** has set a screen behind **A** for the benefit of **Z**. When **Z** cuts for the basket, **C**, who is guarding **R**, shifts to guard **Z**. It now behooves **A** to get into position to guard **R**, because, after **Z** passes **R**, **R** will cut for the free throw line. Unless **A** is very alert and aggressive, **R** will be open for a pass and a shot. As a matter of fact, many coaches who use the screen play hope to force the defense to shift, because then they feel certain that they can spring player **R** into the open. This situation exists whether the screen is longitudinal, as shown in Diagram 67, or whether it is lateral. The longitudinal screen is the more effective and the harder to defend against.

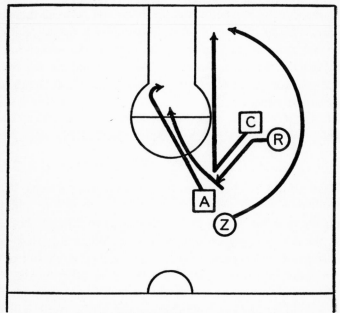

DIAGRAM 67. Defensive Maneuver on Screen Plays

The second situation is one in which an offensive player really plays hide and seek around one or more teammates and their guards. In this situation the player who hopes to elude his guard circles around one or more of his teammates and their guards. Diagram 68 shows the type of situation. **Z** cuts around behind **T** and **E** and then circles back until he gets on a line between **T** and the basket. If **B** attempts to follow around, he will be cut off, and **Z** can break in to the basket. If **E** should shift on to **Z**, with **B** entirely out of position, then **T** would be left unguarded.

The best defensive move (assuming now that **Z** is directly on a line which connects **T** with the basket), is for the inside man, **E** in this case, to fight on out to **Z**. **E** will either be able to cover **Z** or to force him to the side lines and away from the basket. **T** cannot move farther to aid **Z** or by the rules he will be penalized for blocking. As **Z** passes **E** in his diagonal movement, **B** should lag as indicated because he is in a strong defensive position. Then when

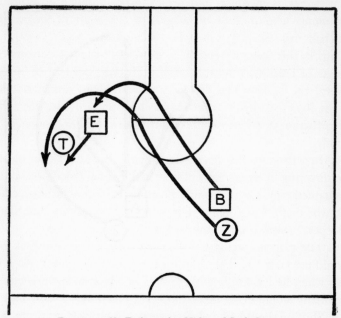

DIAGRAM 68. Defense for Hide-and-Seek Screen

E fights to guard **Z**, **B** is left in position to cover **T** or, should **Z** get away from **E**, **B** is in a position to play both **T** and **Z** until **E** can recover, or until other teammates can come to the rescue.

This same situation prevails when a player in the corner swings around a teammate who is stationed as **T** is in Diagram 68. The same tactics are employed.

FORCING IN THE BACK COURT

When a team defense spreads out to force the play in the back court, the same principles of defense apply as when the defense is massed about the free throw area. The purpose of forcing is to get the ball by hook or crook. Attention is on the ball as always. However, emphasis should be placed on certain specific points of the defense.

1. Each defensive player should take a position that will enable him to make an interception when the ball is passed to the opponent that he is guarding. In general this position will be as follows: opponents who are half the length of the court or farther from the ball may be played loosely (a couple of paces away). The guards in this case may even play in front of their opponents. The danger of breaking toward the ball is greater than that of breaking toward the basket. The defensive player should always be closer to the long axis of the court than is his opponent. In this spread-out situation it is best not to over-rush or crowd an opponent too closely.

2. In setting up the defense for forcing, the safety man must do the directing in seeing that all opponents are guarded. To leave an unguarded player at mid-court, which is the common error, defeats the whole effort of forcing. The safety man must be sure that no "sleepers" sneak back to the basket.

3. The players forcing the man with the ball in the back court should use tactics to delay him for the ten-second count. Rush him only when he has finished his dribble or when he is cornered. The opponent should never be permitted to break by.

4. Shifting should take place at every opportunity. Shifting, when opponents criss-cross, is an effective means of keeping the play in the back court.

5. Chances should be taken to intercept all long passes.

Attempts at Interceptions

When a player attempts to make an interception—and the players should be encouraged to do so—it is the rule that, if the attempt fails and the defensive player has rushed out of position, the teammate next in line must fill in his position for him. The player who has rushed out of position will then take the position left by his teammate as quickly as possible. Experience has shown that, when a player is seemingly maneuvered out of position, the subsequent attack is always at the point thus vacated. The opponents never seem to take advantage of the point left vacant by the teammate who goes to the rescue of the situation. The surprise of seeing the attack stopped so effectively seems to paralyze the opponents for a moment, and in that moment the whole defense has recovered.

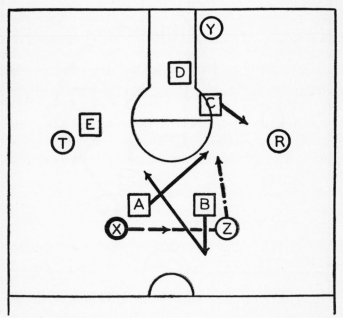

DIAGRAM 69. Defensive Maneuver When B Tries for an Interception

Diagram 69 illustrates a situation of this kind. In this diagram, B has not staggered back as usual. As X passes to Z, B makes a dive for the ball, but misses. Z invariably starts to dribble in. A quickly drops back and in front of Z. B recovers and takes the place vacated by A. What appeared to be a golden opportunity for the opponents has been nipped before it has gotten under way.

This maneuver has been so successful and the players have so much confidence in its effectiveness that they are always eager to gamble for interceptions. **A** and **B** are the players who most often try this type of play. However, **C** or **E** or even **D** will have numerous opportunities to gamble in like manner. When the back line of defense tries for interceptions, then three players are usually involved in the maneuver.

Diagram 70 shows how the back line of defense protects when one of their teammates tries for an interception and misses. **Z**

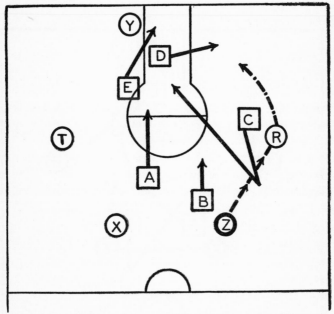

DIAGRAM 70. Defensive Maneuver When C Attempts to Intercept

passes to **R. C** misses in his attempt for an interception. As the pass is made to **R**, all players tend to converge toward the goal. **D** immediately blocks the progress of **R** as he attempts to dribble to the goal. If **R** merely holds and shoots, then **D** must rush out on him. **E** covers for **D**, and **A** is back on the free throw line. These moves come about almost simultaneously to block the offensive thrust. As **C** recovers, his best move is to break for the center of the court which will release **A**. If **Y** had been on the opposite side of the free throw line, the situation would not have been altered in the least. D would have been in a stronger position from the very beginning; therefore, the more difficult situation was shown.

Two-Timing

If a team is taught to play for the ball and not for a man, many opportunities will occur for a defensive player to surprise an opponent by suddenly leaving his regular position and going for the ball. Judgment, of course, must be used when attempts of this kind are made, because it means that two defensive men are attacking one offensive player. This will leave some position and some opponent on the court unguarded. This type of defensive play we have called "two-timing." There are many situations in which players may safely take chances of this kind. Two typical ones are discussed here in detail.

1. The most common situation occurs when a defensive player is dropping back to get between the ball and the basket after the ball has been passed behind him. In such a situation the player with the ball is usually along the side line or in a corner. The offensive player is one who holds the ball and attempts to feint his opponent out of position. It is hardly possible to two-time when a team is a fast passing team and when no player holds the ball in his possession very long. Diagram 71 is an example of a two-timing situation. Z has passed the ball to R. Z cuts for the basket. B drops back to get between the ball and the goal. He sees an opportunity either to steal the ball from R or to cause a held ball, so he attacks R, who is holding the ball. C is closely guarding R, so that the attack from B comes as a surprise.

The same opportunity for two-timing would present itself under conditions in which defensive players would shift opponents, for example, if Z had gone around R, between R and the side line. In this case C would not have shifted to cover Z but would have stayed with R. This two-timing maneuver would have left Z unguarded. Two-timing causes an opponent so much trouble that he usually cannot take advantage of the openings that are presented as a result of these defensive tactics.

2. Another opportunity for two-timing occurs when a defensive player sneaks up behind an opponent or when an opponent whose forward progress is blocked is rushed so that he pivots. The offensive player has usually stopped at the end of a dribble. This may happen anywhere on the court. The time for the second defensive player to attack under these conditions is usually after an opponent has recovered the ball on a defensive rebound or after a guard out

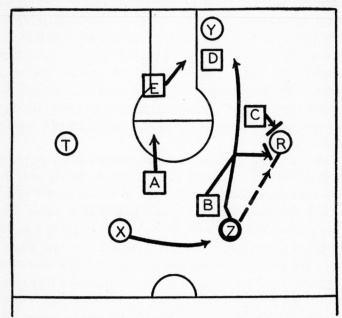

DIAGRAM 71. A Two-Timing Situation

in front of the defense has been thwarted in his attempt to dribble around his opponent. As the second opportunity occurs under an organized defensive situation, it is demonstrated in Diagram 72.

Z passes the ball to X who attempts to dribble, but A stops him and forces him to pivot. B has followed over toward X instead of dropping back. He sees an opportunity to steal the ball and attacks X just as he pivots. Z, of course, is left unguarded, but X seldom has an opportunity to take advantage of this opening. He is lucky to escape with a held ball. Of course, if X is successful in extricating himself from the jam and can pass to Z, the other three

defensive players, C, D, and E—particularly C and D in this case—
are in a position to stop Z until A and B can recover.

There are some who may contend that this method of doubling
up on one offensive player is illegal. They have in mind Rule 15,
Section 13, of 1936–37, which reads: "A player shall not charge in
and make bodily contact with an opponent who is one of two

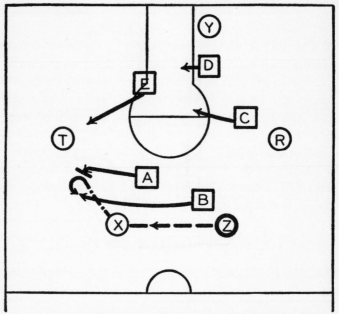

DIAGRAM 72. Two-Timing a Player Who Pivots

opposing players having one or both hands on the ball." It should
be pointed out, first, that the defense is playing the ball and not
the man. Contact in play of this kind should be ruled to be the
same as contact under any other situation. Second, the "two opposing players" seldom if ever have "one or both hands on the ball."
Consequently the play was entirely within the rules, even in 1936–
37. Section 13 of Rule 15 has now been removed, since it is not
even considered as a special situation which would require a rule
to cover it.

CHAPTER XXVI

OTHER DEFENSIVE SITUATIONS

IN CHAPTER XXV defenses against set offensive formations in the front court were discussed. In these situations the ball was always in play and was being maneuvered for an attempt at a setup shot for goal. In this chapter, defenses which start from a dead ball situation will be discussed. Included in these are defenses for out-of-bounds plays, on held balls, at the free throw line, and at the tip-off.

In addition to the above a special type of team defense which is particularly adaptable to small courts and deliberate teams is described. It is called a "box defense."

DEFENSE ON OUT-OF-BOUNDS PLAYS

The defense will need as many setups as there are offensive possibilities on out-of-bounds plays. In general, however, it may be said that, regardless of the offensive formation, the defense should mass itself between the ball and the goal. There are certain general principles which should be followed for all situations:

1. The defense should mass itself around the goal and, where possible, between the ball and the goal. A scoring play can always be stopped this way, even though the ball cannot be intercepted.

2. The defensive players should take their normal defensive positions. They should not be drawn out of position by any offensive maneuver. They should shift whenever possible.

3. No offensive formation should draw the defense out of the position described in 1 and 2.

4. The forward on the side of the court away from the ball may

act as a rover or free agent to make interceptions wherever possible.

5. All players, except the one guarding the man with the ball, should partly face the ball and partly watch the opponent. Their backs should be to the goal.

From the point of view of a team defense, there are a few specific situations that require explanation. Three of these occur in

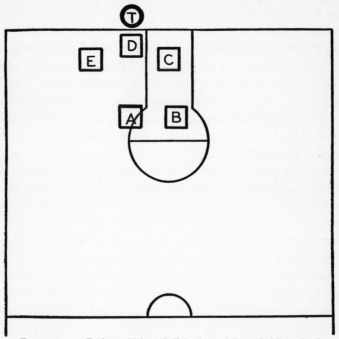

DIAGRAM 73. Defense When Ball Is Out of Bounds Near Goal

the front court: (1) when the ball is out of bounds somewhere along the inner third of the end line, (2) when the ball is out of bounds along the outer third of the end line or between the corner of the court and the point where the free throw line extended would intersect the side line, and (3) when the ball is out of bounds along the side line between the center line and the point where the free throw line extended would intersect the side line.

(1) Diagram 73 shows the position of the defense when the ball

is along the inner third of the end line. No attempt is made here to indicate the position of the offense. It will be appreciated that the defensive players must adjust their positions to specific offensive formations. D, the center man in the defense, will always cover the man with the ball. He should bother him as much as possible. The guard, C in this case, on the side of the court opposite the ball is responsible for play under the goal and on his side of the court. The other guard, E in the diagram, is responsible for the territory between the ball and the nearer corner. The forward (A in the formation shown) on the same side of the court as the ball is responsible for the area back of D. D always faces the player out of bounds with the ball. The other forward, B, either helps his teammate, A, or he may be the gambling member of the defense. He is free to go wherever he chooses in an attempt to intercept the ball. Often he can drop back with the safety man and thus worry the opponents a great deal.

This is not a forcing type of defense, except in the case of one player. It is a defense that has prevented practically all attempts to score and has made necessary a long pass out to the safety man. It has proved much stronger than a man-to-man defense on out-of-bounds plays. When this defense has been met, practically no scoring has been done; but when a man-to-man defense has been encountered, out-of-bounds plays have been repeatedly successful.

(2) Diagram 74 shows the defensive formation when the ball is along the outer third of the end line. The defense would be the same if the ball were along the side line but not beyond the free throw line. In this situation the guard on the same side of the court as the ball covers the player out of bounds. The center man in the defense, D, is between the ball and the basket. The forward, A, on the side of the court nearer the ball, covers the territory along the side line. The other guard, C, guards the area behind A and D. B, the other forward, is again free to take chances. By having the guard cover the player out of bounds, the team has greater strength about the goal.

(3) When the ball is along the side, but beyond the free throw line, the forward on the same side of the court as the ball guards

the player out of bounds. Diagram 75 shows the relative position
of the players. From the explanation given for situations (1) and
(2) the duties of each player should be evident. Again the forward, **B**, on the side of the court away from the ball, may attempt
to make interceptions. When **B** leaves his position as shown, then
C would move slightly nearer to the ball. In this case, long passes
to the far side of the court must be watched.

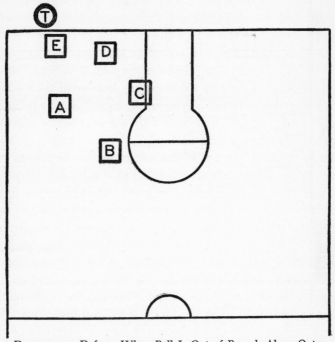

DIAGRAM 74. Defense When Ball Is Out of Bounds Along Outer
Third of End Line

(4) The fourth out-of-bounds defensive situation is in the back
court, particularly at the end line. With one exception the defense
is the same as that described on page 304 under *Forcing in the
Back Court.* When the ball is out of bounds at the end line in the
back court, the player out of bounds is usually not guarded. This
permits five defensive players to cover four offensive men. Most
teams leave·just one player in the back court to receive the ball

from the player out of bounds. The other three offensive men usually retreat to the front court and carelessly turn their backs on the ball. A few scares from defensive forcing will at least keep the opponents awake, and more often than not such forcing has been rewarded with possession of the ball and a subsequent goal.

The three players who retreat to the front court are accounted

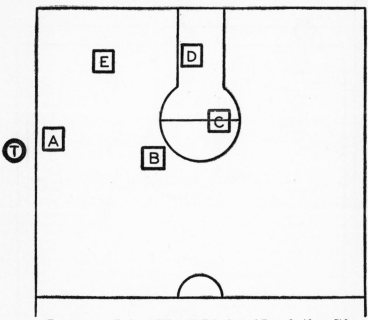

DIAGRAM 75. Defense When Ball Is Out of Bounds Along Side Line Beyond Free Throw Line

for by the three back men of the team defense as described under *Forcing in the Back Court.* The one offensive player in the back court is closely guarded by the two other defensive men. It is best practice for one to play in front or slightly to the side while the other plays behind and slightly to the side. This offsets the quick starts and stops by means of which the player attempts to get into the open to receive the ball.

If the player out of bounds is successful in making his pass into the court, he must be guarded as he comes toward the front court.

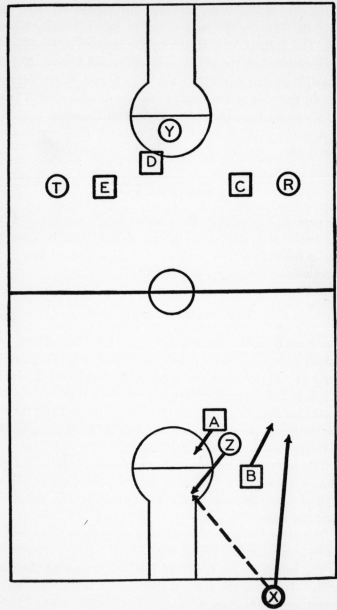

DIAGRAM 76. Defense When Ball Is Out of Bounds in Back Court

It is the duty of one of the two defensive players who have been forcing the play in the back court to be responsible for this player. The illustration as shown by Diagram 76 will explain the method of guarding the player who was out of bounds. X passes to Z and then runs down the court as indicated. B, the defensive player on that side of the court, would guard him while A would guard Z. If, on the other hand, X cuts to the other side of Z, then A would guard X, and B would guard Z. If this procedure is followed, there is never any doubt about assignments.

DEFENSE ON FREE THROWS

On pages 244-47, offense after a missed free throw was described. It was necessary to discuss the defense in this connection, and the reader is referred to these pages and to Diagrams 39 and 40 for the methods of defense on free throws.

DEFENSE AFTER HELD BALLS

The general points in connection with held ball defense were discussed under held ball offense on pages 259-64. Diagrams 47, 48, and 49 will also show the position of the players on defense after a held ball is called. Suffice it to say here that:

1. At least two players should be between the ball and the goal. If the opponents place more than this number in scoring positions, then the defense must match the number.

2. The center and a guard, or both guards, should be the players who are back. If a forward is jumping, then the center and the guard from the side of the court opposite the ball should protect the goal.

3. The other two players may take any positions they choose in order to gain possession of the ball.

4. The ball is usually tipped to the back or toward the nearer side line. Therefore the defense should take chances on making interceptions at these spots.

5. Some teams have favorite stunts for held ball plays or favorite

players to whom they nearly always tip the ball. The habits of teams should be studied, and teams should be played accordingly. It pays to take chances.

6. On held balls near the goal a tall player should always be stationed between the jumper and the goal. He should jump slightly later than the jumpers so that he can block an attempted goal from the tip.

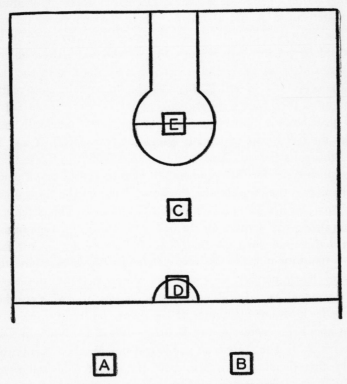

DIAGRAM 77. "Y" Defense at the Tip-Off

DEFENSE AT THE TIP-OFF

Probably the most conservative defense at the tip-off is that in which the players form the letter Y. This defense is shown in Diagram 77. The guards **C** and **E** are placed in tandem. **E** is at the free throw line and **C** is stationed about ten feet from the center circle. By placing them thus in the center of the court, it is not possible to split the defense on the tip. Of necessity all play will be forced toward the side line. There is no chance for confusion on the part of the guards; the positions and assignments are definite.

D, after the tip, will drop directly back toward the goal. **C** always moves to the side to which the ball is tipped. **E** is always the safety man. **A** and **B** usually charge through on either side of the centers. They are, however, free to go anywhere in an attempt to get the ball. If possession of the ball is lost, all five players will be in their regular defensive positions, with the possible exceptions of **C** and **E**, who may be on opposite sides of the court from their regular assignments.

This defense is probably as sound as any, but it practically concedes the ball to the opponents since only two players, **A** and **B**, are fighting for the ball. Also, by lining up definitely in this fashion, it is much easier for the opponents to plan successful tip-off plays.

Because of these objections, the box defense on the tip is much preferred. Such a defense is shown in Diagram 78. This defense is much stronger in fighting for the ball. Also, this is the same formation that is used when the team is controlling the tip, except that when this formation is used and a defensive tip is necessary, the players change position slightly as the centers step into the circle. By agreement between **E** and **C**, one moves up and the other moves back toward the center of the court. To balance the positions about the center, **A** and **B** rotate with **C** as shown in Diagram 78. **A**, **B**, and **C** form an equilateral triangle about the center circle, thus dividing the space about the center. This maneuver leaves three players instead of two to fight for the ball. **E** is back as a safety man so that play will be forced to the side lines. **D** will always drop back directly after the tip to aid around the goal.

This is a more aggressive tip-off defense and certainly more daring. Since the players do not rotate until the centers are ready to jump, it becomes puzzling to the opponents and has proved to be very successful in getting the ball. **E** and **C** may reverse their moves so that the opponents can never be sure which way the rotation will go. The three players, **A**, **B**, and **C**, are free to move anywhere they choose in an attempt to get the ball. Most teams do not try to do more than gain possession of the ball. This defense then capitalizes on the conservativeness of the opponents.

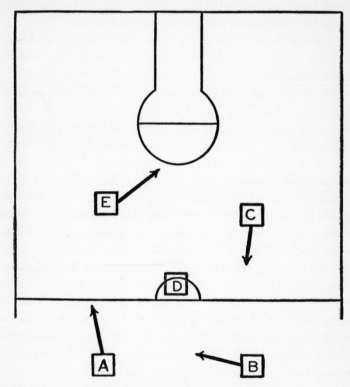

DIAGRAM 78. Box Defense at the Tip-Off

FOUR MAN BOX DEFENSE

A team defense lends itself to many innovations which in no way affect its fundamental principles. There have been occasions, for example, when, for strategical reasons, it was desired to have one player "dog" the heels of another, usually a star player, throughout the game. For a team defense this is rather an unexpected maneuver and therefore most effective. Again, on occasion, one player (always a quick, clever player) has been designated to be a rover. He is free to act as a "sleeper" or to do any other stunt that he may wish to. He may sneak up behind the offense to steal the ball or "two-time" at any moment, etc. He is always ready to quick break for the goal. The strategy of the rover is most effective against a conservative, methodical type of offense.

In any of these situations the other four players form a box about the free throw area. They must work as a unit. They must play a conservative defense, more of a pure zone type of play than would be the case in the regular team defense. The fifth player is free to go "wild," but the other four must not follow suit. The two front men in the defense must not go beyond the outer edge of the free throw circle, because, as the ball shifts from side to side of the court, the player away from the ball must be ready to shift back under the goal. He will be the third man back as an attack is made on the goal. Diagram 79 shows how this defense would form and also shows one movement with the ball. The positions of the players in this defense are almost entirely dependent upon the position of the ball. Since the rover is always behind the offense, long shots are not feared, because for the most part they will be hurried. A is the rover. He will usually play in the center of the court. This places him in a strong position to attack to either side. C and D are the big men on defense. E would be the small guard who is moved out to the front line. With the ball at X the defense favors that side of the court. When the ball is passed to T, the shift is farther to that side. B must be ready to retreat all the way to the goal. This is the reason that the two front men may not go beyond the free throw circle. Because of the hazard of interception by A, the offense cannot proceed with as much speed and assurance as one might expect. For this reason a usually calm and methodical offense becomes erratic and uncertain.

It must be borne in mind that the four men forming the box play as a unit. They disregard the rover, A, altogether. No matter where A may play or what he may do, the other four play their positions as if he were nowhere on the court. This will mean that at times two defensive players may be on one offensive man, as, for instance, if **A** should see a chance to attack **X** at the same time that **E** is guarding him.

This rather unorthodox defense has been most effective when

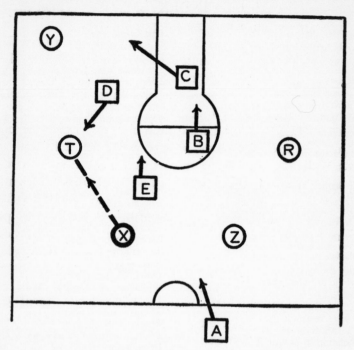

DIAGRAM 79. Four-Man Box Defense with One Man as a Rover

used on occasion during a game as a surprise move, and many stronger teams have been beaten and demoralized as a result of tactics of this kind. Certainly this type of play adds zest to an already exciting game and is very encouraging to a group of eager boys.

It is recommended, however, that a defense of this kind shall not be tried until a team has become thoroughly efficient in its regular team defense.

INDEX

323